The Handicapped Chil

The Handicapped Child

EDUCATIONAL AND PSYCHOLOGICAL GUIDANCE FOR THE ORGANICALLY HANDICAPPED

Agatha H. Bowley
Ph.D., F.B.Psy.S.

Formerly Consultant Psychologist, Cheyne Centre for Spastic Children; and Horsham and Crawley Child Guidance Clinics

Leslie Gardner
B.Sc., Dip.Ed., Dip.Psych.

Principal Psychologist, The Spastics Society, London; and Audiology Unit, The Hospital for Sick Children, Great Ormond Street, London

FOURTH EDITION

CHURCHILL LIVINGSTONE

EDINBURGH LONDON AND NEW YORK 1980

CHURCHILL LIVINGSTONE
Medical Division of Longman Group Limited

Distributed in the United States of America by
Churchill Livingstone Inc., 19 West 44th Street,
New York, N.Y. 10036, and by associated companies,
branches and representatives throughout the world.

First Edition, 1957
Second Edition, 1969
Third Edition, 1972
Fourth Edition, 1980

ISBN 0 443 02084 1

British Library Cataloguing in Publication Data
Bowley, Agatha Hilliam
 The handicapped child.—4th ed.
 1. Handicapped children—Education
 I. Title II. Gardner, Leslie
 371.9 LC4015 79-41013

£ 6.50.

Printed in Great Britain by Butler & Tanner Limited, Frome and London

Preface to the Fourth Edition

The explosion of interest in the field of handicap that has taken place in the last decade is very gratifying. It represents a tremendous step forward in social attitudes towards, and understanding of, handicaps. With this comes a willingness to create the services that handicapped children—and their families—need if they are to have a fair chance of overcoming some of their problems and enjoying life.

New developments in the field have made the task of revising our 1972 edition of this book both exciting and formidable. Our overall aim has remained unchanged: to provide a text on the educational, psychological and social implications of organically handicapped children; but we have endeavoured to meet the obvious need, generated by the recent enormous increase in knowledge, for a compact and yet comprehensive volume which covers all the numerically and educationally important physical and sensory handicaps.

We write as psychologists concerned with assessment, family guidance, educational advice and research, working in close association with medical and teaching professions, with therapists, social workers, administrators—and, not least, parents. By following the progress of a large number of children from early childhood through to adolescence, we have become well aware of the range of psychological, physical and social problems involved in adjustment, learning and employment. The very fact that this book is published under joint authorship reflects the need for a team approach by psychologists whose background, training and experience are by no means identical.

In this edition, we begin with a new Chapter on handicapped people in general and their position in society; we expand the section on children with physical handicaps to include the majority of such conditions, although the major coverage still centres on children with cerebral palsy, which, besides being the most frequent physical handicap encountered in most special schools and units, is one about which a great deal of knowledge has been accumulated in recent years, and one which can, in our opinion, serve as a 'model' for several other handicapping conditions. Therefore, much of what we write under the heading of Cerebral Palsy is often applicable to children and their families described under other headings. We have expanded the section on spina bifida to include the valuable advances in our understanding of the social and educational consequences of this condition in the past decade. The Chapters concerning children with less obvious physical handicaps, those with minimal cerebral dysfunctioning, hearing losses, visual impairments and autism, have also been amended but less extensively so. Although we have had requests to include a separate chapter on mental retardation, we have preferred, as before, in a book of this size, to cover this very important subject (affecting almost half of the children with overt physical handicaps) in the existing Chapters, including notes on recent developments in behaviour modification techniques and parent involvement schemes, but concentrating principally on children with both physical and mental handicaps. We have added a new Chapter on work with the handicapped in developing countries where, in many cases, magnificent work is being done, by very committed staff, 'on a shoe string'.

We hope that this new edition will serve well into the 1980s for a wide range of readers—students and young professionals, including teachers (in ordinary as well as special schools), social workers, health visitors, psychologists, doctors, child care workers, education advisers and the various therapists—and, above all, parents.

Leslie Gardner wishes to acknowledge his gratitude to: the many children and parents involved in our work; to Professor Jack Tizard for wise guidance over many years; James Loring, the Director of the Spastics Society, and the many colleagues whose work and generous support is reflected throughout this book; to Pat Isaac of the Spastics Society, for her general help; to Mary Gardner, of the Charing Cross Child Development Centre, especially for her contribution to sections on children with epilepsy and specific reading retardation; to the Overseas Development Administration for support in extending our work to developing countries; to students at London University and the Bombay Institutes of Education for their constructive comments on many of the themes raised in this revised edition.

Agatha Bowley wishes to acknowledge her gratitude to: Dr Ursula Shelley, Dr John Foley and the staff of the Centre for Spastic Children, Cheyne Walk, London; Dr David Wild, Area Medical Officer, West Sussex; Dr Louis Minski and Dr Henry Rees previously Consultant to the Children's Unit, Belmont Hospital; and to Miss Averil Beevor. Both authors wish to thank Mrs Heather Jones of the R.N.I.B. for her valuable contribution on visually handicapped children.

London, 1980   L. G.
                                                                 A. H. B.

Introduction

The purpose of this book is to set down in terms intelligible to the non-specialist reader, certain facts and findings concerning children with handicaps, based on first-hand experience and from a study of the literature. It is our sincere hope that it will provide factual information which will help to allay anxiety and to build up an informed, constructive and sympathetic approach towards children who are handicapped.

The handicapped child is even more dependent than the ordinary child on the understanding and skill of those adults responsible for his care. His development will be affected if he is handled by uninformed, embarrassed or excessively sentimental adults. It takes courage, wisdom and faith on the parents' part to face the fact that a handicapped child has been entrusted to their care.

Our approach to caring for handicapped children depends on our attitude to the whole problem of suffering and adversity in human life. The various techniques and practical methods are of little avail unless their use is founded on the attitude of compassion.

Our philosophy may be summed up in the following terms: 'to love—to understand—and to help'. In common with all children the handicapped have the right to opportunities of developing their abilities to the optimum levels that are possible. We hope this book will help to enhance these opportunities.

Contents

1

What is handicap? Some old and new orientations

Many people feel uncomfortable in the presence of handicap. Before discussing some of the reasons for this, let us first try to make clear what is meant by handicap, especially in relation to the kinds of 'long-term' physical and sensory handicaps in children that are the main concern of this book.

Some definitions of handicap

A handicap is an interference or obstruction to normal growth, development and/or educational progress. A handicapped person cannot do certain things by ordinary methods or in the ordinary time available.

In the widest sense, handicap is caused by some continuing defect or impairment of the body, intellect or personality. We are all handicapped in some way, in that we lose teeth or need glasses or break a leg, which could leave a slight limp. These are minor organic impairments, unlikely to hold up our daily living unless we happen to be engaged in very special careers or very much in the public eye. What about the loss of a finger through an accident? This would be a definite 'organic impairment', but would not necessarily constitute a handicap. Most of us could continue our lives virtually unchanged by the loss of one finger on the left hand. But what if we were pianists or expert typists? Then we would be handicapped; the impairment would, in this case, affect the execution of our work. This brings out the important distinction between 'impairment', 'disability' and 'handicap'.

An organic impairment is a loss of a limb, or damage to nerve cells or tissues, which can usually be quite precisely defined and measured.

A disability is the loss of function, due to impairment.

Handicap is a wider concept, defining how the impairment affects the person's style of life, and involves a number of psychological and social factors.

In reaching a fuller understanding of what is meant by handicap, we must bear in mind four important points:

1. There is some organic, psychological or culturally induced difficulty compared to the general population.
2. This difficulty leads to some limitations of function, as far as ordinary activities are concerned, comparing the person affected with other persons of similar age, sex, etc.
3. This is likely to affect the individual's psychological development, especially his 'self-image', his view of himself as a competent, managing person, or otherwise.
4. All the above will be affected by society's attitude, and how the majority of people in contact with the handicapped person view his situation. Do they show pity, anxiety or rejection, or do they take the handicap in their stride?

So handicap cannot be defined simply as an organic or medical condition. It is also necessary to define how it affects the person's functioning in life, which, again, is not simply a matter of physical competence, but of the attitudes towards it of the person affected and his peers and associates. It is, then, necessary to comprehend how the four aspects listed above can interact with each other. For example, we have argued that the loss of a finger will not constitute a handicap for the majority of people. But some individuals do 'over-react' even to such a small impairment as this. If physical attractiveness and intactness are very highly valued by a particular family, the family could become very disturbed even by a minor, and mostly cosmetic, impairment. Here is a short case study:

Norma, aged seven, was seen at a child guidance clinic because of her persistent refusal to attend school She was born with a congenital absence of the external ear on the left. Her hearing for speech was quite normal and, although plastic surgery had produced a semblance of a new external ear, the operations were not completely successful and much more work had yet to be done. Her refusals to attend school had occurred from time to time since she was five and were becoming increasingly frequent. Although encouraged to grow her hair long, she said that she was frightened that other children might find out about her 'funny ear' and laugh at her.

The social worker who visited the home reported that the parents were extremely house-proud; they gave the impression of almost being ashamed of any slight blemishes to the decorations of their house, or even on the bodywork of their car, and would immediately take steps to restore a neat and orderly appearance. It seems likely that they were equally ashamed of what they saw as a blemish in their child, and they were, perhaps unwittingly, colluding with the child, in withdrawing from situations in which her blemish might be detected.

Here, emotional factors were more important than the actual organic impairment itself. In extreme cases, very emotionally disturbed people may even act as though they have an organic impairment when, in fact, they have none, or very little. Emotional states can also aggravate organic handicaps that might otherwise remain mild and harmless, as in the case of psychosomatic illness, in which, for example, too much anxiety and stress may contribute to the development of a stomach ulcer.

Not only emotional but also social and cultural factors can induce handicap. For example, in Chinese society during the nineteenth century, there were various groups who were expected to induce physical impairments, which were not regarded as handicaps, although by ordinary standards they would be. Certain groups of women were expected to bind up their feet, thus making their feet very small, which in turn made walking very difficult. This symbolized their membership of a high social caste, whose women were rarely expected to walk.

We should also mention that the significance of a particular handicap will vary with the type of environment surrounding the child. For example, a paraplegic child might manage some mobility, through being able to crawl, provided he remains in an appropriate environment, such as in a typical Indian village, where everything is built on one level. But this same child, if transferred to a crowded block of flats in Bombay or Calcutta, would, no doubt, be rendered completely immobile.

Handicap and child development

A child's handicap cannot be considered in isolation. In order to alleviate his difficulties, it is essential to take into account how well he can function in his physical environment and the effect, not only of his handicap, but also of the cultural environment to which he is exposed.

In recent decades, child psychologists such as Piaget have viewed child development essentially as the result of the *interaction* between the child and his environment, and this is a very useful way of sorting out the mass of factors involved. This interaction is very far reaching. Indeed it is often dangerous to try to separate the two, e.g. to deal with a child in isolation from his social surroundings, or at the other extreme, to consider *only* the child's environment to the exclusion of what he brings to this environment, such as a long-standing organic impairment. The two are inextricably linked.

Handicap can, then, be viewed as something that interferes with a child's interaction with his environment. Our understanding of and efforts to alleviate the handicap must involve not only 'modifying' the child, but modifying his environment as well.

The psychology of handicap

As mentioned previously, many people feel uncomfortable in the presence of handicap, and it is instructive to look at some of the reasons for this. It is also important to do so, since feelings of discomfort, anxiety, fear, etc., can easily be communicated, often unwittingly, to the person with a handicap. Let us look at the psychological effects of handicap, firstly within the handicapped person, and secondly on 'able-bodied' people who are in contact with him.

The handicapped person's feelings

We have explained that a handicap means that one cannot do certain things that are normally expected by ordinary methods or in the ordinary time available, and one cannot keep up with the standards of performance and ways of behaving that are presented by the surrounding society. Since all societies, by definition, care about certain prescribed ways of behaving, most major deviations are almost certain to cause discomfort, and to be 'looked down on', so that the handicapped person often finds himself in a low-status position.

One of the greatest theorists concerning the psychology of handicap was the psychologist Alfred Adler, who in his book *The Neurotic Constitution*, published by Kegan Paul in 1921, wrote that 'the possession of definitely inferior organs, is reflected upon the psyche, and in such a way as to lower the self esteem—to raise the child's psychological uncertainty'.

He went on to argue that this lowered self-esteem leads to a struggle for self-assertion, giving rise to his famous theory of 'compensation for inferiority' which he regarded as a major element in the motivation of people's behaviour (e.g. a man may try desperately to make up for small stature by behaving in a dominating and aggressive way).

Attempts at research studies in the field of 'feelings of inferiority' amongst physically handicapped persons have by no means substantiated Adler's theories. Many of these studies are summarized in Beatrice Wright's (1960) excellent book on the psychological aspects of physical disability. As an example of a typical early research study we can take that of Faterson in 1931, in which a large group of ordinary American students were asked to complete a questionnaire concerning their feelings about their social, academic and physical accomplishments. The scores were then correlated with the students' medical records, mostly concerning relatively minor physical impairments. The correlation between these and reported 'feelings of inferiority' was positive, but quite low, in the region of 0·25. Turning to studies of definitely handicapped persons, the results are equally indefinite, some showing a slight relationship between 'feelings of inferiority' and handicap, others showing no correlation, whilst a few studies, such as Seidenfeld's (1948) study of post-polio groups, suggested that they had *higher* feelings of personal worth, than did the 'normal' groups on which the tests were standardized. Adler, of course, would not have been surprised about this in view of his theory of 'compensation' which would lead him to expect feelings of 'self-assertion' to follow from feelings of inferiority, arising from organic handicap, and he would, no doubt, have argued that more subtle measures would be required for the deeper feelings involved.

The presence or absence of inferiority feelings either at the deeper levels of personality, or at the more superficial, more accessible levels, depends on many factors. One of these is the way a handicapped person has been regarded and treated by his family and other people in close contact with him, especially during his early years. It is this treatment that, to a large extent, determines his 'self-image'—his own conscious and subconscious view of himself—and what situations in life he thinks he can or cannot cope with.

The development of self-image. The development of a child's self-image starts as soon as he begins to distinguish between what is 'self' and what is 'non-self'. He moves his limbs, learns to grasp objects, finds that he can affect his surroundings by his actions and vocalizations. He learns that objects and people have some kind of 'permanence'—as when he first realizes that his mother still exists even when he cannot see her or feel her. He learns to recognize familiar people and distinguish them from strangers, usually by six months of age. At about the same time he begins to show recognition of himself in a mirror, although he is still a long way from actually naming himself. The full use of the pronouns 'I', 'me' and 'my' does not usually occur before the age of three.

In any child, a series of successful activities tends to build up morale and confidence, whilst a series of unsuccessful attempts, leading to little or no recognition or reward, tends to lower his confidence. Severely lowered confidence, of course, affects his chances of success in future activities.

The presence of handicap means that a greater proportion of the early activities of a child are likely to be regarded as 'unsuccessful'. A child with a mild physical handicap, for example resulting in clumsy hands and indistinct speech, is likely to find some of his early sensory-motor experiences, such as learning to control his hands accurately, to co-ordinate hand and eye, etc., quite frustrating—especially if his parents become impatient or critical of his efforts at using a spoon, building with bricks or producing clear speech, or if other children mock his attempts.

The standards of performance expected of a child at a certain age arise largely from parental expectations. These are gradually 'internalized' so that the child develops a set of expectations about his own performance that more or less corresponds to those of the parents. The handicapped child is as likely as a normal child to make comparisons between his performance and that of other children of similar age, assuming, of course, that he is not leading a very isolated existence. As a result, in addition to sensing parental dismay at his 'clumsiness', he is becoming aware that his performance is not matching up to that of other children.

Repeated exposures to such 'failures' can result in a poor self-image, with low morale or confidence, which may be severe enough to decrease the level of performance still more.

Although the effects of morale on performance are very important, we must be careful not to exaggerate the effects of frustration and failure on the handicapped child's self-image. As has been pointed out, the empirical studies so far carried out do not point to any clear-cut relationship between handicap and low morale. The situation is complicated by many other factors, such as the kind of upbringing the child has, the attitudes of people close to him, the standards of behaviour and performance that they expect and the way in which they communicate these standards. We occasionally come across parents whose standards and expectations are too low in relation to what their handicapped child could accomplish, in which case their child is unlikely to feel particularly frustrated or unsuccessful—at least in the short term (although such under-expectation does store up trouble for the future). Other children appear to 'compensate' very well for their handicaps, particularly when parents dwell on their strengths rather than their weaknesses.

The able-bodied person's feelings about handicap

There is a tendency among able-bodied people to dwell on the problems and frustrations associated with handicap to such an extent that the handicapped child ceases to be regarded as an individual with his own personal abilities and contribution to make to society. The psychological process here is one of generalization from one piece of information to a whole set of data—in this case, from a handicap, to a whole child, as if the handicap necessarily permeates his entire being. As one child with spasticity put it, 'Just because my legs are wobbly, people think my mind is wobbly too.' Such a generalization is one of the primary aspects of faulty attitudes towards handicapped people; and the generalization from physical handicap to more extensive mental or emotional handicaps is particularly common.

This preconceived notion of a correlation between physical and mental characteristics is deeply rooted in history. The ancient Greeks, for example, formulated several theories of how a person's temperament might be gauged from his facial characteristics and physique, and in Greek states where such ideas were at their most extreme, children born with a handicap were considered worthless and left to die. The book of Leviticus in the Old Testament of the Bible directs that no 'blind man or a lame . . . or a man that is broken footed, or crook backt, or that hath a blemish in his eye' should be admitted to the priesthood.

The list of possible examples from literature is endless. Shakespeare clearly implied that Cassius was not to be trusted when he commented on the latter's 'lean and hungry look', and, significantly, his Richard III says angrily, and with self-loathing, that he was:

> Deformed, unfinished, sent before my time
> Into this breathing world, scarce half made up
> And that so lamely and unfashionable
> That dogs bark at me as I halt by them . . .

In more recent works we have further examples of the handicapped playing a sinister role, such as Hugo's *Hunchback of Notre Dame* and, in Kubrick's film, *Dr Strangelove*, who was plotting to blow up the world from his wheelchair.

Such literature tends to perpetuate stereotyped ideas linking physical appearance with socially 'threatening' behaviour, although many writers have been at pains to point out that the troublesome behaviour is rarely due to deformity itself. Behind these early suspicions lay primitive ideas that physical deformities might be the work of the devil or evil spirits, and, therefore, persons so marked out should be avoided. There were also fears of contamination (not entirely unreal in times of inadequate sanitation and lower hygiene standards). Such centuries-old 'stereotypes' tend to linger in most societies and provide a breeding ground for current stereotypes, which may be nurtured by new kinds of pressures. For example, for the past 50 years in the West, and now recently in the East, commercial advertising pressures have tended to make a cult of having perfect and beautiful bodies, hair, feet, teeth, etc., and people who have gained such attributes by, for instance, taking the right diet or pills, etc., are portrayed as successful. This cult of 'the body beautiful' works against the handicapped, and handicap tends to become associated with failure and shame.

Face to face with handicap

In addition to these historical ideas, there are also more direct and immediate determinants of negative attitudes. Many ordinary people frequently show discomfort and embarrassment when faced with handicap, and this is partly due to the fact that 'face to face' communication with another person is governed by a fairly strict code of rules. Communication between two people is much more than a matter of spoken words. Other equally important signals are transmitted and received, such as tone and loudness of voice, facial and postural expression, hand gesture, the proximity of speaker to listener, the amount of eye contact and eye avoidance, and so on (see Argyle, 1967).

In physically handicapped people, many of these signals are unusual: there are delays in speaking, difficulty in controlling eye movements, unwanted head movements, perhaps resulting in the speaker coming too close to the listener, unusual grimaces, unrelated to the subject under discussion, etc. Many of these features are common in a person with cerebral palsy, due to poor muscular control, and people unfamiliar with such features can mistake them for signs of mental or emotional abnormality. They may interpret, for example, an over-excited bout of laughter, which is common in the athetoid variety of cerebral palsy, as a sign of 'simple-mindedness' or immaturity, when it is, in fact, a purely 'motor' response. Such attitudes will interfere not only with communication, but with the relationship that might otherwise have been developing. Our self-image is greatly affected by the reaction of other people to the signals we transmit.

A hierarchy of handicaps

Attitudes towards handicap vary from society to society in accordance with cultural, religious and even political background. They also vary with the different kinds of handicap, and in most societies it is possible to construct an approximate 'hierarchy of handicap', ranking each handicap in terms of the public's degree of acceptance on the one hand, or discomfort or dislike on the other. Tringo (1970) carried out a survey in the late 1960s among 455 college students in the USA. The students were asked to indicate their degree of acceptance or rejection of people with various handicaps in terms of whether they would wish to have them as neighbours, would accept them as close kin by marriage, or, at the other extreme, would rather handicapped people were 'kept in an institution'. The approximate 'social' ranking of various impairments and handicaps indicated by this survey is shown in Table 1.

Table 1 A ranking of various impairments and handicaps (from Tringo, 1970)

Disability	Rank order
Ulcer	1
Arthritis	2
Asthma	3
Diabetes	4
Heart disease	5
Amputee	6
Blindness	7
Deafness	8
Stroke	9
Cancer	10
Old age	11
Paraplegic	12
Epilepsy	13
Dwarf	14
Cerebral palsy	15
Hunchback	16
Tuberculosis	17
Ex-convict	18
Mental retardation	19
Alcoholism	20
Mental illness	21

The impairments and handicaps ranked at the top of the list are obviously regarded as relatively mild and unimportant as far as forming a close relationship is concerned, whilst those rated towards the bottom are regarded with considerable dislike, the respondents being unwilling to share activities with persons so affected. Why have the impairments and handicaps been ranked in this way? Clearly, the impairments at the top of the list appear to be purely physical, and relatively circumscribed in their effects. Those at the bottom of the ranking, however, in addition to having a physical component in many cases, are considered to be linked with wider effects on the personality and behaviour of the person concerned. That is, they are viewed as very generalized states affecting the whole person, at least for a time, and, therefore, likely to lead to unpredictable behaviour and possibly lack of self-control and reliability, etc. Such fears are, of course, in many cases very exaggerated, although public attitudes to people with severe personality and intellectual difficulties are becoming much more enlightened. But undoubtedly, in the West at least, such handicaps still disrupt the public's idea of how people should behave, how reliable and predictable they should be if close relationships are to be formed. As for chronic physical handicaps such as cerebral palsy and paraplegia, these are ranked fairly low down the list, suggesting some 'generalization' from the physical to the behavioural characteristics of the people concerned.

Interestingly, the blind are slightly less rejected than the deaf in this study. In most cultures, the blind find much more 'acceptance' than the deaf. The main reasons for this are that:

1. It is easier to *communicate* with the blind than with the deaf. Speech is usually unaffected in the blind, but very impaired for the severely deaf.
2. It is easier to *empathize* with the blind. Simply by having experienced the dark, we all have some idea of what it is like to be blind, whereas we have never experienced the awful silence that deafness brings. This empathy helps us to realize what a blind person's immediate needs may be, such as simple help in crossing a road, whereas so often we fail to realize a deaf person's needs, such as the need to be able to see one's lips, if he is to understand what one is saying.
3. The blind, certainly in the West, have several favourable images, such as the blind poet, or sage, or the war-blinded hero.

Attitudes to handicap are important. If most of the people in a community believe (with no hard evidence) that handicapped people are difficult to get on with, such a belief can turn into a reality, and they may fail to make the efforts necessary to overcome the communication problems that they find embarrassing. This in turn will lead to a feeling of rejection and resentment amongst people with a handicap. As one blind person put it, 'It's not the

blindness that troubles me so much, it's the way people treat me.'
He was referring to the fact that he found himself the subject of
too much pity and over-protection. People were tending to react
not to him as a person, but to his handicap.

We will say more about attitudes to particular handicaps, and
how these attitudes can be improved, such as through encouraging
a deeper understanding of what each handicap actually involves,
in the following chapters.

Who is handicapped?

In what we have written so far, we may be giving the impression
that the population of the world can be neatly divided up into those
people who are 'handicapped' and those who are 'normal'. This
is not so.

Even the concept of 'normal' is a complex one, e.g. it can mean
conforming to a statistical average, or to some ideal standard of
behaviour, or simply being able to stay away from the attention
of doctors and welfare agencies. None of these definitions is fool-
proof; the statistical average is too crude, the ideal too subjective,
and somebody who avoids all agencies may simply be a recluse,
living in considerable pain.

Since we cannot define 'normal' satisfactorily, we cannot be very
definite about the question 'Who is handicapped?' and what
degree of variation from normal can be regarded as sufficient to
constitute a handicap (see Illingworth (1979a and b) for valuable
ideas on 'normality' in children).

Instead of attempting to divide people into the handicapped and
the non-handicapped, it is far more helpful to view impairment
as a *continuum* with almost infinite gradations from the 'normal'
(perhaps most conveniently described as a statistical average),
through mild, just detectable handicaps, to the extremes of severe
and multiple handicap. No one would deny that the latter will lead
to very poor functioning in many areas of activity compared to
mild handicap, but the idea of a continuum helps us to avoid the
dangers of too rigid categorization or labelling of children in an
over-simplified way and regarding handicap as fixed for all time.

However, for the purpose of making estimates of numbers of
persons, nationally or regionally, who are likely to be handicapped
enough to warrant the provision of special help, we must resort
to more simply defined categories.

A large-scale survey of impairment and handicap in the UK
(Harris, 1971) indicated that no less than 7 per cent (approximately
three million) of the whole adult population (age 16+) can be

classified as impaired or handicapped. A large proportion of the handicapped are elderly—a reminder that, if we survive, we are destined to end up handicapped eventually. Not all the three million were severely handicapped, but at least one million were considered severe enough to warrant special help on a long-term basis. These figures may err on the low side since they are based on answers to a questionnaire sent to a large, representative sample of adults (187 000) and it is possible that some respondents might prefer to conceal their disabilities.

Surveys of the incidence of handicap in children have shown equally high percentages. For example, the Seebohm Report, published by HMSO in 1968, used a variety of sources, such as medical records of children and enrolments in special schools, whilst the National Child Development study was based on a particularly large, representative sample, namely all the children born in a particular week in March 1958 in the UK, totalling 16 000 babies, who were then followed up at ages 7, 11 and 16 years.

Table 2 shows the prevalence of handicaps per 1000 of the child population in the UK.

Table 2 Prevalence of impairments and handicaps per 1000 children in the UK

Impairments and handicaps	Appendix Q: Seebohm Report (1968) 5–15 years	National Child Development Study (1958 Cohort) 7–year–olds
Blind and partially sighted	1·2	1·9
Deaf and partially hearing	1·2	1·1
Epileptic	7·2	6·2
Speech defects	27·0	23·3
Cerebral palsy	3·0	2·2
Heart disease	2·4	3·6
Orthopaedic condition	3·4	4·6
Asthma	23·2	27·4
Eczema	10·4	24·7
Diabetes	1·2	0·2
Other physical handicaps	6·7	6·7
Severely subnormal	3·5	2·7

These two sets of figures show considerable agreement, the slight differences being due to differences in sampling, and in the criteria used for defining certain handicaps. They revealed that a substantial percentage, in the region of 10 per cent of children, have impairments and handicaps, and although some of the impairments are quite mild and unlikely to affect a child educationally or socially, many did call for some form of special consideration and special services. At least 2 per cent of the National Child Development sample were described as having severe handicaps, needing special help on a long-term basis.

Another approach to gaining information about the numbers of children with handicapping conditions is to look at the numbers of children who have actually been recommended for special schooling. In 1977, in England and Wales, just over 175 000 children, or 1·8 per cent of the school population, were attending special schools or special classes (or awaiting admission), but according to the figures of the Department of Education and Science, there are large variations in the provision of special schools from area to area. So the figures are telling us more about the actual provision that has been made, which is not necessarily the same as the numbers of children actually needing special help.

None of the studies mentioned so far, useful as they are, can give a fully satisfactory estimate, e.g. they have had to rely on considerable 'second-hand evidence', from a variety of sources, which does not always give a consistent or reliable picture.

The most direct and comprehensive study of the prevalence of significantly handicapping conditions in the UK is that of Rutter, Tizard and Whitmore (1970). This was a very carefully planned study of all the children between the ages of 9 and 11 years on the Isle of Wight, who at the time of the survey totalled 2199. All long-term handicaps (defined as being of at least 12 months duration) likely to affect the child's educational progress were studied, divided into four carefully defined categories, with exact criteria for each—intellectual retardation, educational retardation, psychiatric disorders and physical impairments and handicaps. Besides collecting existing records, group tests were carried out on all the children, and questionnaires sent to their parents and teachers. This was followed up by individual interviews by teams of doctors and psychologists in order to arrive at a more accurate estimate of those children suspected of having an impairment or handicap.

This study showed that at least 16 per cent of the children had one or more of the handicaps. The percentage of those with physical impairments and handicaps, which is the main concern in the present book, was very close to 4 per cent, ranging from those with chronic handicaps such as cerebral palsy, deafness, blindness, of major educational significance, to those with relatively mild conditions such as asthma and diabetes, which, although interrupting a child's schooling periodically and calling for some special consideration, do not usually present serious educational and communication problems. Studies of more adverse environments than the Isle of Wight, which in the 1960s was relatively stable and prosperous, show even higher rates for conditions such as psychiatric disorders and retardation in reading, e.g. Berger and Yule's (1975) study of school children in certain Inner London areas, using the same measuring techniques. However, the Isle of Wight studies are representative of the majority of areas in the UK. There is another striking point about the findings: they highlight the extent to which children have more than one handicap. Of the children with handicaps (354 out of 2199 school children age 9 to 11) approximately 19 per cent had two handicaps, and 5 per cent had three or all four.

The Isle of Wight study is one of the best examples on record of a well-planned and systematic attempt, in both breadth and depth, to discover the prevalence of handicapping conditions, not merely in terms of simple medical and educational categories, but also involving the measurement of children's actual social, educational and physical functioning. These very detailed measurements exemplify the idea of handicap as a 'continuum', with many gradations from near normal to severely handicapped, that can be effectively measured. These measurements are essential if proper services are to be planned, and the resulting proportion, that of 1 in 6 of school children at any one time, having special educational needs, is an estimate that can be useful to experts in many countries.

New orientations towards the handicapped

Children with special needs
This expression has come into common usage in recent years as a result of the general realization that handicapped children can best be helped if one looks beyond their primary handicap (usually defined medically in terms of blindness, deafness, orthopaedic handicap, etc.) to their wider educational, social and environmental needs.

For example, the child might be classified as 'spastic left hemiplegia' and this could be a valid description of his medical condition, indicating impaired motor functioning on the left side of the body due to brain damage in the right hemisphere. This is useful knowledge of the physical and neurological basis of his impairment, but may not be the most significant information about the child, from the point of view of his educational and social development. Our 'left hemiplegic' may have other impairments, less obvious, but more important educationally, such as special learning difficulties (see Chapter 2 for examples of these) due to poor visual perception, affecting his skill in reading. Our thoughts about how to help such a child should concentrate less on his physical category, and more on what are his special educational needs, and how can we provide a remedial service to meet these needs.

In the UK, the Warnock Committee of Enquiry, set up by the Department of Education and Science, recommended (HMSO, 1978) that single categories labelling a child as handicapped be abolished and replaced by detailed descriptions of the child's special educational needs. This approach, which has been gaining recognition in the last decade in this country, has much to recommend it, although the system of recording exactly what a particular child's special needs are will need further development to avoid the danger of *vagueness* in recording that might lead to needs of very severely and multiply handicapped children being overlooked.

Unless the records clearly indicate the extent of such a child's special needs, he may find himself grouped in a class with children with far less severe handicaps, and be unable to cope. The older categories tended to lead to over-specialized and separate education for many children. The new proposals emphasize the need to consider a variety of educational and special needs which, though helpful in breaking down the rigid demarcation between the handicapped and the non-handicapped, carry some danger of neglecting the very severely handicapped and their very special needs. The Warnock Committee, for example, suggested replacing the term 'educationally subnormal' with a new descriptive phrase, 'children with special learning difficulties', which could be either mild, moderate or severe. The new phrase needs further elaboration since 'special learning difficulties' could be due to a wide variety of factors: to severe deafness, severe cerebral palsy, severely limited intelligence, or even to a serious lack of schooling. For many purposes these conditions cannot be lumped together and each requires a large measure of specific understanding and treatment based on the following major principles:

1. Handicapped children should be regarded as *children* first, some having special needs. The handicap should not take precedence.
2. A suitable educational programme which will be most suited to the child's particular needs must be established.

3. Children may have several needs which must all be met. The older categories tended to classify children in terms of one single handicap, which could obscure some of his other needs. More children than we realized have 'multiple' handicaps.
4. A child's needs are likely to change over time. Handicap is not necessarily static, and the treatment should be accordingly flexible.

Integration
The logical outcome of blurring the dividing line between 'normal' and 'handicapped' is that, wherever practicable, handicapped children should be educated alongside their able-bodied peers, rather than segregated in special subgroups or institutions.

'Integration' is the goal of parents and professionals who have a real concern for children with physical handicaps. It means the realization of one's ultimate aims for the handicapped (or for any under-privileged group): namely that they be *accepted* as people in their own right, with the same degree of autonomy, position in the community, rights to education, citizenship, career, marriage, parenthood, and so on, as are enjoyed by their able-bodied contemporaries.

In this country, as in many others, there is a history of complete segregation of the handicapped from normal society. In Victorian times, for instance, many people with physical handicaps and quite sound minds spent their entire lives in vast institutions which also housed the mentally subnormal. Such traditions die hard, and there is a tendency for large institutions, even though founded with the best intentions, to resist new ideas and practices.

Nevertheless, even in Victorian times, certain philanthropists, including Dr Barnardo, Lord Shaftesbury and Mary Ward, were concerned about the situation of handicapped children, particularly their lack of education. The normal schools of the day were overcrowded, understaffed, under-equipped and ill-informed to such a degree that they could not possibly cope with physically handicapped children.

The first day school for such children was started in London, on a voluntary basis, by Mary Ward in the 1890s; and other pioneers, including teachers in the state system, such as Jessie Thomas, followed her example in the early 1900s (see Thomas, 1950). From these early beginnings, a large network of special day and residential schools, run both by voluntary societies and the State, has developed in the UK. By 1972 over 200 schools for physically handicapped and delicate children were in existence, able to provide excellent education and therapy even for the most severely handicapped children.

The question arises: are such specialized schools now out-moded, and do they have a segregating effect, tending to work against the new ideas of treating the special needs of handicapped children and integrating them into society as much as possible? The enthusiasts for integration would argue that this is indeed the case. The extreme integrationist would go further and say that prejudice against the handicapped exists largely *because of* segregated schools, and that such schools prevent contact between the handicapped and the normal, so that the latter never have a real opportunity of getting to know a child with a handicap—a situation likely to lead to prejudiced attitudes.

The extreme integrationists' argument *sounds* plausible, and the ideal of integration is unchallengeable: all children are equal morally, spiritually and legally. However, from a functional viewpoint, children with handicaps are *not* equal to normal children (in respect of speech, educational attainments, physical movements, etc.). If they are to be helped to full advantage, they require a modified environment—which, in turn, necessitates *at least a degree* of segregation from normal children, who have other abilities and needs.

In some early attempts at integrating children with handicaps into normal schools, these basic considerations, of what treatment the child needs, and what help the school needs, were ignored. Here is a brief case study:

Jennifer has a right hemiplegia, with some involvement on the left, leading to poor fine hand control, which impairs her writing. Speech moderately indistinct, but mostly intelligible. Occasional petit mal attacks, usually well controlled by drugs. Youngest in a family of four girls, she attended ordinary primary school at age five years.

By age eight, her educational progress was noted to be 'fair' rather than 'good' and she tended to be taught and to mix socially with rather younger children. Her writing was slow and untidy – she was given extra time (in place of P.E.) to 'catch up', whilst at home her parents and siblings were allowed to write her essays and other homework at her dictation. Since her speech was indistinct and she was embarrassed by this, she was rarely asked to read aloud by her teachers.

At age 11 the school reports still noted low average achievements, but she appeared socially well adjusted, and although the parents were becoming anxious about her progress, especially compared to her siblings, they agreed to try her in the local comprehensive school.

By age 12 many difficulties became apparent. Jennifer complained that the frequent changes of classroom and teachers confused her. A few incidents of children 'teasing' her had greatly upset her. The biology mistress noted her enthusiasm for her subject, and her quick and accurate 'oral' responses—and was intrigued by her failures in written work. She completed very few written assignments, although her parents were still allowed to write them out for her homework. When pressed she began to complain of 'feeling faint', her complaints of sickness and fatigue rapidly increased over the months and she showed reluctance to go to school. The school doctor suggested referral to the Spastics Society for advice and the parents agreed.

At age just under 13 years she was seen by the Spastics Society's Assessment Panel in London, and the psychologist reported:

'Jennifer's physical handicaps are fairly mild. Her general intelligence is above average (Terman Merrill I.Q. 115) and she thoroughly enjoyed the oral tests. When presented with a list of words to read, she showed marked anxiety and complained of "feeling faint and sick". After sympathetic encouragement and discussion, she finally agreed to attempt the reading tests—apparently responding to the suggestion that she probably needed help with her reading.'

Her reading age on the Schonell Word List was $7\frac{1}{2}$ years, at age nearly 13. In short, she was practically illiterate, and her deficits had not been detected in the normal system—which had tended to over-protect her, and to make too many concessions to what was considered to be the effects of her physical and speech handicaps.

Her basic problems were related to a 'visual-perceptual' handicap, which had been overlooked, and in view of the late detection of her severe reading difficulties and her urgent need for special help, special schooling was recommended.

This is an example of 'pseudo integration'. A child with handicaps was placed in a 'normal' classroom, where her special needs were largely ignored due to ignorance and over-protection (which led to too many 'concessions'), rather than through rejection or neglect. In spite of the teachers' very sympathetic approach to her physical handicaps, Jennifer was exposed to repeated failures, as she inevitably compared her attainments with those of her peers, and this led to a progressively poor self-image and eventually to attempts to withdraw from normal activities.

Of course, many children with physical handicaps have been successfully integrated into normal schools. The earlier work in this field in Scandinavia (Anderson, 1971) and more recent studies in the UK (Anderson, 1973; Cope and Anderson, 1977) show many examples of this. However, such researchers, together with the Warnock Committee Report (1978), also highlight the fact that in recent years there have been many examples of ill-prepared, half-baked attempts at integration, showing that the authorities concerned failed to appreciate the extent and nature of the problems of integration.

Some of the main considerations are as follows:

1. Have the child's educational, therapeutic and social needs been thoroughly assessed over a reasonable period of time, with particular reference to one of the chief obstacles to integration—communication difficulties (such as the extent to which his handicap affects his speech and writing)? A profile of the child's physical, intellectual and emotional strengths and weaknesses must be carefully constructed.

2. To what extent can the normal school, that may be receiving a handicapped child, be helped to modify its environment to facilitate his adjustment to it? This involves consideration of:
   a. The physical location of the child (should he be placed with his peer group or in a special class within the school?); physical alterations to the building and its furniture (e.g. ramps instead of stairs, special desks and chairs).
   b. The need for special equipment, such as typewriters and other communication aids for children whose writing and speech are poor.
   c. Adequate staffing, not only in respect of the high staff/pupil ratio essential for children with special needs, but in terms of the teacher's understanding of the special help required, for a child with a particular profile of abilities and disabilities, who is likely to benefit by a modified curriculum.
   d. How much specialized help will be needed, and how can the work of the therapists, remedial teachers, psychologists, school doctors, and others be fitted in with that of the class teacher? Unless the work of such specialists is carried out unobtrusively, integration will not be achieved as well as it might.

3. The monitoring of the child's progress must be carefully arranged, in close consultation with the parents, embracing his physical, social and academic adjustment.

4. Work may be required on the attitudes of the able-bodied children and their parents—who may feel that too much attention is being paid to 'special needs' at the expense of their children's ordinary needs. This calls for careful discussion, as well as adequate staffing.

Research studies of the integration of children with physical handicaps in normal schools, such as those of Cope and Anderson

(1977), have shown that, despite the fact that many attempts at integration in the UK have so far been rather poorly planned, in terms of the dimensions listed above, some success has been attained. Cope and Anderson's studies are particularly promising in respect of children quite markedly handicapped, and indicate considerable social and academic progress within units (or special classes) attached to normal schools, the children spending time in both settings. The educational progress, for example, in their group of 87 children in special classes, was virtually equal to that of children attending traditional special schools. It is also important to note that their social relationships with the able-bodied children in normal school were fairly satisfactory, at least within the school setting. (Distances between homes tended to prevent the children meeting out of school hours.)

Nevertheless, there is still a great deal of room for improvement. As the Warnock Committee Report (1978) emphasizes, detailed planning and adequate resources are a pre-requisite for more widespread success in integrating handicapped children in normal schools. And not only would handicapped children benefit, but also normal children would have a better opportunity to develop a realistic, constructive attitude towards children who happen to have a handicap.

Although integration is now feasible for a much larger proportion of children with handicaps than previous generations found possible, it must be recognized that this advance is largely due to the efforts of both voluntary and state agencies, including special schools, over many decades, in building up our knowledge and understanding, and spreading 'know-how' throughout the community.

Special schools, both day and residential, will probably always be needed for a minority of handicapped children, such as those with severe and multiple handicaps, those whose families cannot cope, and those living in remote rural areas where there are not enough children with handicaps to allow the setting up of adequate provision in the normal school. The Warnock Committee underlined another future role for the special schools: that of acting as 'resource centres' to back up the services being offered in ordinary schools. We will say more about the various schooling arrangements in the following Chapters, in terms of the various needs of children with important handicapping conditions.

A dilemma

Inevitably, by trying to meet both the handicapped child's special and normal needs, a dilemma arises. On the one hand we want our handicapped child to be equally accepted and not marked out in any way; on the other hand, we must come to grips with the handicap, and in doing so, we cannot avoid marking him out.

There is no easy way out of this dilemma. Exhortations to 'treat the handicapped child as normal' are no more helpful than clichés like 'he'll be happier in an institution with his own kind'.

This subject will be broached again in greater detail in later Chapters, where all the educationally significant 'organic' handicaps will be discussed in turn.

REFERENCES

Anderson, E. M. (1971) *Making Ordinary Schools Special*. Guidelines for Teachers No. 10. College of Special Education, London.
Anderson, E. M. (1973) *The Disabled School Child, a Study of Integration in Primary Schools*. London: Methuen.
Argyle, M. (1967) *The Psychology of Interpersonal Behaviour*. London: Penguin.
Berger, M. & Yule, W. (1972) *Cross Cultural Survey of Educational and Psychiatric Disorders in School Children*. Final report to Social Sciences Research Council, London.
Boswell, D. M. & Wingrove, J. M. (1974) *The Handicapped Person in the Community*. Milton Keynes: Open University Press.
Cope, C. & Anderson, E. M. (1977) *Special Units in Ordinary Schools: Provision for Disabled Children*. University of London Institute of Education/N.F.E.R.
Davie, R., Butler, N. R. & Goldstein, H. (1972) *From Birth to Seven*. The second report of the National Child Development Study (1958 Cohort). London: Longman.
Harris, A. I., Cox, E. & Smith, C. R. W. (1971) *Handicapped and Impaired in Great Britain*. London: HMSO.
HMSO (1978) *Special Educational Needs: Report of Committee of Enquiry into the Education of Handicapped Children and Young People, headed by H. M. Warnock*. London: HMSO.
Illingworth, R. S. (1979a) *The Normal Child*. Edinburgh: Churchill Livingstone.
Illingworth, R. S. (1979b) *The Development of the Infant and Young Child, Normal and Abnormal*. Edinburgh: Churchill Livingstone.
Rutter, M., Tizard, J. & Whitmore, K. (Eds.) (1972) *Education, Health and Behaviour*. London: Longman.
Seidenfeld, M. A. (1948) The psychological sequelae of poliomyelitis in children. *Nervous Child.*, 7, 14–28.
Thomas, D. (1978) *The Social Psychology of Childhood Disability*. London: Methuen.
Tringo, J. L. (1970) The hierarchy of preference towards disability groups. *Journal of Special Education*, 4 (3), 295–306.
Wright, B. (1960) *Physical Disability—a Psychological Approach*. New York: Harper & Row.

2

The child with physical handicaps

In this section we will discuss physical handicap, referring to those children with overt physical difficulties, affecting their motor performance, and marking them out as visibly different in some way, from ordinary, able-bodied children. The discussion centres principally round two groups of children:

1. Those with limb deformities or absence of limbs, amputees, post-poliomyelitis paralysis, muscular dystrophy, and rarer diseases affecting muscular control.
2. Those with cerebral palsy and spina bifida. Unlike the first group, these conditions may involve, in varying degrees, what may loosely be termed 'damage to the brain'. These conditions are usually present at birth, whilst some of the conditions in our first group, such as polio, can obviously occur at any time in life, and lead to special problems of adjustment to a changed status.

Within these broad groupings of physically disabled children, our main interest here is with those children whose physical handicap is of such severity as to affect their social and educational functioning. Those particularly affected are usually those whose condition also involves some degree of 'brain damage': all children with cerebral palsy and the majority of those with spina bifida fall into this category. These latter two groups are in fact the two largest single ones in the field of physical handicap receiving special educational provision in the UK.

CEREBRAL PALSY

Cerebral palsy (C.P.) is a complex condition. The one thing that all children with cerebral palsy have in common is a difficulty in controlling certain muscles. They differ from other children who lack control of their limbs in that these difficulties are not due to any damage or paralysis to the limbs themselves, as in the case of polio or dislocated hips, but to faulty development in part of the brain that would normally control movements of the body. Apart from this common feature of poor control of limbs, which may vary from a degree that is hardly detectable to an almost complete lack of voluntary motor control, cerebral palsied children have little else in common. Indeed it is difficult to find two C.P. children who are alike, for the impairments in their brain development can take so many different forms, sometimes affecting, in addition to motor control, their intelligence, vision, hearing, speech, and their emotional state. In a few children we find all these capacities affected greatly. In others some capacities are affected greatly and others only slightly. In yet another child we may find none of these areas affected significantly.

One can formally define C.P. as a 'disorder of movement and posture resulting from a permanent non-progressive defect or lesion in the immature brain', but we must be careful not to obscure the fact that people with C.P. differ very widely from one another. Much confusion could be avoided if the *diversity* of C.P. conditions was properly understood: for example when two groups of children with C.P. are being compared in respect of say, rates of progress, we must be sure that the two groups are comparable at the outset: they may all be C.P., but those in one group could be very different to those in the other. Formal definitions and classifications have their uses, particularly for research and administrative purposes, but they tend to concentrate on the *obvious* physical feature of the child's condition, whereas the less obvious features, such as the intellectual and emotional features, may be the most important ones in reaching an understanding of his needs and ways in which he may be helped.

It is this complexity and diversity of cerebral palsy that has contributed to the delay, until recent decades, in setting up proper facilities comparable to those, for example, for the blind and the deaf child, for whom facilities such as special schooling have been in existence for centuries. Although cerebral palsy was described in medical terms as early as 1843 by a certain Dr Little, and Sigmund Freud showed an early interest, writing on C.P. in 1891, the condition was regarded largely as a medical and surgical matter, and its implications for training, therapy, education, social and vocational work, remained unexplored. It was commonly assumed that the condition was associated with severe mental retardation and it was not until the 1930s that more accurate assessments showed that at least half of these children had an intelligence that was more or less within normal limits and that the great majority were capable of benefiting from training, therapy and education.

The incidence of cerebral palsy

It has been estimated that there are around 100 000 persons with cerebral palsy in the UK, of whom about 40 000 are under the age of 15 (based on 1970 data). Estimates of the incidence of C.P. births have varied from 1 to 5·9 per thousand live births in various studies, the difference being due in part to differing techniques of case-finding and differing definitions of cerebral palsy which is not always easily detected at very young ages. The very high figure of 5·9 per thousand emerged from the Schenectady County Study (Levin *et al.*, 1949) which was based on very intensive case-finding techniques, including not only the usual techniques of searching school rolls and clinic lists, etc., but an actual house-to-house survey of 16 per cent of the county. Although thoroughly carried out, the incidence is twice as high as most other large-scale surveys have indicated. The most recent of these is by Rutter *et al.* (1970), and it probably offers the most reliable incidence figures: 2·9 per thousand based on studies of 11 869 children aged 5 to 15 living in the Isle of Wight, including post-natal cases, such as those children who had become cerebral palsied because of encephalitis. Thus, in any large city one would expect to find approximately 290 C.P. children per 100 000 children of school age. As for persons with C.P. over the age of 15, the numbers might be slightly less, due to the higher mortality rates amongst cerebral palsied compared to ordinary people. These mortality rates are over ten times higher, and this probably accounts for the slightly lower incidence of C.P. people aged 15 and over. In Ingram's study (1964), the incidence for the age group 15 to 39 was two per thousand, giving a total of about 37 000 persons in the UK in this age group. Mortality rates amongst older spastics are not yet reliably known, but Crothers and Paine's (1959) study suggests that although these mortality rates are higher than normal, the majority of these occur under the age of 20 and they conclude that the majority of spastics who survive to the age of 20 have a considerable life expectation—perhaps normal in many cases. Until further studies have been completed, a prevalence rate of about 1 per thousand seems a reasonable assumption for C.P.s aged over 40—giving an estimated total of 24 000 in the UK for this age group. These estimates of the size of the problem (in 1970) can be summarized as follows:

Ages	Prevalence rate per thousand	Estimated approximate total
0–14	2·9	39 000
15–39	2·0	37 000
40 plus	1·0	24 000
		100 000

In recent years there have been encouraging signs that the incidence of C.P. in Western countries may be decreasing. Hagberg (1978), for instance, carried out a survey in the Göteborg area of Sweden which indicated that the incidence of C.P. per thousand live births dropped from 2·24 to 1·34 between 1954 and 1970. The reasons for this decline are not clear, and no further decrease has been noted since 1970.

Results of further studies being carried out in other countries are pending. This includes studies begun by the Spastics Society in the UK in 1978 as part if its major 'prevention' campaign.

Improved care of mothers during pregnancy and labour has tended to increase the survival rate of C.P. infants, but there is some evidence (Davies and Tizard, 1975) that, given a high standard of prompt treatment in intensive care units, a large number of new-born babies can survive *and* escape injury.

The incidence of handicap in children could be further reduced by raising the general standard of health education, improving maternity services and increasing the number of intensive care units. The incidence is generally slightly lower in societies with higher standards of prosperity, hygiene and nutrition and where, contrary to the practice in some developing countries, women do not continue to bear large numbers of children well into middle age.

Resources for detailed surveys of the situation in developing countries have so far been lacking, but experts in urban areas of India and Africa believe that the incidence there corresponds roughly to that of the West in the 1960s—i.e. approximately 2·5 per thousand births. Little is known of the incidence in rural areas of these continents. In 1966, however, Margulec carried out an interesting study amongst various cultural groups in Israel, comparing cases from immigrants born in Afro/Asian countries, with Israel-born cases. There were slightly lower rates of C.P. amongst the Afro/Asian groups, but this might be explained by extra difficulties in case-finding and by higher mortality rates amongst the poorer Afro/Asian immigrants rather than any major differences in the actual incidence. No study so far has shown significant differences in the rates of C.P. amongst different ethnic or social class groupings.

The causes of cerebral palsy

Although a great deal is known about the causes of C.P. in general, the causes in any one particular case are often difficult to determine because so many environmental and genetic factors may be implicated. Environmental factors are normally of greater importance, the term 'environment' being used in a wider sense than usual to embrace the baby's pre- as well as post-natal environment.

There is rarely, if ever, a single cause of C.P.; rather, it is caused by a combination of contributory conditions. It is known that certain cells and connections in the baby's brain are impaired in some way either before, during or after birth. One of the commonest causes of such impairment is lack of oxygen (anoxia) to the baby's brain, for even a short period of time. This, then, begs the question of what causes the lack of oxygen. There are many possible factors: premature, prolonged or unduly difficult births can be associated with anoxia. About a third of C.P. children are born prematurely and have a low birth weight, and the incidence of an abnormal labour history is four times as common as in the normal population. Fortunately, the majority of premature babies and those who had a difficult birth turn out to be quite normal; however, there are always a few who suffer injury.

We do not know why some premature babies are cerebral palsied whilst the majority are not, but recent evidence (Neligan et al., 1976) suggests that being born prematurely and given intensive medical and nursing care is not as dangerous as being born 'small for dates' and underweight.

Forceps delivery is four times more common than amongst the normal population. This is not to suggest that forceps necessarily cause any injuries: their use is merely an aftermath of other difficulties that precluded a normal birth. In view of the frequency of difficult births amongst first-born children, it used to be assumed that more cases of C.P. occurred in the first-born. Subsequent research has not confirmed this, e.g. in Hopkins' (1954) study of 654 birth histories of C.P. children, no particular birth order showed a higher correlation with C.P. Twins, however, are more common amongst C.P. children: around 5 to 10 per cent in several surveys, including Henderson's (1961) study of 240 cases, and there is a slight tendency amongst twins for the first-born to be more often affected than the second-born twin.

Excessive jaundice after birth, such as that due to blood group incompatibility, occasionally causes athetosis, but in recent years great strides have been made in preventing this type of brain damage by means of prompt blood transfusions very soon after birth. Maternal rubella during the first two or three months of pregnancy is another causative factor in brain damage, which has become increasingly rare as more and more girls are immunized against rubella. However, a recent outbreak of maternal rubella in the UK showed that such preventive measures can only be successful if prolonged efforts are made to educate the public about their importance and to ensure that *all* girls are immunized. Although the great majority of cases of cerebral palsy are caused by factors which are operating during pregnancy or at the time of birth, about 10 per cent become affected during the early years of life, due, for example, to severe infections, such as meningitis or encephalitis, or obvious damage to the brain.

Hereditary causes are rare, and only in a small percentage of families do we find more than one child affected, or any marked history of relatives being affected. Extremely young or old mothers are slightly more 'at risk' than others. All social classes are equally at risk as far as C.P. is concerned. Males are more common than females (61 per cent of Ingram's sample were males).

Some of the important causes of and conditions associated with C.P. are summarized in Table 3.

Table 3 Summary of some causes of C.P.

Hereditary	Probably not important in C.P.: abnormalities in chromosomes, resulting in C.P., are extremely rare: however, there may be a few inherited 'predisposing' factors (such as a biochemical abnormality harmless in itself but becoming important if other difficulties occur during pregnancy, affecting the blood supply to the fetus).
Pre-natal	Infections, e.g. maternal rubella; diabetes; poisons such as lead; excessive exposure to X-rays; extreme malnutrition. Poor general care of mothers during pregnancy and lack of medical advice may lead to complications—more commonly in lower than higher socio-economic groups.
At birth	Difficult prolonged delivery leading to birth trauma. Prematurity and 'small for dates'. Anoxia, such as due to disturbances of the placenta.
Immediately after birth	Infections. Jaundice.
After birth	e.g. infection affecting brain development such as meningitis, accidents involving serious head injuries.

It must be emphasized that none of the factors listed in Table 3, taken singly, is certain to cause C.P.—indeed the majority of babies survive them. However, research to date indicates that most cases of C.P. are probably the result of several such factors, operating together at a crucial period. A great deal of further research is necessary to pin-point the causes more accurately, so that our preventive measures can be effective.

Prevention

It has been estimated that if all the current knowledge about dealing with the causes of C.P., during pregnancy and birth, were put into practice, at least 40 per cent of cases could be prevented in future. As we have mentioned, a decline in the incidence has already been demonstrated in Sweden, and although all the reasons for the decline are not yet understood, there are several measures that undoubtedly play their part.

1. Health education for girls and young mothers-to-be, emphasizing the dangers of excessive use of drugs, excessive smoking and alcohol consumption, the need for proper rest and exercise.
2. Regular routine medical check-ups especially during pregnancy, with prompt referral to a more specialized unit if any complications are noted.
3. Specialized units must be adequately equipped to monitor the condition of both mother and fetus, particularly in 'at risk' cases. Modern techniques permit accurate checks to be carried out on the condition of the placenta, heart rates, temperature and fetal growth. In addition, with the ultrasonic scanner, the size and position of the fetus and the placenta can now be accurately monitored with no harmful effects to either mother or baby; and samples of the fluid surrounding the fetus can be obtained (by a technique known as amniocentesis) by which conditions such as spina bifida and Down's syndrome can be detected. Unfortunately no such technique has yet been developed for the detection of C.P.
4. Highly qualified staff and specialized equipment for monitoring the fetal condition are necessary, as are intensive baby care units for very premature and 'small for dates' babies or those who may need some emergency treatment such as an exchange transfusion. Since most small maternity units are unlikely to be able to afford such an array of sophisticated equipment or the staff needed to use it, some concentration of the services into high-powered units, on a regional basis, will be necessary,

together with efficient transport and other facilities, for transferring mothers 'at risk' to such units very promptly. Although such units are expensive they will actually save money in the long run, since reduced numbers of handicapped children reduces the costs of the long-term treatment and care that would otherwise have been necessary.

The large-scale monitoring of mothers and babies during pregnancy may seem a far cry from 'natural childbirth' and perhaps tends to increase anxiety and 'medicalize' what for the vast majority of mothers should be a perfectly natural occurrence. However, these anxieties are a small price to pay for the reduction of the incidence of handicap; and if the monitoring is carried out with due regard to the mother's anxieties, and becomes a more or less standard routine in future, such anxieties will lessen.

Over the next decade or so the number of children born handicapped could, by these methods, be halved—an exciting and encouraging prospect (see Wynn and Wynn (1977) for an excellent review of recent progress in prevention work in Europe). Nevertheless, the effect on the community would not be instantaneous: it was estimated, for instance, that there were 100 000 people with C.P. in 1970 in the UK; but even if the incidence of new cases at birth had halved immediately, it would still take 30 years in all to reduce the total number to 50 000.

The scope for prevention in many Third World countries in terms of elementary care of pregnant mothers, nutrition, hygiene and control of infection rather than sophisticated equipment at this stage still represents a tremendous challenge.

Types of cerebral palsy

There are four main types of cerebral palsy:

1. Spastic. This is the largest group; about 75 per cent of C.P. children show spasticity, that is marked rigidity of movement and an inability to relax their muscles, due to damage to the cortex (see Fig. 1) affecting the motor centres. The extent of the handicap varies. In monoplegia, only one arm or leg is affected; in hemiplegia one side only is affected, the right arm and leg or the left arm and leg; in paraplegia the legs only are affected; while in quadriplegia (sometimes called diplegia when the legs are more affected than the arms) all four limbs are spastic.

2. Athetoid. In this condition the child shows frequent involuntary movements which mask and interfere with the normal movements of the body. Writhing movements of the limbs, the face and the tongue, grimacing, dribbling, and slurred speech commonly occur. Hearing defects are fairly common (over 40 per cent) in this group, which interfere with the development of language. Damage to the basal ganglia of the brain appears to be the cause of this condition. Less than 10 per cent of C.P. children show athetosis (which is sometimes referred to as 'dyskinesia').

3. *Ataxic.* In this condition the child shows poor body balance, an unsteady gait, and difficulties in hand and eye co-ordination and control. Injury to the cerebellum is the cause of this type of cerebral palsy, and it is comparatively rare.

4. *Mixed and others.* Nearly 10 per cent show mixed types of C.P. and a small percentage show special kinds of muscular tension, such as dystonia, hypertonia, hypotonia, rigidity and tremor.

Figure 1 shows a very simplified diagram of the three main sections of the brain. For more detailed studies see Bleck and Nagel (1976).

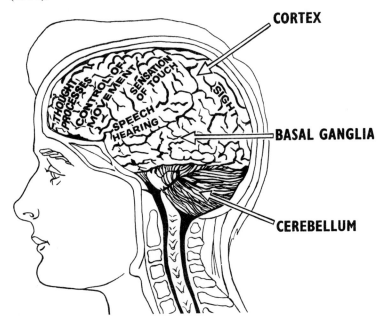

Fig. 1 Simplified diagram of the brain.

The type of cerebral palsy that a child has tells us little about how handicapped he actually is. It is important, therefore, to know, in addition to the type and the number of limbs affected, the *degree* to which his motor control is impaired. The degree of handicap can be classified as mild, moderate or severe.

Mild handicap. This term is used of children who can walk and talk and whose physical movements are just a little clumsy.

Moderate handicap. This refers to children whose speech is indistinct, who have some difficulty in controlling their hands and who can walk only unsteadily.

Severe handicap. The independence of severely handicapped children is very limited since they have little control of arms, hands and legs. The muscles controlling speech are also likely to be affected.

Most studies of large representative groups of C.P.s have indicated that almost one-third of C.P.s are mildly, one-third moderately, and one-third severely handicapped—the variations between different studies being due to differing methods of rating the degree of handicap. Objective measures of degrees of physical functioning are available (Holt, 1965; Holt and Reynell, 1967; Lindon, 1963) and these are very useful for recording progress over time. Having classified a child in respect of the type of cerebral palsy, the number of limbs involved and the degree of physical handicap, we have made a beginning, but only a beginning, in understanding his condition and working out the best ways of helping him. As we have mentioned, the majority of cerebral palsied children have other handicaps in addition to their motor difficulties.

Additional handicaps
It is often found that the brain damage has affected not only the development of movement, but also, in varying degrees, the development of intelligence, vision, hearing, speech and other factors important to the child's progress.

It is imperative that parents, teachers and therapists be aware of these factors, since in some cases they affect the behaviour of the child. The major additional handicaps associated with C.P. are as follows:

Epilepsy
Epilepsy has been found to occur in 25 to 35 per cent of cerebral palsied children. Woods (1956) reports 38 per cent out of 301 cases, and Henderson (1961) found 25 per cent in 240 cases and regarded this as an under-estimation. In a survey of 104 children at the Cheyne Centre, London, one of the authors (A.H.B.) found an incidence of 36·5 per cent. The definition of epilepsy mostly used in these researches was the occurrence of more than one fit after the first two weeks of life—and in fact the majority

of spastics have very few fits. Less than 10 per cent of Henderson's sample of 240 C.P. children and adolescents were having regular fits (more than one per month). Approximately 15 per cent of the sample were on anticonvulsant drugs, which are very efficient in controlling fits. Oversedation can of course lead to drowsiness. In a few children it is difficult to strike the balance between eliminating the risk of fits on the one hand, and maintaining the child's normal state of alertness on the other. Epilepsy is more common among quadriplegics and hemiplegics than other types of cerebral palsy and in Rutter's (1970) study it was noted that amongst children excluded from school on account of severe physical and intellectual handicaps, epilepsy was found in as many as 70 per cent, compared to 28 per cent amongst the children with C.P. who were attending school. In severe cases, epilepsy interferes seriously with learning and frequent fits may result in some intellectual dysfunctioning, but this may be only temporary, and such cases are very rare. See Chapter 3 for further information on epilepsy.

Visual defects
A high proportion of cerebral palsied children suffer from *visual defects*; poor visual acuity, nystagmus, restricted field of vision, strabismus, refractive errors, and other oculo-motor defects. The educational implications of these are not always fully understood. Asher and Schonell (1950) noted 25 per cent in their series of 400 children, especially among the quadriplegics. Douglas, in 1961, reported squint in 37 per cent of 160 C.P. persons under 20 years of age. In the Cheyne Clinic survey of 104 cases, 35 per cent showed ocular defects. Many of these defects are comparatively minor and many can be successfully treated in early childhood.

Hearing losses
A partial degree of *hearing loss* is frequently found in these children, more especially with athetoids where the loss is often one of high-tone deafness. Fisch's (1957) detailed study of 427 cases found 25 per cent, and in 16 per cent the defect was serious. A figure of approximately 15 per cent is probably the most reliable estimate of the number of C.P.s having an educationally significant hearing loss requiring the use of a hearing aid, and the regular help of a visiting teacher of the partially hearing, and in some cases, the facilities of a partially hearing unit. Without such help their language development would be seriously impaired.

Speech defects

Speech defects occur if the control of the facial and respiratory muscles, the tongue or lips is poor. These defects range from very minor articulation defects to a complete absence of speech. Approximately 50 per cent of Henderson's (1961) sample had some degree of speech defect, and almost 20 per cent had no intelligible speech—the majority of the latter being also of impaired intelligence and their lack of speech being due to a combination of factors. Feeding is difficult in many such children but early physiotherapy and speech therapy may do a great deal to improve the situation.

Intellectual impairment

There have been a number of surveys showing the *distribution of intelligence* among cerebral palsied children. It has been found that, usually, children with the greatest physical handicap have the poorest intelligence, which in view of the extent of the brain damage is understandable. Usually children with spastic quadriplegia are less intelligent as a group than the hemiplegic group, although of course there are startling individual exceptions to this general group finding. Some severely motor handicapped children have an extremely high intelligence and some mildly motor handicapped children have very limited intelligence, or many specific

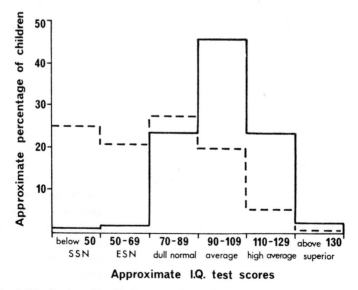

Fig. 2 Distribution of intelligence test scores comparing cerebral palsied and normal children.

learning difficulties. It is unwise to infer mental status from the degree of motor disability. The difference between the athetoid and the spastic group is negligible. Most surveys report a figure of between 40 and 50 per cent of cerebral palsied children to be of subnormal intelligence (approximately 25 per cent severely subnormal, I.Q.s 0 to 49, approximately 21 per cent E.S.N.(M), I.Q.s 50 to 69).

As for those with higher intelligence, approximately 47 per cent score within normal limits (dull, average and high average), leaving about 6 per cent in the upper intellectual ranges, most of whom can and do pursue academic education, sometimes with considerable success in spite of severe physical handicaps. The distribution of intelligence test scores is summarized in Figure 2 (p. 33), based on many studies in recent years, comparing C.P. with ordinary children's scores.

The fact that the range of intellectual functioning is found to be so wide amongst these children, with nearly 50 per cent showing some degree of subnormality compared to about 3 per cent amongst children in general, raises some interesting questions about the extent to which the subnormality is due to:

1. The early damage to the child's brain.
2. The cumulative effects of the limitations in the child's opportunities for learning.
3. Bias in psychological testing, owing to the fact that many of the tests in use are designed for ordinary children and sometimes demand more hand control, visual skills, and speech than the handicapped child can easily produce in the test situation.

Whilst the first factor, that of actual damage to the higher neural structures, no doubt accounts for some of the subnormality, we are learning a great deal about the long-term effects of limited experience and opportunities for learning.

Special learning difficulties
Some children with cerebral palsy have no difficulty in keeping up with ordinary children in the long process of learning to become mature, independent and responsible adults. Indeed their handicap may spur them on to greater learning than they might otherwise have achieved. Many children, however, do learn slowly. Amongst the obvious reasons for this are the effects of their physical and sensory and speech impairments which limit the degree to which the child can explore his surroundings and gain understanding of his world. The effects of limited experience, if allowed

to continue over many years, can be profound and the task of parents and teachers and therapists is the urgent one, as far as the very handicapped young child is concerned, of providing maximum stimulation at the right level, of bringing stimulation to the child in situations where he cannot reach out for it, as early as possible.

Other limitations are gradually becoming clearer. A considerable number of children whose physical and sensory handicaps are really quite mild have special learning difficulties which are quite distinct from general intellectual retardation.

Visual perceptual and visual motor disorders
Disorders in *visual perception* are exemplified by difficulties such as in matching shapes, distinguishing shapes which appear alike, distinguishing the outline of a drawing from its surrounding background, in recognizing the different directions of certain shapes such as the letters 'b' and 'd'. Other children appear to perceive shapes satisfactorily for their age, but have enormous difficulties in constructing patterns out of bricks, completing jigsaws, and writing and drawing. These are known as *visual motor disorders*, and appear to be more common amongst spastics than athetoids. Excellent surveys of visual perceptual and visual motor disorders are to be found in Abercrombie (1964) and Wedell (1973).

The fact that these disorders can be seen in some children whose hand control and vision are quite near to normal, and whose verbal and social reasoning may be at a very high level, suggests that these are special learning difficulties, possibly due to unevenness in the development of certain parts of the brain and the higher central nervous system.

Distractibility
Another kind of special learning difficulty encountered in some children is that of *distractibility*, which causes children to have great difficulty in controlling or focusing their attention. For example, they are easily distracted by slight sounds or movements in a classroom that ordinary children would have little or no difficulty in ignoring, and this results in a short span of attention which frequently interferes with their learning at school so that their attainments are eventually very patchy. Distractibility does not only occur in cerebral palsied children. Indeed it is often seen in children without external signs of physical handicap, such as those who have suffered from meningitis and whose general behaviour is overactive and restless. Psychologists and educationalists, whose

work in the field of special learning difficulties has been extensive in the past decade, include Marianne Frostig (1973), Cruickshank (1966, 1973) and Kephart (1971) in the United States, Tansley (1967) in the United Kingdom, and Brereton (1975) in Australia, who are concerned not only to produce more accurate techniques for measuring such features as visual perceptual disorders and distractibility, but to devise training techniques that may help to overcome some of the difficulties. Scientific studies of the long-term results of such training programmes are not very encouraging and this is partly because of the tremendous complexity of these learning difficulties. These points are discussed in more detail in Chapter 3.

Multiple learning difficulties

A child rarely has only one kind of difficulty, such as in confusing left and right directions or in co-ordinating his motor and his visual responses. He is more likely to have a *combination* of several of the difficulties we have mentioned, which may be quite mild when looked at singly but which *multiply* into a formidable learning handicap when combined in one child and affect him right from birth. Effective learning depends on the gradual building up of the ability to combine various motor and sensory and perceptual impressions. For example a baby of 12 months exploring a box of bricks is engaging in a wide variety of learning experiences. He is learning that bricks have shape, colour, texture, that they can move in various directions, can be put together to make a shape, and will fall if pushed from an upright position but not if they are already lying flat. Bricks can disappear into a box and be made to reappear again. Large bricks will not go into a small box, and so on.

To a baby these are new discoveries. To pursue them he must be able to combine what he sees and feels and hears and what he perceives and remembers. His later learning, for example of reading and writing, depends on much the same processes at a more advanced level, and without these earlier experiences he will run into difficulties. Piaget's work describes the development of these skills as a continuous interaction between the child, his past experience and his immediate situation. All children, according to Piaget's theory (1956), pass through four stages of learning ability, from the early sensory motor phase to the mature adolescent phase of abstract formal and logical thought, the child 'graduating' through these four stages in sequence, the later stages being dependent on the successful mastery of the earlier ones. It is therefore not surprising that many spastic children do run into diffi-culties which become very apparent when they reach school.

All children, perhaps with the exception of some who are ex-tremely subnormal or autistic, have a strong drive to explore their environment. What happens to this in-built curiosity, these ex-ploratory drives, depends on what kind of environment surrounds the baby, such as whether opportunities for movement, manipula-tion and mastery of objects are available, and in the case of the handicapped, what actual help can be given with the physical diffi-culties that impede expression of his exploratory drives. This is one of the major tasks of parents, teachers and therapists in provid-ing for the handicapped child. They must continually modify the environment so that it suits the child's handicaps—which will change over time.

Lastly we must mention the *emotional barriers* to learning. Children who show the special learning difficulties we have de-scribed are sometimes quick to realize that their efforts do not match up to what their parents expect or to what other children accomplish, hence their self-confidence and morale are likely to suffer; they become over-anxious about failure, and give up so quickly that their learning advances only at a very slow pace.

It is therefore important to detect these learning difficulties as early as possible so that we can avoid aggravating the child by pressing him too much with tasks that he finds very difficult, and taking steps to introduce very gradual training, much of which can be carried out by parents at home, with the help of occu-pational therapists and teachers.

Psychological assessment
The purpose of psychological assessment is to measure how far the handicapped child has reached in his learning, so that advice can be given about the type of training most likely to be helpful during the next few years. We have described the very wide range of different levels of intelligence and different kinds of special learning difficulties that are found amongst cerebral palsied child-ren. How does the psychologist measure these? Let us first con-sider the *measurement of general intelligence.*

For the majority of C.P. children, the standard individual psychological tests are of considerable value, such as the Stanford-Binet, Wechsler and Merrill-Palmer Scales. In the Stanford-Binet Scale, the child is presented with a wide variety of problems to do with the meaning of words, sentences and pictures, the matching of shapes, copying of shapes, remembering a series of numbers, and patterns on a card, etc. The Merrill-Palmer, consisting primarily of practical rather than verbal problems, is of special interest to children under five. The method by which the child solves the practical problem is often a valuable indication of his intellectual functioning. As with all psychological tests, the child is given standard instructions about the problems and his responses are scored in accordance with given standards. The standard procedures allow us to compare the performance of a particular child with that of a large group of typical children of his age, on whom the test was originally constructed. Can such tests, based on the responses of ordinary children, be considered fair for handicapped children? We have mentioned the many ways in which handicapped children are deprived of ordinary experience and in any case they are sometimes unable to express their thoughts, because of limited speech and hand control. In a sense then, ordinary intelligence tests are unfair, but in the hands of an experienced psychologist, accustomed to communicating with very handicapped children and able to interpret the results carefully in the light of the child's background, the results are of considerable value in exploring a child's special educational and training needs—whether these should be met, at least in the short term, at a level that is more or less normal for his age, or at a slow-learning (ESN) level. This helps parents, teachers and therapists to match the educational and training programmes to a level appropriate to the child, having regard to the stage he has reached in his intellectual development.

For example, a six-year-old who scores on the tests at about a $3\frac{1}{2}$-year level and falls within the slow learning educationally subnormal group will need to continue with play material that will help him to build up his basic ideas of size and shape, with simple jigsaws, nests of cubes, and brick building, rather than attempt more complex and abstract material, such as letters and numbers, that the average six-year-old can manage.

The results of general tests of intelligence, provided the child's handicaps are not severe, are also of use in helping to decide what kind of school or special unit will be most helpful for the next stage in his learning.

A more recent test, the new British Abilities Scales (Elliott et al., 1978), has been developed to give not only an assessment of general learning ability, but a more detailed *profile*, indicating particular strengths and weaknesses a child may have in a comprehensive battery, made up of 24 scales. This kind of 'learning profile' is important in generating new ideas about the teaching strategies that a particular child is likely to need. Although devised for physically able children, aged $2\frac{1}{2}$ to 17 years, some of the scales are applicable to physically handicapped children, and their usefulness is being explored.

Most psychologists would agree that there is nothing sacrosanct about general test results and their interpretation of them, especially with young handicapped children, and there are dangers, as we have discussed in Chapter 1, in attempting to classify and label children. On the whole, the intellectual ratings of children remain fairly constant over the years, e.g. in Nielsen's (1966) review about 70 per cent of the children's scores remained more or less constant when they were retested. In Gardner's (1970) study, about 80 per cent of 203 C.P. children studied over a five-year period remained in roughly the same intellectual level of schooling. A small percentage changed, such as from an E.S.N.(S) to E.S.N.(M) level, some unaccountably, some because of being essentially borderline in the first place, and some because of therapeutic and educational help, and increased emotional maturity due to improved family circumstances. In a few cases the changes were artificial, due to errors in assessment procedures. This emphasizes the need for frequent reassessment and a flexible approach to training, education and therapy, starting early in the child's life.

Special tests for the severely handicapped

So far, we have mentioned tests of general intelligence of the type constructed originally for ordinary children. These are useful to the majority of cerebral palsied children, but clearly inappropriate to the severely handicapped, such as those who have no speech, no useful hand control, and whose posture and head control may be so poor as to need constant support. In such cases it is impossible to assess general intelligence with any great accuracy, not only on account of the child's enormous difficulties in communication, but because one cannot be sure of the extent to which his sheer lack of experience in so many spheres of life has held up the development of his intelligence. What we can do is to try to establish a base line—an estimate of the minimum level of learning ability, usually expressed as a 'mental age' below which the child is unlikely to fall—above which he may rise, given plenty of experience of the right kind to make up for what he has missed.

To assess this base line for the very handicapped child, the psychologist uses tests of a 'multiple choice' type (Fig. 3), to which a simple sign for 'yes' or 'no' can be given by the child. For

Fig. 3 Example of multiple-choice test card.

example, the Columbia Scale of Mental Maturity (Burgemeister, 1972) has several pictures on a large card, one of which differs from the others by virtue of its colour, shape, size, class of objects, etc. The psychologist points to each picture in turn and the child has to give any kind of sign when the correct picture is being pointed to. The sign can consist of any kind of response, a murmur, a lifting of the head, or even a generalized body movement. The test contains 92 large cards, covering an age range of approximately 3 to 10 years. There are not enough items at each age to make it a very accurate test so it usually forms part of a larger battery.

Another test which can be administered in a similar way is the Raven's Progressive Matrices Scale, from age six onwards, although a poor performance may indicate visual perceptual disorders rather than low general intelligence, so again one has to rely on a battery of tests and never on a single one.

A test which is less dependent on visual perceptual skills is the English Picture Vocabulary Test (Brimer and Dunn, 1973) in which the child has to indicate which of four pictures on each card corresponds to the word given by the psychologist, e.g. 'Which is table?', 'Which is horse?' at age two, graduating to quite complex pictures and words, such as ones depicting 'astonishment', 'communication', for older children up to age 18. The test can be administered to children who lack speech and hand control but, of course, it demands adequate hearing.

A more comprehensive scale of language development on both the receptive and expressive sides of language has been produced by Joan Reynell (1977) for ages six months to six years. It uses familiar, everyday objects and toys which are usually of greater interest to children than pictures, and has the great merit of not only measuring a child's expressive speech, from his early vocalizations to quite complicated sentences, but his *inner* language—his understanding of speech—and these measurements are particularly important in our assessments of children who have no speech or are too shy to use it. Since the tests have been specially developed for handicapped as well as for ordinary children, their administration has been arranged so that children can show their understanding of language by means of whatever minimal motor responses they can make, such as by simple pointing to objects in response to instructions, or by 'eye glance' if they cannot use their hands. The toys are large and well-spaced enough to allow such responses, in such a way that the examiner can, in nearly all cases, determine exactly what the child means. For the partially hearing, the Columbia and Raven's Scales are useful, and the Nebraska Scale has been specially designed with the deaf children in mind but demands rather too much hand control for many cerebral palsied children.

For the partially sighted, the Williams Scale for Blind and Partially Sighted Children is of considerable value, provided the child's speech and hearing are adequate.

The assessment of specific abilities and disabilities

So far, we have dealt with tests of *general* learning abilities, of the verbal and non-verbal types. There are also tests of *specific* abilities and disabilities which analyse in great detail a child's particular strengths and weaknesses. Often in the process of testing general intelligence, such as on the Stanford-Binet or Wechsler Verbal and Performance Scales, the psychologist notes an unevenness in the child's test scores that suggests special learning difficulties. We have mentioned the special learning difficulties in respect of the visual perceptual and visual motor areas; a large discrepancy between a child's verbal and performance scores of over 20 points on the Wechsler Scale may suggest these. Special tests such as the Marianne Frostig (1964) Developmental Test of Visual Perception can be used to throw some light on the difficulty. Here is an example of one of the Frostig subtests (spatial relationships). In Figure 4 the child simply has to join the dots on the right, to match the given pattern on the left. The boy (aged nine, mild spastic diplegia, Wechsler Verbal I.Q. 125, Performance I.Q. 70) has little idea of how to plan and execute the movements required— although his fine hand control itself is almost unimpaired. If, on the other hand, the child's verbal scores are markedly below his scores on visual perceptual tests, a more detailed analysis of his understanding and expression of language, his abilities to communicate without words, and other aspects of communication can be explored by the Illinois Test of Psycholinguistic Abilities (Kirk

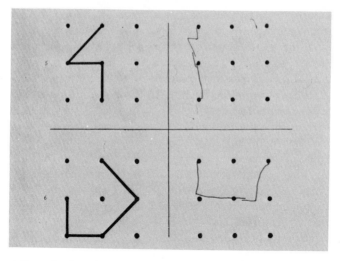

Fig. 4 Example of specific learning difficulties indicated on part of the Frostig Scale.

and McCarthy, 1961). Both these tests can be used for children aged approximately 3 to 10 years. They are still in experimental form, the reliability of the various subtests being low, but they have served a very useful purpose in promoting remedial education and therapy.

A test particularly devised for use by teachers is the Aston Index (Newton, 1977), giving a profile of specific abilities and disabilities, such as in sequencing, immediate memory, sound blending, etc., that are likely to be relevant to reading and writing difficulties. A useful general guide to tests of abilities and attainments is to be found in Jackson (1972).

Social and behavioural development

Psychologists have also constructed measures of the social and behavioural development of handicapped children, and this aspect is just as important as the child's intellectual and educational development. Rating scales such as the Vineland (Doll, 1947) and Gunzburg's Progress Assessment Charts (1966) give useful pictures of the C.P. child's daily living skills, such as his capacities for self-help, play, and social activities. For very handicapped and retarded children, a more detailed scale, the Behaviour Assessment Battery, has been developed by Kiernan and Jones (1977). This covers all important areas of development—motor, perceptual, social, self-help, communication, etc., in meticulous detail, not with a view to simply arriving at a general estimate of the profoundly handicapped child's learning abilities compared to other children, but to assess precisely what a child can and cannot manage, in respect to particular tasks—leading on to the setting up of teaching and training goals for the particular child. Finally, we must mention the development of rating scales for use by parents, such as those devised at the Hester Adrian Research Unit in Manchester (Jeffree and McConkey, 1976) as part of a wider programme of parent involvement in the teaching of their handicapped child.

The ideal tests and rating scales are not those that merely measure abilities and disabilities but those which point to some areas in which extra help should be given to the child, setting reasonable short-term targets for the child and the adults concerned with him, and providing a series of accurate measurements of progress over the years. Parents have a vital role to play in this area.

The need for continuous and comprehensive assessment

In assessing the learning abilities amongst C.P. children, with their wide range of assets, handicaps, backgrounds and experience, the psychologist can never rely on a single test and he must have at his command a wide range of tests, some of which we have mentioned, and must be constantly on the alert in discovering the reasons why a child has failed a particular test item. He must constantly ask whether the failure was due to poor vision or poor hand control, attention or visual perceptual difficulties—or did the child perceive the problem correctly but fail to express the answer correctly? Has fatigue set in or has the child become negative or uncommunicative? It is essential to consider all such questions before forming an opinion about whether or not the child's intelligence is seriously impaired. We cannot rely on assumptions such as that heavily handicapped children are likely to have seriously impaired intelligence (on the whole they have, but there are exceptions) or that lightly handicapped children necessarily have only minor learning difficulties (some lightly handicapped children, with high aspirations, develop major emotional problems which affect their learning) or that athetoids are more intelligent than spastics (the difference is very slight). The complexities of cerebral palsy are too great for any simple assumptions and reliable assessments are best based on repeated observations over long periods. The ideal setting for assessments is one in which the response of a child to various types of training and teaching can be closely observed over many months, as was pioneered in the UK at such centres as the Cheyne Centre (Bowley, 1967; Blencowe, 1969) and at the Spastics Society's long-term Assessment Centre at Hawksworth Hall (Gardner and Johnson, 1964).

Since the incidence of cerebral palsy is not high enough to warrant long-term day-assessment units in areas other than large cities, there is an advantage in establishing assessment units that can provide for many types of handicapped children. Child development centres are available in certain health authority regions in the UK, providing the comprehensive, long-term, multi-disciplinary approach that is essential for young handicapped children and their families. For older children (say, over age five), unless their medical needs are very complex, a school rather than a hospital setting is usually preferable, and in the UK most local authorities are now providing assessment classes, sometimes attached to normal schools, sometimes to special schools. The Department of Education and Science (1970) surveyed 33 of these in 1967 and 1968. The standard of assessment work in some units was reported to be low, chiefly because of lack of expert staff, such as visiting psychologists, doctors and social workers. Nevertheless, the establishment of proper multi-disciplinary services within an educational setting where long-term observations and experimental trials of various educational methods can be carried out should be strongly encouraged. Every area should have community-based assessment classes where parent co-operation with teachers, therapists and social workers can be furthered. Parents should insist on their child's assessment being followed up with practical guidance, treatment and good early educational opportunities.

The UK Warnock Report (1978) emphasized the importance of early detection and assessment of handicap, and recommended several stages in this process, starting with health visitors, who are in a unique position to spot that there may be something wrong with a particular child's development. At a later stage, teachers will refer to educational advisers and psychologists if necessary, who will in turn refer to multi-disciplinary assessment teams, including doctors and social workers, if the child and family's problems appear serious. At all stages the parents must be brought into partnership with the professionals and this means that the great majority of their reports must be made available to parents.

The problems of parents

The parents of very handicapped children have very real practical and psychological problems in the upbringing and care of their children. The arrival of such a child is usually a shock, and many find it very difficult indeed to accept the facts, and to plan care and training constructively. Often they feel in some measure to blame, and feelings of guilt are very natural and fairly common in such cases, though usually quite unfounded. It seems something of a slur on the family name, a stigma and an embarrassment to all concerned. Sometimes, though this is rare, the parents find it hard to love their disabled child fully and feel resentful and hostile towards the world and everyone who tries to help. But usually a very close tie grows up between the mother and child. In a few parents, this tie becomes so extremely close that they refuse to consider outside help, even in cases where the child's physical and intellectual handicaps are so severe as to dominate the entire family's life. Obviously the mother is emotionally involved to an extreme degree, and to fail to recognize this is to court disaster. Once a mother has accepted the cruel fact that her child is severely and permanently handicapped, a second stage of adjustment has to follow, that of coming to terms with the long-term implications, in respect of family life, feeding, playing, social activities, education, health, job prospects and marriage; in short all aspects of the life of the whole family for many decades. The very phrases 'acceptance of' and 'coming to terms with' severe handicap only superficially describe the tremendously complex and subtle adjustments that parents of a very handicapped child are expected to make. The balance of all these, with pessimism and hopelessness on the one hand, and over-optimism and denial of reality on the other, must be very difficult to maintain, and professional workers are sometimes presumptuous in the advice that they give parents. For example, glib advice to 'treat him as normal' is clearly out of the question in the case of a very handicapped child. The reality of handicap is that there are some things the child cannot and never will do, for example walking or writing. This is not to deny that there are many things he *can* do: and that there are many substitutes and alternative skills that he can develop, given expert help, that will make a great difference to his life, such as using a wheelchair, or typing efficiently. Some parents need almost as much help as the child, to come to terms with the facts, to accept the limitations imposed by the handicap realistically, and at the same time to appreciate the amount of ability and independence that the child can achieve. Long-term support from a social worker can be very valuable to such families: intensive case-work is necessary when the parents strongly deny reality.

The effects of handicap on the family

Some studies of the impact of handicap on family life have helped
to throw light on some of these problems. Sheila Hewett's (1970)
study was based on a representative sample of 180 families in the
Midlands which had a C.P. member. Although on the whole many
of the families were coping well (better than many professional
workers might have expected, the point being that the latter's experience is usually confined to those families who cannot cope),
some were showing extreme tension. This tension was exacerbated
by factors such as a lack of information about cerebral palsy (40
per cent did not know their child was spastic till past the age of
two, and 17 per cent had never been told), difficulties in obtaining
suitable equipment and gadgets, particularly wheelchairs, poor
assessment and nursery facilities (62 per cent of the under fives
had no nursery day-care of any kind), lack of schooling or training
for the retarded child (37 per cent of the over fives had no education or day-care of any kind provided by the local authority), extra
financial burdens and a lack of any single agency to whom parents
felt they could easily turn when they needed advice. This last
point was also emphasized in the National Children's Bureau's
study *Living with Handicap* (Younghusband *et al.*, 1970). Parents
in many areas were confronted by bewildering, complex, differing
but overlapping services, such as hospitals, clinics, local authorities, voluntary societies, schools and so on, so that even for relatively simple needs such as for a special wheelchair, many different
agencies had to be contacted. Such studies show the need for co-
ordination at both national and local levels. They also show that
it is imperative that parents know precisely who to turn to for
immediate help. One person in the team of professionals must be
singled out, for a certain period, as the 'named person', to whom
parents can refer at any time, if and when difficulties arise.

The family as a unit

It is important, as social workers have emphasized, to consider
the family as a unit, so that the needs of the rest of the family,
the husband and brothers and sisters, are not neglected, and the
spastic child is not allowed to become the centre of attention in
the home. The other children should be taught not to give in every
time to the disabled child, and the more rough and tumble he
can take the better. Sometimes it is wise for the family to go on
a short holiday without the handicapped child, who may spend
the period in a children's hospital or family help unit, and often
enjoy the experience. It is most important to keep things in the

right perspective. Voluntary societies, such as the Spastics Society and its local groups, can provide important support to parents, who particularly appreciate the special experience and insight that perhaps only being a parent of a handicapped child can bring to the situation. Given such support many families have built up a very satisfying life, including their very handicapped child—sharing his care and letting him join in with family activities as much as possible. In some cases, it is found that the presence of a handicapped child in the family has proved enriching and most rewarding, but of course it is important not to allow the older children to feel too responsible for him, to the detriment of their other interests. The care can be a shared responsibility between the parents, the brothers and sisters, the relatives and the teachers, therapists and doctors attached to the school and hospital which the child attends, the voluntary agencies, and the social services of the local authority. The growth of these services increases the possibilities for children to remain within the normal community and share ordinary family life.

Early care and treatment
The Spastics Society (UK) publishes a number of excellent pamphlets which give practical guidance and scientific information to parents. The names of several are listed at the end of this Chapter. In recent years a great deal has been done to educate public opinion, to give them factual knowledge about cerebral palsy and the ways by which these children can be treated and educated. A tremendous interest and concern for the problems presented by these children have been shown in recent years, and it is rare to find a case of cerebral palsy undetected at school age.

It is generally agreed that early diagnosis and treatment are of the utmost importance. If the spastic condition is not evident at birth it usually becomes clear in the first few months, when instead of beginning to lift his head or move his limbs freely the baby remains passive. By six months, if the baby is making no attempt to sit up, the doctor should be consulted. Early treatment, training and advice are important, as is enlisting the help of physiotherapists, speech and occupational therapists, teachers and the like. The trend in recent years is to encourage parents to carry out treatment in the natural setting of the home, rather than putting a child through a series of formal exercises in a clinic—although these may have their place when the child is older in conjunction with treatment at home and within the school. Parents feel relieved when they find they have a vital part to play in treatment.

Physiotherapy

Ideally physiotherapy should start during the child's first year, as soon as the mother is ready to accept advice and practical demonstrations on handling.

In cerebral palsy, the part of the brain which controls the movements of the muscles has been damaged and the physiotherapist's aim is to provide systematic training that will help the child to make correct and useful movements. Left to himself, the child would choose the easiest way, using the strongest muscles and letting the weaker ones atrophy. Contractions and tensions thus develop and these constitute a 'secondary handicap' which must be prevented wherever possible. The whole process of training is very slow and the child has to pass very gradually through the normal developmental sequence of physical growth and locomotion—to lift and hold his head erect, to sit supported in a suitable chair fitted with a tray for his toys, to roll and gradually to crawl (see Fig. 5), supported by a crawler perhaps, and he will need space on the floor to practise these activities. We know of a three-year-old in a nursery school who is allowed to take messages to the kitchen by rolling, which he does with great pride. As the return journey usually takes some 20 minutes, urgent messages are sent by speedier routes!

Some children will never be able to walk, but they may learn

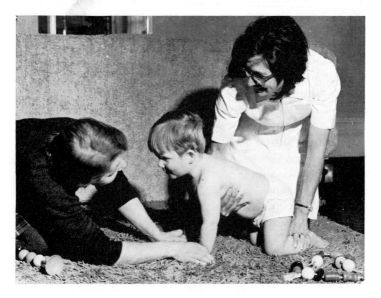

Fig. 5 Physiotherapy—a mother being shown the correct position for crawling.

to ride a tricycle with skill and safety. A triplegic boy at seven was accepted in a normal primary school, and used to ride his tricycle alone along the avenues to school with his calipers strapped on behind. His mother had great faith and great courage and knew when to let go and let him prove his independence. Many children will be able to use braces and crutches and we often witness the child's great delight when after much coaching he finds he can move about alone, and will convey his calipers home with great pride and delight, demanding almost that they should go to bed with him. Sometimes rapid skill in their use is expected and much disappointment experienced when immediate success is not forthcoming. It is most important to teach him that he can only hurry slowly. Some parents find great difficulty in allowing their handicapped child to meet normal hazards and to do much for themselves. An important part of the educational work of a centre is to suggest to parents what are reasonable expectations and what are necessary limitations for their particular child. The staff at a centre also need to review, from time to time, the strengths and limitations of the treatment they are offering. A most valuable practical guide to parents, *Handling the Young Cerebral Palsied Child at Home*, has been written by Nancie Finnie (1974) based on the methods of the Bobaths at the Western Cerebral Palsy Centre. A more technical description of the latter's pioneering work is to be found in their monograph (1966). *Treatment of Cerebral Palsy and Motor Delay* by Levitt (1977) is also helpful, advocating a more eclectic approach.

Speech therapy
Speech therapy proves necessary for many of these children. Once again, an important aim is to foster correct muscular control (see Fig. 6)—this time of the lips, the tongue and the throat, which if left alone may not learn the correct movements. First, the child must learn correct voicing and breathing; next sucking, swallowing and blowing; then babbling and the gradual introduction of syllables and words with meaning; finally simple phrases and sentences. The therapist's approach is one of constant encouragement for the young child to communicate in ways that have meaning to him, and, of course, the parents' encouragement at home, where countless opportunities arise for the child to use speech with understanding, is very important. Feeding is often difficult for spastic children, but speech therapy can help in teaching the child to swallow and to suck and to chew. We know of one speech therapist who usually commences her sessions with iced lollies as a

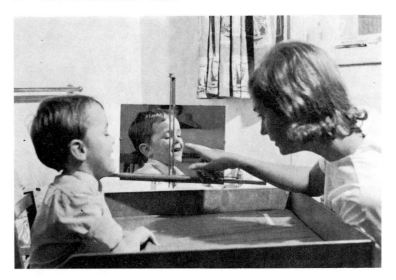

Fig. 6 Speech therapy.

sucking and swallowing exercise, which is deservedly popular! This will also help control the dribbling which is so common with many athetoids.

Occupational therapy

A great deal of help can be obtained from cerebral palsy centres with adapting furniture, potty chairs, and equipment to suit the child's particular needs. He may need a wheelchair which he can learn to propel himself. He may need a play chair with wooden beading fixed round the edge of the tray so that his toys will not constantly roll on to the floor. His play table may need to be raised on wooden blocks to the right height and he will need toys which he can control and handle. Discreet choice of radio and television programmes can also help a busy mother with normal household care to attend to. Home care is nearly always best for the handicapped child and if parents feel they have plenty of support and expert guidance at each stage of growth they will be able to tackle this tremendous task of caring for their child intelligently and courageously. Some will need constant reminders that the child with cerebral palsy is first and foremost a *child* and needs, therefore, to be treated as such, and not as a poor disabled invalid or a tender greenhouse plant!

Occupational therapy is a method of treatment which is closely allied to teaching in the pre-school period especially. Its purpose is to improve fine motor skills, develop self-help and daily living activities such as feeding or dressing, and to undertake, together with teachers and psychologists, training in many aspects of learning, such as improving visual perceptual skills and specialized methods of communication (Fig. 7).

Many cerebral palsied children have special difficulties in understanding spatial relationships, in discriminating shape or direction. He may be confused about the position of his body in space. Hand dominance may not be fully established and confusion in reading and writing correctly, e.g. by reversing letters such as b, d, p, q, n, u, may occur and impede later school work. Skilled occupational therapy in these early years coupled with good nursery school experience may do a great deal to prevent some of the learning difficulties commonly reported of older brain-damaged children.

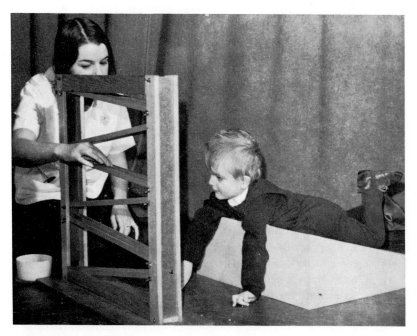

Fig. 7 Occupational therapy: training correct eye movements and weight bearing on hands.

The occupational therapist works with one child alone or with small groups. Matching of shapes and colours, sorting similar patterns, fitting puzzles or form boards, tracing shapes and letters, drawing in sand, copying bead or matchstick patterns, learning parts of the body by simple games, learning to button or tie shoes, and learning to persist in a simple task are invaluable aids to improving perceptual ability and prepare the way for more formal learning later. Looking, listening, touching, and naming reinforce learning and help to compensate for the restrictions of learning imposed by the physical handicap and a sheltered environment.

The use of appliances and supports is another important part of occupational therapy—wrist supports, head support, the right type of chair, the proper utensils to aid independence—and the occupational therapist co-operates with speech therapists, psychologists and teachers in the important field of communication aids.

Communication aids

Of all the problems of severe handicap, those of communication are the most serious. Is there anything more frustrating than having ideas and feelings and no means of expressing them? Without adequate speech or writing, we are isolated, cut off, not only from sharing ideas with other people but from social and emotional interaction as well. Fortunately, there is now a wide range of mechanical and electronic aids, and alternatives to speech, developed over many years to enable even the most grossly handicapped children and adults, whose motor control is too seriously impaired for speech or writing, to achieve considerable levels of communication.

Mechanical and electronic aids
Indicators. The simplest and cheapest aids are letter or word boards, the child simply pointing to the required symbol, using the head pointer if his hand control is too poor. Alternatively someone else can do the pointing, the child signalling an agreed sign for 'Yes' in response to the pointing. Electronically operated boards are also available in which the words and pictures light up in turn, until the child operates a simple switch, stopping the light at the required symbol. Switches which can respond to very crude or weak types of movement can be arranged. The board can also have the shape of a clock face, with a large hand that the child can stop at the required symbol—this is known as a rotary pointer.

These aids are usually limited in that only a small number of pictures and words, say about 100, can be contained on a reasonably sized and viewable board. Children over mental age six can begin to use more sophisticated devices, such as typewriters.

Typewriting aids are the main form of communication for the majority of severely physically and speech handicapped children. Machines such as IBM electric typewriters are the communication lifeline for thousands of people who would otherwise spend their lives in isolation.

Many severely handicapped children are able to use an ordinary electric typewriter given such considerations as correct positioning of the machine, correct setting and arm supports; keyguards, in the form of metal or wood plates with holes which are placed over keys, make it easier for a child to press one key instead of two at once. An alternative to using hands is to use a pointer attached to the head or to the foot.

Other modifications and extensions of typewriters for the severely handicapped are available.

Expanded keyboards. There are several forms of expanded keyboards available, providing an easier target for the child to hit, and keys which are sensitive to the slightest touch. In addition to making it easier on the input side of the typewriter, enlarged visual 'outputs' are also available, such as in the Toby Churchill desk writer in which the typing appears on an electronically based screen in large clear letters.

Electronic typewriting system. Fully electronically operated typewriting systems have also been developed following the invention in the 1960s by R. G. Maling of the 'Possum system'* originally designed for severe ex-polio sufferers, with extreme paralysis. Given only a capacity to blow or suck down a tube the Possum apparatus can be set up to operate a whole variety of equipment, including an IBM typewriter. For example, the blowing and sucking can be thought of as the dots and dashes in the Morse code. The Possum and the later Electraid apparatus use various codes and activating mechanisms—hand switches, joy-sticks, foot pedals, etc. (see Fig. 8), depending on the particular pattern of handicap a particular individual has. Electrical equipment enables grossly handicapped and speechless children to communicate with simple head movements. A child with a mental age of six can learn some of the simpler codes, e.g. the machine makes a series of clicks, pressing any kind of switch after say four clicks, followed by pressing a switch after three clicks, will always give a particular letter. It is astonishing how rapidly a reasonable rate of typing can be produced by using these methods, and adult experts can, using several switches and complicated codes, reach 20 wpm in spite

---

* The word 'Possum', which in Latin means 'I am able', is derived from the full title of the equipment—Patient Operated Selector Mechanisms.

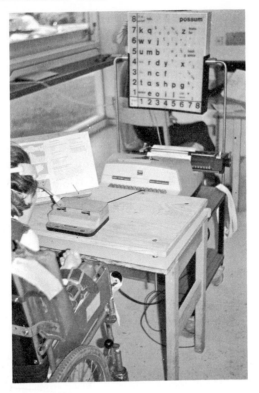

Fig. 8 Electraid equipment.

of gross physical handicap. (See Boydell's chapter in Bleackley, 1974. For details of existing communication aids for various kinds of handicapping conditions see Wilshere's (1975) excellent compendium.)

New developments in communication aids
The recent developments in micro-electronics hold out exciting prospects for the further development of communication aids aimed at:

1. Much wider *availability* of these aids, as large-scale production costs are reduced.
2. More *portability*. The earlier aids were large and heavy, and 'miniaturization' has already led to the development of what is virtually an electric typewriter—little bigger than an ordinary hand calculator, small and lightweight enough to be strapped to the wrist. This work has been pioneered by the Canon com-

pany of Japan with the help of their Dutch colleagues, producing a machine measuring only 70 mm × 90 mm, and giving a very clear typed output on a paper strip. It is completely portable and even has a plastic cover to keep off the rain (see Fig. 9).

3. Computer-based aids: the recent development of micro-processors (which are really small computers) has opened up further possibilities. The micro-processors can be used to store words and phrases which can rapidly be recalled, and displayed on a screen, such as by using a modified coloured T.V. set. This can gradually increase efficiency in communication—for example, hundreds of standard phrases can be stored, such as 'Dear Sir, Thank you for your letter'.

4. Speech synthesizers: a next step is to transfer the typed words into a spoken voice. This can be done, although at present the vocabulary involved is limited to only a few hundred words.

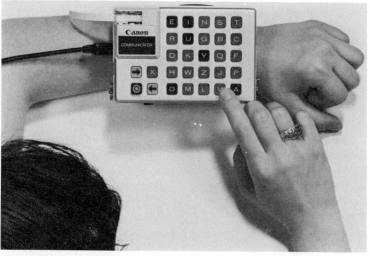

Fig. 9 A Canon communicator. It is portable and can fix to a wrist or wheelchair. It provides a print-out on thermo-sensitive paper.

Training in the use of aids
These sophisticated aids offer exciting possibilities to the severely handicapped, but they must not be regarded as panaceas for all our ills, and applied indiscriminately to people who do not really need them or who cannot even properly use them. Detailed

assessment, trial periods and step-by-step training programmes are essential if these aids are to be properly used. A child's special learning difficulties, which may interfere with the use of such aids, have to be taken into account, e.g. visual difficulties which may prevent the child from seeing what he is trying to type and perceptual motor difficulties that lead to confusion over which keys to press. It is also important to consider not only means of expression, but the content—the level of ideas and inner language, and the silent reading and spelling levels that the child has reached.

If these levels are limited, due to limitations in intelligence or educational opportunities, then they must be tackled before sophisticated means of expression are offered. Some children's 'expressive' difficulties are due to learning difficulties that cannot be solved by communication aids, and call for a more basic approach.

Alternatives to speech and writing

Most of the typewriter-like aids presuppose a knowledge of letters and words. A small percentage of children, such as those with particular damage to the language centres of the brain (discussed in the section on 'Aphasia' in Chapter 3), will have peculiar difficulty in comprehending and producing language in its conventional form. The letters and words that they see and hear make little sense to them. However, it is possible to express ideas and feelings through non-verbal means, such as through pictures, gestures and signs, and several sign languages are available, based initially on work with the deaf.

The 'finger spelling' traditionally used by the deaf, involving hand and finger movements for each letter, is too complicated for many physically handicapped children and for many with special learning difficulties, and a simpler system is necessary, using hand-signs to indicate a whole word; e.g. 'food' can be represented by imitating the use of a knife and fork. There are many such systems, developed in various countries, often with regional variations in the gestures used. One of the most 'standardized' systems in the UK is the Paget Gorman system (Gorman and Paget, 1970) which, in a simplified form, has been found useful for children with considerable physical and mental handicaps. A simpler system, devised more specifically with the retarded in mind, is the Makaton. However, some of the more grossly physically handicapped children cannot produce the necessary hand and finger movement for any of these forms of sign language, and a return to a special form of communication board becomes necessary.

The Bliss system meets the needs for some grossly physically handicapped children. It was particularly devised for C.P. children by workers at the Ontario Crippled Children's Centre, Canada, and extends the idea of the communication board, on which are printed, not merely pictures or letters, but a new system of symbols, systematically and logically devised, so that young children can learn the basic symbols, extending their vocabulary as they mature, so that eventually quite complex sentences can be transmitted and received. Many of the symbols are more easily learned than the ordinary letters of the alphabet because some visual cues are given, e.g. the symbol for 'man' looks something like a human figure, as shown in the following examples (Fig. 10).

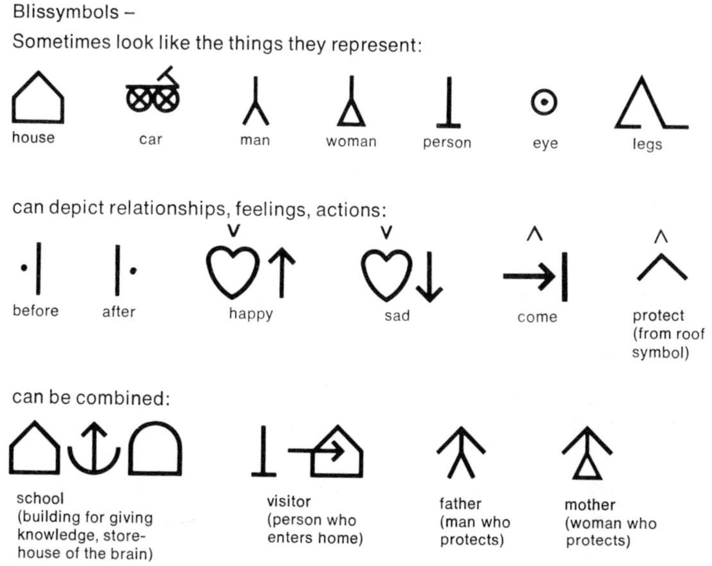

Blissymbols –

Sometimes look like the things they represent:

house   car   man   woman   person   eye   legs

can depict relationships, feelings, actions:

before   after   happy   sad   come   protect (from roof symbol)

can be combined:

school (building for giving knowledge, store-house of the brain)   visitor (person who enters home)   father (man who protects)   mother (woman who protects)

Fig. 10 Example of Blissymbolics. © Blissymbolics Communication Institute (1979) Toronto, Canada. The comments in the text are those of the authors, not the Institute.

The symbols also have the English word equivalent written underneath, which is helpful to people who have not learned the system. This is an advantage over other systems like the Paget Gorman system, which has to be learned by everyone concerned. The presence of the English word equivalents also help the child towards the process of ordinary reading, if this is possible later on. Once a child can read he no longer needs Blissymbolics, but the system is proving useful for many children with severe and multiple learning difficulties, through which they are unable to master speech, writing and reading, in spite of many years of help.

A useful review of the strengths and weaknesses of the various 'alternatives to speech' can be found in Kiernan *et al.* (1978). The same author is completing a major research on communication systems, which will help to clear up the confusion caused by the emergence of several systems that appear to be in competition with each other.

New systems of treatment and early education

We have described the traditional methods of treatment by physiotherapists, occupational and speech therapists, developed over the past 50 years. In recent years some new, radical and comprehensive methods have been developed: these break away from traditional treatment carried out by several separate therapists and teachers, and advocate instead a *unified* approach that aims to deal with all aspects of the handicapped child's development, not only his motor development, but his perception, attention, language and early educational skills, etc., in accordance with the carefully devised strict programme of step-by-step sequential training. Two large-scale systems of treatment are currently being practised in several countries, the Peto method and the Doman-Delacato method.

Conductive education

The Peto method is of particular relevance to the treatment and education of severely handicapped cerebral palsied children. It has been developed in Budapest at the State Institute for Conductive Education of the Motor Disabled under the direction of Professor Peto, who died in September 1967. The Institute continues to admit children for one to two years' intensive treatment on a residential basis and trains 'conductors' who act as physiotherapist, speech therapist, occupational therapist, teacher and nurse. The Spastics Society has encouraged trials of these new techniques in this country and research on the outcome is being completed (Jernqvist, 1978). The children are educated in groups of 10 to 20 children under one conductor and an assistant. All the daily activities are carried out in the group which obviates handling by many different specialists in different places and reduces the 'fragmentation' that most very handicapped are subjected to, such as when, in the course of one day, their speech, motor activities, daily living skills, and formal education are dealt with by different personnel of different disciplines, in different settings, often with little real link-up between all these various activities. The room has the minimum of distracting material, but visual aids, occupational therapy materials, charts and pictures are produced at the appropriate time. The room is furnished with slatted wooden plinths used for eating and sleeping on, and for the required exercises. Special chairs without arms are used for sitting and as walking aids.

The training programme is a highly structured one and the day is carefully programmed. General training to promote general body control, e.g. lying still, turning over, sitting with feet on the ground and hands on the table, etc., comes first. As the child attempts to perform the exercise he repeats loudly and slowly his intention, e.g. 'I join my hands together', and counts rhythmically to five, all the children in the group performing the same action and saying the same words. This is known as 'rhythmical intention'. Continuous verbalization in simple language accompanied by the appropriate movement no doubt aids concentration and helps him to exclude other activities, thus possibly enabling the cortex to form new neuro-physiological pathways. Rhythmical speech and counting reinforce the action necessary to move a limb and a new movement pattern is developed (see Fig. 11). This theory has some basis in the work of Pavlov and has been described by Luria (1961).

This general training in body movement is followed by specific

Fig. 11 Conductive education. The child can improve his sitting-balance by learning to control and tolerate hip flexion and abduction, with the aim of touching the floor between his knees, saying 'Down, down, down'.

programmes of exercises devised to develop particular skills, e.g. pre-writing exercises, perceptual training, body image training, independence in eating, drinking, dressing and undressing and using the pot. The exercises are carefully worked out to perform the sequences leading to the performance of a functional task.

Detailed descriptions of 'conductive education' can be found in articles by Esther Cotton (1967, 1975). A number of special schools and centres have been using the Peto method in modified forms and in many ways it has revolutionalized their educational approach. Cerebral palsied children need a more structured, more repetitive programme than ordinary non-brain-damaged children. They need more reinforcement by verbalization and bodily activity, by seeing and hearing and touching and linking their sensations to form percepts and later concepts. In this way they may gain greater control of their movements and actions and organize their thought processes more effectively.

The important features of the Peto method are: (a) its emphasis on group treatment, which produces high motivation amongst some children; (b) it is a well-thought-out programme, largely of motor training for the severely handicapped; (c) it is applied intensively at an early age (often starting at age three full-time, all day and every day for a couple of years); (d) by one expert conductor trained in several disciplines, so that she can act as an important focal point in the child's life. Such radical and intensive methods certainly deserve close study, since conventional methods of helping the motor development of very handicapped young children are by no means always successful.

The Doman system

Another radical and intensive system of motor treatment is that propounded by Glen Doman and Carl Delacato in the Philadelphia Rehabilitation Centre, established in 1955. In 1963 this became part of the Institutes for the Achievement of Human Potential, and the Doman-Delacato methods of treating cerebral palsied and other types of brain-injured children have the aim of producing movement patterns by means of an intensive programme of repetitive movements to be carried out largely by parents (in contrast to the Peto method). The movements are patterned in accordance with the sequences of movement that normal children go through, in for example the various stages of locomotion (rolling, crawling, creeping, standing erect with support and so on until normal walking is achieved). The theory is that the child's damaged central neurological organization can be enhanced by such procedures, and substantial improvements are claimed, provided the parents can carry out the very intensive and continuous training. Careful records of neurological development are kept, and the use of these for evaluative studies are described by Doman and his colleagues in Wolf's (1969) study of the results of treatment in C.P. Large-scale studies of the effectiveness of such methods are still awaited, no definitely positive results being available so far: the Institutes and their offshoots in various countries tend to claim high success rates in general, and these claims must be regarded with caution until more evidence is available.

The difficulties of mounting such studies are enormous. Comparable groups of untreated children, for the purposes of contrasting their spontaneous progress over the years with the treated groups, are hard to find. It is also difficult to find large enough groups of treated children to allow statistical comparisons.

The advantage of the more systematic intensive programmes of treatment, such as the Peto and Doman-Delacato, is that they do have definite aims and methods, which can be subjected to precise measurement, preferably by independent researchers. They are also important in turning our attention to the possibility that very early and very intensive motor treatment may lead to greater progress than we have hitherto thought possible. Part of this progress might be due to the enthusiasm that is generated amongst the staff by having a systematic method, rather than the intrinsic merits of the system. This remains to be seen. We can only find out the answers to such questions by continued research.

Emotional development

Children with cerebral palsy are sometimes described as 'emotionally labile', which means that their feelings are strong, easily aroused, difficult to control and very fluctuating. They may show quite violent anger at frustration which they have to experience so often. They may show acute fear in a new situation or when unsteady and afraid of falling. They may show depression and tearfulness. In her study of fear and frustration of such children in a residential hospital school, Maureen Oswin (1967) gives some vivid examples of behaviour problems encountered in school due to the frustration of the physical handicap. Depression, withdrawal from people, refusal to work or co-operate may occur and the reasons for this must be fully understood. It seems likely that some C.P. children may have an extended period of the natural emotional instability that is found in ordinary young children, due to their impaired neurological condition. For example, their capacity to inhibit strong feelings may be delayed in its development by several years, after which they will show greater stability and less fluctuation of mood. In Rutter's (1970) sample, nearly 40 per cent of the C.P. children were rated by teachers as psychiatrically disturbed and the authors conclude that this very high rate, over five times that of the general population, must in part be due to brain dysfunction and could not be wholly attributed to environmental influences, such as faulty reactions by parents and the community to the handicapped child. Capacity to learn will be affected by moodiness, fear of failure and of social incompetence. Later, during adolescence, a return of moodiness and difficult behaviour may be expected as the young person has to begin to face up to the demands of community life and contend with normal physical changes and increased frustrations, including a feeling of rejection by non-handicapped peers. A very stable, consistent, and regular routine with the minimum of excitement or stress will increase stability and reduce emotional disturbance and distractibility.

It is not surprising that these children, sometimes well past babyhood, give way to tantrums when one remembers how dependent the child is on the whim of the adults around him and how frequently he will have to face frustration. His toys roll out of reach, his bricks constantly fall over because he cannot control his movements sufficiently; his pencil will not move in the direction he wishes. He has to wait for an adult to fetch what he wants, to give him his food, or take him to the toilet. It is remarkable that so many show such cheerfulness, patience, and dogged determination in the face of so many obstacles. It is a healthy sign when a handicapped child can show occasional defiance and rebellion. Sometimes he is resistant to physiotherapy; sometimes he tries to deny the existence of a spastic arm or leg and resents treatment which forces the disabled limb on his notice. It is wise to suspend treatment for a period in such cases. Sometimes he will draw a bizarre type of man with one arm much smaller than the other or one leg left out altogether. This seems an attempt to express strong feelings about his disability.

Obviously, the more independent the child can become, the more skills he can acquire, the greater his sense of achievement and feeling of self-confidence will be. Depression and anxiety may occur in adolescence, but in childhood, given good therapy, good teaching and an accepting, supporting home behind him, the cerebral palsied child can enjoy life at school and at home.

Early education

The education and training of a young handicapped child cannot begin too early. He has to be taught skills that an ordinary child picks up more or less spontaneously or incidentally during his early years, such as speech and locomotion. Children start to learn, right from birth, to organize the mass of impressions they receive from the outside world, to make sense out of the sight and sounds and the feel of things around them, exploring, manipulating, vocalizing and generally gaining an increasing measure of understanding and control of their surroundings. The handicapped child in contrast tends to miss out on much of this early experience, and to become bored and frustrated if he continually fails to reach a satisfying degree of control.

The early stimulation and experience that parents, and only parents, can normally provide is, of course, tremendously important, for they are the child's first teachers and are in constant close contact with him during his most impressionable years. Further discussion of how parents' teaching skills can be improved may be found on pages 72, 73.

Ordinary pre-school play groups can normally accept one or two handicapped children. However, more specialized help for the handicapped child and support for parents are given in the hundred or so 'opportunity groups' which have been set up in the UK. These groups provide for both normal and handicapped children, with the emphasis on the latter (see Fig. 12). The

Fig. 12 Nursery group for able-bodied and handicapped children.

Pre-school Play Groups Association sponsors a range of ordinary, opportunity and specialized play groups, and it has also published some helpful literature on the subject (Pre-school Play Groups Association, 1978).

Most handicapped children, if emotionally ready by, say, age three or four, are capable of benefiting from the wider experience of an ordinary nursery school, provided that the staff are adequately briefed. However, the more severely and multiply handicapped children who need regular therapy as well as educational and social interaction will probably do better in a specialized nursery group, such as one of the Spastics Society's local day centres or local authority special nursery groups (which may share some of the facilities of a school for the physically handicapped).

One of the great advantages of this type of early education, within a special group, is that the child can spend part of the day in an atmosphere where his severe disability is accepted as a matter of course. While his difficulties are fully understood, he is expected to measure up to certain standards of independence and skill often not demanded of him at home or within a normal school. It is a great deal easier for the trained staff of such a centre to treat the young, severely handicapped spastic child with reasonable, kindly, firm, and even detached care, than a mother who is intimately involved or a teacher with a class of 20 to 30 able-bodied children.

The gradual learning of independence in simple routine matters is of great importance for the child, both for his self-respect and his self-confidence in community life. Sometimes it is well nigh impossible for him to help to feed himself, to dress himself, or wash his hands or fetch his toys. All the comparatively simple skills that an ordinary four-year-old can achieve quite easily, such as undoing coat buttons, turning on taps, threading beads, using a crayon or paint brush, or moulding clay or plasticine into shapes, are virtually impossible to many children with cerebral palsy until they have been able to learn, by constant training and therapy, some degree of control of their hands. Washing, toilet and feeding processes are not hurried at the special unit; the child will be provided with special equipment which will make feeding and toilet training easier, and both speech therapists and occupational therapists may help with this. He may have a hole cut for his plate and mug, and spoons and forks with large handles easy to grasp. Drinking through a straw may help to develop correct swallowing movements and indirectly control drooling which is such an impediment to some of these children.

Manipulation of material, which will increase motor skill, is made more possible by fitting a tray with a raised edge to the child's chair if he cannot sit in an ordinary chair at a table. He can then use many of the usual nursery school educational apparatus, sorting and matching games, puzzles, bricks, beads, dough, clay, and manage sit-down painting or drawing at an easel. He can enjoy a sand tray and a water trough if adequately supported in either a sitting or a standing position.

Locomotion, which provides little difficulty for the ordinary two-year-old, is often something which the cerebral palsied child has to acquire slowly. In the special unit he is given opportunity to hitch or roll or crawl, whichever is possible and most beneficial for him. Close co-operation is necessary between the teacher and the physiotherapist so that the right type of movements can be encouraged in a free environment. He can be encouraged to clamber on the climbing frame, to push wheel toys around, to climb up steps and slide down the chute if he is able. He gains confidence and courage, and learns to disregard the occasional tumble.

Creative activity is of immense importance to a child who is frustrated in so many ways on account of his motor disability. Sand and water, clay, dough, or other modelling materials provide good opportunities. Finger painting may be possible when the control of paint brush or crayon is beyond his powers. Brick building and constructional toys can be a great delight unless manual control is too limited or uncertain and then such activities become merely irritating and unrewarding. Athetoid children experience special difficulties because involuntary movements constantly interfere with such activities and cause his bricks to be scattered all over the floor. Many valuable special toys for the handicapped, which can be borrowed from toy libraries, have been designed at the Nottingham Child Development Research Unit (under the direction of John and Elizabeth Newson).

Imaginative play is part of the young child's means of communication, of expression, and his method of relieving feelings of fear, of hostility and frustration. In pretending games, family games, bus driver, engine driver, cowboy, policeman, and hospital play especially the child reflects and interprets his experiences in his environment. By this type of play he learns to express, re-direct, and modify his feelings. The play, with other children in the group, helps in this process which is so valuable for emotional development. By this means too he learns to make a more satisfactory relationship to other children near his age. At home he may be always competing with active and able brothers and sisters and feel always a little inferior. Or he may be always sheltered and protected from showing initiative and independence. In the special unit for cerebral palsied children, his companions have similar handicaps, similar problems and similar frustrations. He can compete on more equal terms and can even assist a child more handicapped than himself. A great deal of healthy social growth goes on in the group. He learns to combine efforts for a definite purpose such as playing at shops, to accept leadership, to make a good partner, sometimes engage in healthy mischief, and to enjoy all the fun and enrichment of personality from playing and quarrelling together. Active play out of doors has been encouraged amongst the C.P. children at Cheyne Centre by the use of the special Adventure Playground for Handicapped Children in Chelsea.

Group activities. Some time is also given for simple organized activities. The children listen to stories and rhymes. They enjoy action songs and just listening to music. A percussion band is a popular feature of the programme, and some suitable instrument can be found for most of the children, however disabled they may be. Such social activity is immensely stimulating to a young cerebral palsied child who may previously have remained much of the day in his cot or pram while his mother busied herself with the housework and the rest of the family were at school or at work. As a result he is more contented, less irritable, sleeps and eats better, and is generally more happy at home as well as at school.

Although in some areas of the UK, notably the large towns, there is adequate provision of special nursery units for handicapped children (too severely handicapped for anything like realistic integration in normal nursery schools), there is still a lack in the smaller towns. With greater provision, more handicapped children could have a chance to overcome some of the special learning difficulties that we have previously mentioned, such as the difficulties in visual perception, attention span, and the emotional barriers that spring from repeated early failures, before these difficulties have become ingrained. It is to be expected that, with early special unit help, a greater proportion of cerebral palsied children will be able, at ages five or six, to pass on to the type of school that almost every parent hopes for—the ordinary school within their community, achieving a degree of integration that is more than just a façade.

Education after age five

At five, as with the ordinary child in the UK, a decision usually has to be made about the type of schooling that will be most helpful for the handicapped child. This decision has to be taken with great care. Between 25 and 50 per cent of cerebral palsied children attend normal schools in many areas, according to surveys by Hewett (1970) and Henderson (1961), although there are great variations, depending on local circumstances. In most areas, children with mild physical handicaps and average intelligence can usually attend the ordinary school, but it must be clearly established whether they have the subtle kinds of special learning difficulties that we have mentioned, and whether the needs arising from these can be met in the normal school.

The decision to place a handicapped child in an ordinary school must rest on many factors, such as the presence or absence of special learning difficulties, the degree to which his speech is affected, the personality of the child, notably whether he is over-sensitive and over-anxious about failure, or resilient and well able to stand up to emotional as well as physical knocks. Another important consideration is the attitude of the staff at the ordinary school, who vary in their abilities to cope with the presence of a handicapped child. As we mentioned in Chapter 1, more thought needs to be given to how ordinary schools can be assisted in making better provision for handicapped children.

As for the more significantly handicapped children, a halfway house between the normal school and the special school is a very useful provision. For example, the provision of *small special units* for the physically handicapped, attached to the normal school, along the lines of the partially hearing units, which in the main have been successfully attached to normal schools. A few such units exist in the UK, and they allow opportunities for at least partial integration of ordinary and handicapped children, the experience of which can be as fruitful to the ordinary child as it is to the handicapped. We can hardly expect ordinary children to develop sound and realistic attitudes towards the handicapped if they never have opportunities for meeting them. The disadvantage of such integration is that the competition can become too great. There are dangers in asking a very handicapped child to attempt too much, to struggle all the time to keep up with ordinary children.

Studies so far of special units attached to normal schools (Cope and Anderson, 1977) report only marginal difficulties amongst a sample of 55 physically handicapped children at primary-school age. This sample, however, included very few children with severe and multiple handicaps, such as those with very severe speech and hand control and other difficulties affecting their ability to communicate. For the more handicapped children, a more sheltered school career, in a day school for the physically handicapped, for instance, is often necessary, at least for a period.

One of the great advantages of such specialized groups is that they can offer all the necessary services 'under one roof'— assessment, treatment and therapy services, as well as education, plus close attention to aids and equipment, especially for those children with communication difficulties. Although specialized schools for children with cerebral palsy are required on a lesser scale than before, in most Western countries (given that knowledge and expertise concerning their special needs are now more widespread), there will always be some children in some areas who will need them. It is too idealistic to hope that the expertise needed to help children with very severe learning difficulties can become so widespread as to end the need for specialized centres altogether.

For example, a typical Spastics Society school as described by Loring (1965, 1968) has a high staff to pupil ratio, which can call upon many trained and experienced professionals, in education, therapy and care; small units can also be provided for children with additional handicaps, such as those with hearing losses or

Fig. 13 Overcoming multiple handicaps: hearing, speech and physical impairments.

with disturbed behaviour, or who require intensive academic facilities.

The teaching staff are able to specialize in developing ways of minimizing the many barriers to learning that we have mentioned, such as the difficulties in hand control, in speech, in eye movements, in co-ordinating hand and eye, in visual perception, and in problems of distractibility and emotional instability (Fig. 13). Full use is made of special equipment such as adjustable desks and chairs to allow a proper sitting position, mechanical and electronic aids to communication (see pp. 52–58).

Given attention in respect of these all-important means of communication, most children can follow an ordinary curriculum, although at a slower pace than in an ordinary school. Many of the ordinary experiences and informal opportunities for learning that ordinary children enjoy and which form a basis for later school learning, have to be carefully provided for the very handicapped child, within a school time-table that is already interrupted by the needs for the various therapies. Experiments in new techniques of teaching are usually more easily carried out in specialized C.P. schools, since many of the staff have accumulated a great deal of experience, on the basis of which they can evaluate some of the latest advances in educational techniques and contribute to research in new areas.

The question of residential schooling

This is less in demand these days, with the increasing availability of day schools (ordinary and special) for handicapped children in the UK. However, there will always be a need for some boarding schools, e.g. for children living in very remote areas, those needing more specialized help than a local day school can be expected to muster, and those whose families are very unsettled and under stress.

Parents occasionally feel guilty about placing their child in a boarding school—as if it represented a failure on their part to cope with their child's needs. These feelings should be discussed openly and are usually found to be greatly exaggerated. Most parents accepting a boarding-school placement for their child have genuinely tried to manage, often with considerable local professional support, but simply cannot continue to meet their child's needs at home, and feel that the local community services and day school are inadequate. In many cases the problem lies in the extreme severity of the child's handicaps and the continuous demands that this makes on all members of the family. The idea that the burden can be *shared* between the family and a boarding school is useful in such a situation. Most head teachers would agree that a child should not go to a residential school, however, before the age of seven unless family circumstances are exceptional or the child is greatly frustrated through lack of expert teaching and therapy. Close contact must be maintained between the home and the child. Letters, telephone calls, frequent visits, including overnight stays by parents and the long holidays at home, all help to preserve the vital link between the child at boarding school and his family life. Frequent contact between home and school also helps the staff and parents to arrive at a united plan for helping the child, such as continuing treatment during the school holidays.

A wide variety of day and residential schools is necessary to deal with the whole range of severe and multiple handicaps. Fortunately, through the efforts of voluntary and state workers, a sufficient number of school places is now available in this country—except, regrettably, for children of nursery school age and those with additional handicaps (e.g. a combination of severe physical and mental handicaps). This not to say, however, that we can relax our efforts to improve the *effectiveness* of the education that exists, through research and experiment to find, for example, the best ways of teaching reading and arithmetic to children with perceptual disabilities, the best ways of teaching speechless children, of helping those who are overactive and distractible and those with disturbed behaviour. At the lower end of the intellectual scale, there is an enormous job to be done. The services for severely subnormal C.P. children (who represent nearly 25 per cent of the C.P. group) are far from adequate in quantity or quality.

Severe subnormality and C.P.
This large group has been relatively neglected in the early days of building up facilities. Priority was given to the more intelligent 'educable' children who appeared more likely to profit than the very retarded ones, and more likely to produce results that would help to break down public indifference. Facilities for the so-called 'ineducable' children (i.e. those whose mental levels tend to be below half of normal, and who are unable to learn reading, writing and arithmetic and other basic academic skills sufficiently to use them effectively as tools) have therefore lagged seriously. This was indeed unfortunate since it meant that parents who were faced with caring for a child who has two major handicaps (subnormality

and C.P.) received less help than those whose children had only one major handicap. The strain of caring for and educating a child with two major disabilities at home is enormous. An extreme and very moving example of the family disruption that such a strain can provoke has been portrayed in Peter Nichols's play *A Day in the Death of Joe Egg*. A delicate balance has to be struck between the needs of the child, and those of his brothers and sisters, his mother and father: the relationships between all members are affected.

Clearly, care and training for such very handicapped children must be shared between the family and the wider community. Properly staffed day schools and local spastic group day centres are available in some areas. Here they learn the rudiments of self-help in eating, dressing, toilet, and in mobility so far as they are able. They gain stimulation from play activities, from simple group activities, and from direct training in perception using the nursery school type of occupations. The social experience is of tremendous value to them and they can receive daily physio-therapy if they will respond. The parents at the same time gain a much needed respite from their daily care. Even three attend-ances a week is a very great help to the families concerned. In some cases the child responds so well that he can be upgraded to a formal school, and some of the older children may learn the rudiments of numbers and reading. The following case history exemplifies how well the subnormal can be helped to adjust:

One quadriplegic boy of 20, known since 10 years of age, was attending a day centre regularly. His capacity was about the level of a $4\frac{1}{2}$-year-old. He could match colours and pictures, grade sizes, count in an automatic way, copy a circle, a cross but not a square or a star. He made an attempt to write his name. He echoed everything said to him, whatever was asked him. He named pictures and could carry on a simple conversation, using phrases, simple sentences and single words. His verbal comprehension was assessed at about the level of a five-year-old. He was cheerful, co-operative, contented and most amenable. His father said he was most helpful at home in the house, enjoyed the day centre and spent a good deal of time living with his aunt in the country during holiday periods. He was learning basket-work, swimming and football. He was able to feed, wash and dress himself (with the exception of tying his tie) as his quadriplegic condition was com-paratively mild. He was said to be well liked in the centre and the neigh-bourhood and would accompany his father on many trips and drink orange juice in the pub on a Saturday night with him. He was an only child and appeared to be well accepted by his kind, understanding parents. His father was in a skilled job as an electrician. The general adjustment of this boy with severe subnormality and some spasticity was very good.

There is still a shortage of properly staffed units; in Sheila Hewett's (1970) sample, nearly one-third of the subnormal children over age five had no unit whatsoever to attend. In the UK since 1970, however, the new section of the Education Act has improved the quality and quantity of such services, since it placed all subnormal children, including the severely subnormal, within the framework of the local education authorities, clearly recognizing that their prime need is for special educational not health facilities. The new Act has led to an increase in the number of trained teachers and assistants, and thus to a higher standard of schooling for the handicapped. Much-needed research into the best means of promoting progress by using scientific ways of measuring outcomes, and by new training techniques including behaviour modification techniques, is now being carried out.

Parent involvement in educational programmes

An important development in recent years in the West has been the growing recognition of the important part that parents can play in their handicapped child's education, as well as in his general upbringing. This, as Mittler (1974) has pointed out, calls for a new relationship between teachers and parents, in which both collaborate to mobilize all opportunities at home and at school that are available to further a child's development. With handicapped children, one cannot rely so much on 'spontaneous' or 'incidental' learning, as one can with ordinary children. For example, the normal baby needs little encouragement to play with a rattle, whereas the severely handicapped child often does. Parents need training in the following areas:

1. The systematic observation of their child's behaviour.
2. Recording skills on a prepared chart.
3. Selecting certain special goals or tasks (and the toys and other equipment relevant to them).
4. Breaking down the tasks into simpler steps, and allowing plenty of practice.
5. Giving plenty of praise for success—breaking down the tasks even more if success is not achieved.
6. Monitoring progress and selecting further tasks.

Such training can be given in the form of practical workshops to small groups of parents, with their children, described by Cunningham and Jeffree (1974); another organization that has pioneered work in the field of parental involvement is 'Kith and Kids' (Collins, 1976). Kiernan's (1978) contribution is also very important, providing very specific guides on teaching techniques that can give very practical answers to parents' urgent questions about their young and severely multiply handicapped children, e.g. 'How can I get my child to pay attention, to show more interest in toys, to start feeding himself, to communicate more?' These very practical forms of help, involving the parents in the day-to-day teaching of their child in a much more systematic way than hitherto, can greatly increase the capacity of a family to cope, given local support facilities. However, residential schooling will be needed for some.

Residential facilities

Residential facilities are needed for children whose handicaps are particularly severe and when home conditions are very difficult, and this can be provided in some hospitals for the severely subnormal. A few of these provide excellent training, but, unfortunately, many are understaffed, badly housed and poorly equipped and thus able to provide little more than custodial care, which many parents find unacceptable. Parents are rarely given any part to play in the upbringing of their child under such circumstances. Such hospitals should be closed to make way for residential schools and hostels.

A model residential school (Meldreth) for 120 severely subnormal children, excluding those who are so grossly retarded and physically handicapped as to need full-time nursing care, was

Fig. 14 Independence training: senior Meldreth pupils on weekend boat trip.

opened and staffed by the Spastics Society in 1966. The primary aim of this unit is to promote the child's social development. Towards this end, the children are placed in small, family-type units, within which their capacity for self-help and some degree of independence (such as dressing) is developed (Fig. 14). They also contribute to the running of the community by helping other children, delivering messages, feeding pets, etc.

Behaviour modification

Behaviour modification is a technique for changing behaviour resting on the simple proposition expounded by Skinner that behaviour is altered by its consequences. Our behaviour patterns are affected by what the outcome happens to be, whether we find the outcome rewarding or not. Unfortunately, we spend much of our time unwittingly rewarding behaviour that we really do not wish to see repeated. This happens, for example, when a child in a classroom screams for attention. We usually end up giving it to him, which is just what he wants, and this tends to reinforce the screaming behaviour. It used to be thought that simply ignoring the screaming would cause it to die away, but this is really not the case.

Behaviour modification aims at a more effective approach by encouraging a child to behave in ways that we would wish and rewarding his efforts immediately when he does so, having first found out what will act as a reward for him.

Such techniques are proving successful, particularly with mentally handicapped children. Jones (1976, 1977) has carried out research into techniques for increasing the attention span of mentally handicapped and cerebral palsied children in the classroom setting at the Spastics Society's residential school, Meldreth. He is currently engaged on a larger project involving six multi-handicapped, overactive, aggressive children, using behaviour modification techniques, including token economy, which are intended to improve their behaviour. Special monitoring devices record their behavioural responses at all times for a period of months, which allows an objective appraisal of teaching and training techniques and points to the most effective reward systems.

Although behaviour modification is sometimes criticized as being 'too mechanical' in its approach, tending to manipulate people too much, its usefulness in freeing children from behaviour that severely reduces their social acceptability (such as aggression and destructiveness) is unquestionable.

A useful introduction to the subject is to be found in Patterson's (1968) book, and more detailed studies are available by Kiernan (1973) and Bricker (1973).

Community services

The alternative to a large hospital institution is the small home or hostel intended to house about 25 severely subnormal children, some with severe cerebral palsy. In such homes, the less physically handicapped majority can help the more heavily handicapped, and all the children, regardless of whether they are full-time residents or weekly boarders, can retain links with the ordinary life of the community instead of being completely segregated from normal society. These concepts of community care have been developed by Tizard (1964) and Kushlick (1965). Some authorities are providing hostel care of this kind with considerable success and at reasonable cost. Community-based homes and hostels are unlikely to provide for all very severely physically and mentally handicapped children, some of whom need very intensive care and treatment that is better provided in a larger unit, subdivided as far as possible, with medical and nursing help. But the majority do not need this, and every effort should be made to provide family- and community-type facilities, which will allow at least some measure of integration with the non-handicapped. It is to be hoped that this work marks the beginning of an era in which our generation faces up to some of the tremendous problems that previous generations have shamefully neglected.

The intellectually gifted C.P. child and the aims of education

What of the children at the other end of the intellectual scale, those of sufficiently high intelligence to profit by academic schooling, examinations and higher education? As we have noted in a previous section, something like 5 per cent of C.P. children are of high average to superior intelligence (I.Q.s above 110) and just under 1 per cent are exceptionally bright (I.Q.s above 130). When the accompanying physical, sensory or speech handicaps are mild, no particular problems may arise, provided the pupil's aspirations are realistic; for example, it must be appreciated that even a slight speech defect could be very troublesome to a would-be linguist. Particular stresses arise when high intelligence is accompanied by severe spasticity or athetosis, affecting many avenues of expression and communication. Then we have the special challenge of 'a mind imprisoned in a defective body'. Consider the following case:

David was a rhesus baby, jaundiced. Described as floppy: athetosis suspected at age six months, not feeding, sitting properly. Good attention and drive noted in his pre-school days but no speech developed. Hearing proved normal. Condition on entering special school for cerebral palsied children at age seven described as 'very severe athetosis: no speech, very little control of hands and legs: virtually helpless'. Yet he was determined to communicate and could nod and shake his head in response to questions and showed good comprehension. By age 12 he was reading well, and could indicate the correct answers to complicated questions about what he had read. Psychologist estimated his intelligence as at least I.Q. 125, and noted good mathematical skills. Beginning to use electric typewriter well, using a headband with a pointer attached: could also 'converse' by pointing to letters on a board. Gained entry into specialized secondary school: grasp of English, maths and history reported excellent but means of communication too slow for 'O' and 'A' level exams. Wide interests including travel and classical music. Transferred to higher education centre: worked extremely hard for examinations. Some emotional difficulties: unco-operative and irritable at times, especially with houseparent staff on whom he was completely dependent for washing, feeding, toileting, etc. Psychologist commented: the gap between his superior intelligence and his negligible motor and speech skills is so vast that he has, in a sense, rejected his body as worse than useless—merely a source of frustration. Experiments with the Possum equipment attempted, but his headband method of typing developed sufficiently for him to sit 'A' levels in several subjects. He passed and is considering university entrance: the practical daily care and social life problems will be tremendous. Hopes eventually to become a journalist, in spite of almost complete physical and speech handicaps, and has already published articles.

Fortunately, such cruel combinations of extremely high intelligence and extremely limited physical, speech and general communication abilities are rare, yet we can learn a great deal from extreme cases in understanding and planning facilities for the less extremely handicapped concerning, as we have seen, their need for careful assessment and extra help in at least partially overcoming some of the communication difficulties such as by the use of special equipment. As electronic engineering and computers become more highly developed in the next few years, it is likely that more special equipment to supplement impaired speech and hand control will become available.

Extreme cases also give us clearer insight into the emotional conflicts that are more likely to arise in a sensitive, highly intelligent spastic than in a duller one. In David's case the discrepancy between his adult intellectual status on the one hand, and his almost infant-like dependence on near-by people for daily care on the other, often led to conflicts, not only within David but within the persons relating to him. His behaviour at one moment was that of a very mature adult, the next as a dependent helpless child. The transitional period from the role of the dependent child to an independent adult through which most children slowly pass seems never-ending for David.

Similar problems affect less extremely handicapped persons though fortunately to a much lesser degree in most cases. In a follow-up study of 20 C.P. children with I.Q.s ranging from approximately 115 to 140, one of the authors (A.H.B.) found that the majority were making satisfactory progress socially and educationally over the 5 to 10 year period that they were under review, in various schools, both normal and special.

Follow-up notes on two of these children were as follows:

J.P., a very intelligent little girl (I.Q. 127, paraplegic), with excellent verbal ability, attended a normal school and was very advanced in reading and outstanding in arithmetic. She wrote an expressive poem at the age of nine. She can use her left hand effectively. But writing remains a problem because at 10 years of age she cannot keep up with the rest of her class. It has been arranged for her to use a silent typewriter to help her. Speed of movement is also a difficulty, and the school is taking the view that undue allowance must not be made for her if she is to remain in a normal school. She has good sticking power and I think will win through. She has a lively sense of humour and seems well adjusted to her disability. She remarked when the class were preparing a nativity play, 'Funny if you made *me* an angel. Fancy an angel on crutches!' Her school commented, 'A charming and intelligent child, who, by her unfailing cheerfulness in face of her disability and by the amount of enjoyment she extracts from everything, is an inspiration to grownups and children alike.'

J.C. (I.Q. 119, athetoid) was a most interesting boy. He made good progress in a P.H. school, using his high intelligence effectively, learning to type and doing especially well in mathematics. He achieved a place at the Thomas de la Rue School for Spastic Children and made good, working for 'O' and eventually 'A' levels. He also is a boy of great determination, battling against all odds and determined not to let his twin normal sister outshine him. He is very eager to prove his capacity and shows almost a dare-devil attitude. He insisted on going on a pony trek, on riding in a chair, unstrapped, up Glen Shee in Scotland and is now determined to learn to drive a car, and this despite quite severe athetosis and high tone deafness! He is rather strained and at $17\frac{1}{2}$ one felt he was setting himself rather impossible standards. He is now beginning to think of a job and is determined to find one for himself when he has completed his examinations. He recently wrote to the G.L.C. to enquire prospects and is interested in the possibilities of working for London Transport, planning new trunk roads and traffic improvements. One feels sure this boy will make good and find some satisfactory use for his good intelligence, and good practical ability. He is quite determined to help himself, and shows impatience at maternal solicitude.

The important factors that promote satisfactory adjustment appear to be:

1. Good drive, persistence and resilience on the part of the child.
2. Parental support.
3. Special advice and attention regarding communication difficulties, such as in writing and speech in their early school years, followed up by considerable ingenuity on the part of the teachers in later years, such as by encouraging the use of typewriters and dictation to class-mates in cases where writing was impaired.
4. Everyone concerned with the pupil is able to strike a reasonable balance between overprotection on the one hand and underprotection on the other, i.e. neither showing too much concern over his handicap so that he is more or less carried along as a passenger in the school, nor at the other extreme of making impossible demands such as subjects demanding quick and accurate motor control (P.E., craftwork, etc.).

Fig. 15 Busy classroom in secondary school for pupils with cerebral palsy.

Some of the difficulties that intelligent C.P.s have in adjusting to normal secondary school are outlined in an article by Gardner (1968) discussing the case of an athetoid girl whose difficulties were more in social-emotional adjustment than educational progress: the girl was eventually transferred to an academic stream in a secondary school for C.P. pupils and settled well to the less demanding atmosphere there. Specialized secondary schooling is available through the Spastics Society for very handicapped, bright pupils and the success rate in academic examinations is high, partly through the skill of experienced teachers who not only know their subjects but who have grasped the more difficult art of communicating with very handicapped pupils.

The aims of education

For the not too severely handicapped, the aims of education can be very similar to those that are advocated for ordinary children— a blend of aims: of self-fulfilment, of the development of potentialities, intellectual, physical, emotional, the aims of working towards a career and of service to the community. These various aims are not always completely compatible for ordinary children: for the handicapped pupils even greater difficulties are apt to arise. The presence of a considerable handicap means that achievements are bound to be low in certain areas. Self-fulfilment aims (such as an interest in art or poetry) may conflict with vocational and economic aims. Ordinary children can usually compromise, pursuing both aims and managing tolerably well in both. But the handicapped spastic has less scope: his range of alternatives is limited, such as by the simple time factor for example (the fact that he may need five times longer to type an essay than it takes an ordinary child to write one). Should he therefore abandon the self-fulfilment aims such as his interest in art, and concentrate solidly on academic work such as English and maths that may lead to 'O' and 'A' level exam successes and a professional career later? But there is a further problem: academic examinations are often the key to a professional career for ordinary pupils; but they are not necessarily so for very handicapped pupils. So the very handicapped pupil may have to aim at a less demanding career, such as a semi-skilled or technical one, rather than a professional post. Should the curriculum, therefore, be altered accordingly, devoting less time to English, for instance, and more to technical drawing and workshop experience? Does this also mean that he should spend more time on improving his motor skills, such as through some of the intensive methods of training that we have mentioned, like the Peto method? Follow-up studies of school children in various types of special schools suggest that their motor skills do not improve significantly as they go through the school and perhaps more intensive motor training would pay better dividends than certain academic subjects. But if the pupil is very severely handicapped we might in any case expect very little motor improvement, even through very intensive training. Should we in these cases abandon the idea of working towards employment for gain—and concentrate on self-fulfilment aims?

Many of these questions were debated at a multi-disciplinary Spastics Society seminar, including groups of psychologists, social workers, teachers, medical officers, Y.E.O.s and others (Gardner, 1969): no simple answers emerged and there is still some uncertainty about the aims of education for the severely handicapped pupil and what 'style of life' we might envisage following certain aims.

However, an increasing number of severely handicapped C.P.s are following academic careers at university level with some success. Some universities have been extremely helpful in providing the necessary extra facilities: York, for example, has been built with a view to providing easy access for physically handicapped students. Fellow students have, on the whole, been helpful with matters such as transport, accommodation, providing copies of lecture notes for students whose writing is too slow, and so on. In a US study (Muthard, 1968) it was noted that the attainments of a sample of 80 handicapped students were, on the whole, somewhat lower than those of ordinary students and that subsequent careers were quite satisfactory; but some problems remained in that although most of the handicapped graduates obtained jobs, these were seldom at the level or salary to which they felt entitled. As Mary Greaves (1969), who has first-hand experience of problems herself, points out, better counselling services are needed (as indeed they are for ordinary students) including the pooling of experience by appointments officers so that further lessons can be learned about providing the best opportunities for handicapped graduates. Some of their problems are very well described in the personal accounts by several very severely handicapped persons and their training and career achievements in a book entitled *Despite Disability* edited by Bleackley (1974).

Further education, training and employment prospects
We have touched on the difficulties of transition from school to work that beset very handicapped adolescents, as they leave the

relatively planned and ordered atmosphere of school and are often suddenly thrust into the wider world. For many, whether they be mildly, moderately or severely handicapped, additional help is usually needed over the transition period, particularly in respect of their need to develop some degree of social and emotional independence. A period of further education and training is often essential, such as those provided by the Spastics Society which runs residential centres of various kinds, some providing scope for further academic studies, some for general education and social training, some for vocational training, either technical or commercial, and there are, of course, schemes available through other agencies that provide for a variety of handicaps. For the less severely handicapped, ordinary Further Education Colleges are increasingly able to offer courses, and the Warnock Committee Report (HMSO, 1978) strongly emphasizes the need for such facilities, together with the necessary assessment, counselling and advisory services. Education does not stop at age 16 for any person—and certainly not for those with a handicap, who may have much 'leeway' to make up.

Ingram (1964) and Hellings (1964) carried out surveys of representative groups of people with cerebral palsy—i.e. including mildly, moderately and severely handicapped people—which showed that about 40 to 50 per cent obtained open or sheltered (earnings near normal) employment. Many are helped by an early assessment of their employment potentialities by attending a Spastics Society assessment course (Morgan, 1966). Those too handicapped for employment or special vocational training can attend work centres. The Spastics Society has over 25 such centres, where a variety of simple work opportunities are available even for the very handicapped, who can at least earn considerable pocket-money. Some work centres have hostels attached for those with homes in relatively isolated areas, or whose families can no longer provide for their care.

Clearly great efforts have to be made to ensure reasonable employment prospects for handicapped persons, by the many agencies involved, state, local authority and voluntary agencies. Mary Greaves (1969), in her very useful study of the employment of the disabled, emphasizes the need for some degree of integration of these services. Much also depends on the attitudes of employers and fellow workers. These are influenced by a variety of factors, ranging from the general state of employment in the economy, to the deeper attitudes of the community towards handicapped persons in their midst. Some of the older ideas of segregation of the handicapped still persist and in a sense handicapped persons form a 'minority group'.

Organizations

The parents' first consultation is likely to be with their family doctor, but since cerebral palsy is not a common condition, the advice of a specialist, particularly in the growing number of child development centres in the UK, will also be necessary.

As the child becomes older his needs become less medical, and more social and educationally orientated. The local Social Services and Education Departments can provide a wide range of advisory and support services, and in addition to these, the services of voluntary societies, such as the Spastics Society, are available to all.

The Society is a voluntary organization founded by parents in 1952, which has nearly 200 local groups and is run by a partnership of parents and professionals, providing a large network of day and residential services, including assessment and advisory centres, day treatment centres, schools, further education, careers advice, staff training, library, film and research units, help with holidays and family emergencies, clubs for teenagers, aids and appliances, including a mobile visiting aids centre.

These and its other services are described in various pamphlets obtainable from the Resources Division of the Spastics Society, 12 Park Crescent, London W1N 4EQ (Tel. 01-636 5020). Other relevant organizations are listed at the end of this Chapter.

SPINA BIFIDA

Spina bifida, which means 'split spine' and results in paralysis of the lower limbs, is a congenital condition from which babies rarely survived until about 20 years ago. By the early 1970s, new methods of treatment were available which ensured survival but did not cure the paralysis and other effects. It became necessary, therefore, to make urgent provision for the increasing numbers of children who could now survive, including help with management for parents, long-term medical and surgical coverage and special education. Research into ways of improving the effectiveness of such services was also urgently required. (See Anderson and Spain (1977) for an excellent summary of their own work in the field, especially in respect of social and educational consequences of spina bifida.)

Incidence

The incidence varies from area to area, unlike in conditions such as cerebral palsy and deafness, and it also varies over time. As we have mentioned, few affected babies survived before 1958, when new surgical measures, including the Spitz-Holter valve, which, combined with a shunt, helped to control the effects of the hydro-cephalic condition that troubles a large proportion of the children. The incidence of children surviving reached at least two per thousand live births in certain areas in the early 1970s. The prevalence is now estimated at about one per thousand live births in many regions of the UK (Lorber, 1977), although there are some so far unexplained regional variations. The recent decline in the numbers is largely due to the smaller number of cases selected for surgical treatment. The severity of spina bifida is usually readily evident at birth (unlike conditions such as cerebral palsy). The worst cases are subject to severe and permanent paralysis, in-continence and frequently some brain damage due to hydro-cephalus (an excess of cerebro-spinal fluid, which causes the skull to enlarge), all of which demands considerable surgical, medical and nursing care and expertise for long periods, if survival is to be ensured. Given this prospect, some surgeons no longer recom-mend the immediate and complicated surgery which is needed after birth, and without which the vast majority of such severely affected babies would not survive. It goes without saying that this involves very difficult ethical decisions, distressing to parents and doctors alike.

In future it will be possible to reduce the incidence consider-ably, since spina bifida can now be detected during the early months of pregnancy. Thus, if religious and moral views permit, an abortion may be carried out. Prenatal diagnosis of spina bifida is established by a technique known as amniocentesis. This in-volves taking a sample of the fluid surrounding the fetus, prefer-ably around the sixteenth week of pregnancy. In all except mild cases of spina bifida, this fluid will be found to contain a substance known as alphafetoprotein (AFP), due to the 'open wound' in the spine of the fetus. Unfortunately, the procedure is too elaborate for mass screening and in any case it carries slight risks, but it is available to mother's 'at risk' such as those who have previously had an affected baby. Intensive work on levels of AFP is being carried out in many countries, attempting to detect signs of it in the blood stream of pregnant women. If this search is successful, it could lead to very simple, inexpensive and safe methods of detecting spina bifida during early pregnancy.

Description of the condition

Spina bifida results from the failure of the protective bony arches in the baby's backbone to develop adequately at some point along the spine, thus leaving part of the spinal cord unenclosed. In mild cases (meningocele) treatment is simple and effective. Unfortunately, in over 90 per cent of cases the lesions are more extensive (myelomeningocele) and part of the spinal cord and its delicate nerves are malformed and exposed to further damage at birth.

The result is that a swelling containing cerebro-spinal fluid develops soon after birth and there is paralysis of the lower limbs (paraplegia), skin insensitivity and incontinence of the bowel and bladder. Hydrocephalus is an additional complication in the majority of cases. This is due to the fact that the cerebro-spinal fluid cannot be fully absorbed because of a partial block in the circulatory system. Internal pressure is thus increased, and an enlarged head may result.

Causes

The causes are not yet known for certain. There is a slight tendency for the condition to run in families, which suggests a genetic factor. Girls are affected more often than are boys, which is the reverse of most handicapping conditions, the ratio being 1·3:1. It is more prevalent in some ethnic groups than in others—in the UK, for instance, and northern parts of India it is more common than among Mongolians and Negroes. Environmental factors are also likely to be important, but no relevant ones have been identified yet. Earlier studies of the diets of affected families suggested that consumption of blighted potatoes or large amounts of tea might be contributory factors, but the theory has not been substantiated and seems unlikely. The condition is more common in lower than in higher socio-economic groups, which points to a complex pattern of interacting causes, both genetic and environmental.

Treatment

Early surgical treatment is usually essential in the great majority of cases if the baby is to survive. Usually this consists in removing the lump on the child's back and covering the area with a skin graft. This highly skilful operation should be carried out in the first 24 hours of the child's life. Later operations achieve less satisfactory results.

If hydrocephalus is present, surgery is undertaken at two or three weeks of age to insert a pressure valve known as the Spitz-

Holter just beneath the skin, behind the ear, connected by a plastic tube to the head's reservoir of fluid at one end and to the right receiving chamber of the heart at the other. At a given pressure the valve automatically opens and the excessive fluid is drained off and absorbed into the blood stream. It this is done early enough and if other brain damage has not occurred, there will be no damage due to compression and the child's intelligence should develop normally.

Early physiotherapy is arranged which the mother can carry out under expert guidance so that frequent long journeys to hospital with a heavily incontinent child can be avoided. The purpose of physiotherapy is to keep the child's muscles strong and in balance and to prevent contractures especially in the hips, knees and ankles. Before the crawling stage the child can start moving around by pulling with his arms, sitting on a trolley such as a 'Chailey Chariot' or a 'Surfskater'. These are easily propelled and cannot tip easily and the child can be strapped in for safety. This activity encourages exploration and provides first-hand experience of size, shape, texture, position in space, colour, movement and sound. These experiences may well reduce later visuo-spatial difficulties in learning which are common among children with brain damage.

When the child is on the threshold of walking the right type of caliper may be supplied with hand sticks or 'plonks', and he can be taught the right gait. Later he will manage a tricycle or kiddicar perhaps. Mobility should be given every encouragement. Walking without aids is rare among these children, but later they can learn to play football, stool ball, learn to swim, enjoy badminton or even a tug-of-war in calipers.

The valve inserted in babyhood must be periodically checked, for intra-cranial pressure due to a faulty valve may result in convulsions or even blindness. Early symptoms of distress are irritability, loss of appetite, sickness, headaches or drowsiness and the parents must continually be on the alert for these warning signs. They may mean that the valve is blocked or infected or come unstuck. The cause can readily be detected by X-ray and medical attention provided.

Incontinence management

The spina bifida child does not achieve continence of bowel or bladder, naturally, as an ordinary child does between two and three years of age. He does not receive warning signals from the bladder or rectum and consequently does not know when they need emptying. If the bladder is not emptied when full it will tend to stretch, enlarge and by back pressure can compress and damage the kidneys. Waste products will circulate into vital organs and serious illness will result.

Allen Field (1970) gives details about the regime necessary to control incontinence which can, if not dealt with, make the child's life a misery and prevent admission to a school. The child needs to drink a great deal of water, between 5 to 7 pints a day, and this should be established as a habit. The bladder should be emptied every two hours and twice during the night. For males a penile urinal attachment can be used, made of soft rubber and easy to take to pieces and to clean. With the female an operation is usually necessary to insert a stoma, often called 'a red cherry', attached to a collecting bag which must be emptied every two hours. Very careful attention to hygiene is essential if infection is to be avoided. These routines have to be learnt by the child and managed by him as soon as he is old enough. Naturally the problems of incontinence weigh heavily on the school staff and for this reason it is difficult for even a very intelligent child with poor continence control to be accepted in a normal school. Moreover he might well become miserably self-conscious and anxious about accidents.

Skin insensitivity
The spina bifida child has an insensitive skin, particularly in the lower limbs. He does not receive normal sensory messages indicating heat, cold or pain. Consequently he is especially prone to skin hazards such as burns, pressure sores or ulcers. Specially sensitive skin areas on the buttocks and on the ankles, elbows, knees and other bony prominences can be toughened by massage with soap, then rinsing, drying and applying surgical spirit and powder. Any red areas which may develop should be treated with appropriate ointment and very careful examination of his body surface should be made twice a day. Damage can so easily be done by getting too close to a fire, leaning against a radiator, stepping into a too hot bath or friction from use of calipers. Foam rubber mattresses or cushions should be used to protect the surface of the skin from friction.

Intellectual development
The intellectual development of spina bifida children varies widely. This is scarcely surprising, however, in view of the combination of hydrocephaly (which is found in many and impairs the intelligence of some) and the accompanying physical handicaps

with all the time-consuming medical and surgical attention that these require.

Whilst children without hydrocephalus may show a virtually normal level and range of intellectual functioning, those with a sufficient degree of hydrocephalus to warrant the use of a shunt show a range that is mostly below average. In Tew's (1975) study, the intellectual level of children with a shunt averaged around I.Q. 70, which means that almost half were in the subnormal range. It must be stressed, however, that these figures refer to the scores of *groups* of children, telling us nothing about any particular individual, who, in spite of the need for a shunt, may nevertheless be of normal intelligence or higher. In Spain's (1974) sample, the shunted children also scored predominantly in the dull to low average ranges (mean I.Q. 83). They also showed signs of special learning difficulties, similar to those we have outlined in our other sections, on children with cerebral palsy, and 'minimal cerebral dysfunction'.

1. On the whole verbal abilities tend to be higher than non-verbal ones.
2. Visual perceptual and visual motor skills are frequently impaired in similar ways to those we have described in previous sections (see pp. 35–36) and require similar educational intervention.
3. Fine hand control may also be slightly impaired according to some observers (Anderson, 1977) sufficiently to affect accuracy and speed in writing.
4. There is also an interesting tendency for some (but certainly not all) spina bifida children with shunts, to show a superficial precociousness in their speech. This tendency was first noted in hydrocephalic children without spina bifida, and is sometimes described as the 'cocktail party' syndrome, referring to excessive, superficial chattering, on unrelated and often irrelevant topics, with often very little understanding. In Spain's (1975) study about 40 per cent of the children at age six showed some degree of hyper-verbal speech, and many tended to be physically restless and distractible. The picture suggests a difficulty in inhibiting irrelevant responses, similar to some of our descriptions in Chapter 3, Minimal Cerebral Dysfunction. These special learning difficulties in children with spina bifida have been intensively studied by Anderson and Spain (1977).

Education

Education, in its broadest sense, begins at home with the parents, and it is particularly important that the parents of handicapped children be given help and advice. They need advice at the clinic on the child's medical and nursing needs, from physiotherapists on treatment, from health visitors on general management, and from social workers and teachers. The latter need to be specially skilled in communicating their teaching skills to parents and handicapped children, in the way we have described in 'Parental involvement projects' (p. 72). Unfortunately, there is a shortage of teachers who are adequately trained in this area. Furthermore, more training facilities where parents can be given advice and practical demonstrations to help with their children's early education are urgently needed.

Nursery education is also needed for most handicapped children, and with a condition such as spina bifida, only just over half receive it in the UK at present. Nursery education can help make up for the restricted social life and limited range of experience that many children suffer on account of their handicaps. Provided the mobility and incontinence problems are not too great, many children with spina bifida can attend a normal play or nursery group. It is important, however, that the staff should receive some expert advice about the children's special needs; and then all the usual free activities of a nursery—painting, building, hammering, sand and water play, chasing, fighting, dressing up, and constructive imaginative play—can be made available. Speech, bodily control and social skills are more likely to develop quickly in this sort of environment and, as a rule, it is helpful if the majority of children with handicaps can start school life in the company of ordinary children, learning about the normal world.

However, if the handicaps are severe and multiple, as with severe cases of spina bifida, the amount that they gain from such experience can sometimes be outweighed by the anxieties produced and by the widening gap between the very handicapped children's responses and those of ordinary children. This gap cannot always be bridged, without curtailing the normal children's activities. Therefore, the need for some specialized nursery groups will continue.

Ordinary schools are often willing and able to provide for spina bifida children's special needs when they reach formal school age (age five in the UK), but again, more advice and support from experts should be forthcoming. Woodburn (1973) found in one study that about one-third of the children with spina bifida were in normal school at age five, but the figure varies from area to area, depending on factors such as the amount of special provision that is available, and the amount of support for the normal school staff.

Some special provision after the age of five is certainly needed for children with severe and multiple handicap, including those with severe intellectual impairments, some of whom need special schooling, others a special unit attached to a normal school. We have already mentioned studies of such units (Cope and Anderson, 1977) in the section on children with cerebral palsy, and the majority of units are shown to be successful in providing for the educational, medical, social and some of the therapeutic needs of children with spina bifida, just as they are in providing for the needs of children with cerebral palsy—provided the handicaps, particularly in communication, are not too severe.

The staff in such units need to be alert to the special learning difficulties that children with shunts show, in particular, e.g. uneven intellectual ability, poor visual perceptual and visual motor skills, slight but sometimes significant fine hand control problems, affecting handwriting in some children, and difficulties due to distractibility. The remedial measures needed to combat these will be similar to those we have outlined in other Chapters.

Residential schooling may be a necessity, owing to the lack of day schools near at hand, but this should be the exception rather than the rule, especially for children under 10 years of age. It is so important for them to know a normal home life, to mix with their normal contemporaries and cope with the ordinary hazards of life rather than to grow up in a more sheltered environment with a handicapped population. There are a few excellent schools for spina bifida children only, which provide all the necessary care and treatment as well as a satisfactory education, but again this involves segregation and lack of contact with ordinary children.

The future

Though the numbers of severely handicapped children with spina bifida are likely to be less in future, there are several thousand affected children in the UK with significant problems that call for careful consideration and long-term support. The sensitive period of adolescence, for example, is made doubly difficult by such problems as embarrassment over toileting difficulties. Dorner (1975) found evidence of depression in teenagers with spina bifida, particularly amongst the girls. Mobility problems impair social life, and cause some teenagers to remain very dependent on their families and, at the same time, resentful of this dependence, so that they are angry and sullen towards the parents.

Most of all, with adolescence comes the problem of the stark realization that the handicap that they have at that stage is permanent—and will have a lifelong effect on their prospects for jobs, sex, marriage and having children. Many of these problems, and the kinds of support, counselling, further education and vocational training that are required to help with them, are fully discussed in the works of Anderson and Spain (1977). Elizabeth Anderson also initiated a study of 119 young persons, 89 with cerebral palsy and 30 with spina bifida, age 15, and still at school. It is proposed to follow up their progress after school, in respect of their self-image, problems of special adjustment, work prospects, etc.

As we have previously mentioned, many of the problems are not so much within the handicapped person, but in the attitudes of people coming into contact with them. Fortunately these attitudes are changing.

Organizations

The main organization serving the interests of people with spina bifida and their families is the Association for Spina Bifida and Hydrocephalus (ASBAH), Tavistock House North, Tavistock Square, London WC1H 9HJ. This organization publishes a variety of literature on the subject, including a regular journal.

Other organizations for the handicapped are listed at the end of this Chapter.

OTHER PHYSICAL HANDICAPS

These include a wide variety of physical conditions, some temporary, some permanent, affecting the child's health or energy, or control of certain limbs, etc., in varying degrees, and therefore having varying effects on his educational, social and emotional development. Fortunately in most cases, the extent of the handicap is mild enough for the child to benefit by ordinary schooling.

Asthmatic conditions, for example, are very common, affecting over 2 per cent of children in the UK, but, providing the teacher is aware of the child's condition and its occasional effects (such as coughing and wheezing, fatigue due to nights without sleep as he struggles for breath, and the anxieties these produce in him and his family), the great majority of children with asthma can enjoy a normal school career.

Likewise, the great majority of children with heart diseases, diabetes, epilepsy, can cope with most ordinary demands, given minimal and occasional 'concessions' based on the teacher's understanding of the condition and its effects.

Turning to children with handicaps that are sufficient to warrant more close attention, those severe enough to lead to special educational needs, that cannot be met by ordinary common sense, we can consider some of the various kinds of handicapping conditions that are typically found in special schools for physically handicapped children. These figures are based on a Department of Education and Science Survey of England as a whole, in 1970, when there were approximately twelve thousand children attending, or waiting to attend, special P.H. schools.

The most numerous groups were of children with cerebral palsy (33 per cent) and spina bifida (17 per cent), involving not only physical handicaps, but 'brain damage' in the majority of cases, giving rise to special educational needs, that we have already considered, especially in respect of communication difficulties.

The remaining 50 per cent of children in special schools very rarely show complications due to brain damage, but a sizeable group will, of course, have difficulties with communication, mobility, hand control, etc., that can be helped by some of the measures that we have described in previous sections.

Heart disease, either congenital or due to rheumatic fever, accounts for about 8 per cent of the children in special schools; activity levels must obviously be curtailed when the child shows signs of feeling faint, chest pains, shortness of breath, unusual fatigue, etc.

Muscular dystrophy accounts for approximately 6 per cent in special schools, and this is unfortunately a 'progressive', i.e. deteriorating, inherited condition, largely affecting boys, and resulting in a steady deterioration of muscle cells. The condition is usually first noticed as 'clumsiness', by the age of about three, and in the commonest (Duchenne) type, the majority of children need a wheelchair by the age of ten and are likely to die in their late teens, especially if their heart muscles become affected. No treatment is yet known, and the aims of teachers, social workers and other professionals can merely be supportive—to ensure that the child has as full a life as possible, whilst he can, and whilst the search for a cure continues. Fortunately its occurrence is rare, about one in thirty thousand births in the UK.

Congenital deformities and disorders affecting limbs and skeletal growth account for approximately 10 per cent of the children in special schools, including talipes (club foot), dislocated hips, scoliosis (curvature of the spine) and absence of limbs, usually congenital, but can also be due to amputations.

Rheumatoid arthritis can result in severe stiffening of the child's joints (wrists, knees and ankles, etc.) accompanied by considerable pain. Causes and cures of this condition in childhood are not yet known, but treatment to relieve some of the pain and stiffness, including physiotherapy and hydrotherapy, etc., is essential, plus plenty of rest periods. The degree of inflammation of the joints varies over the years and fortunately usually becomes less as the child gets older so that the majority can eventually lead a normal adolescence and adult life.

The remaining 20 per cent of children in special P.H. schools have a wide variety of conditions, too numerous to describe here, in any detail, e.g. haemophilia (failure in blood clotting), Perthes disease (a deterioration in the hip end of the thigh bone), cystic fibrosis (an inherited condition affecting the pancreas and the lungs in particular, sometimes severe enough to cause lung damage and death).

For a comprehensive description of the great majority of such conditions see Bleck and Nagel's (1975) *Medical Atlas for Teachers*.

Conclusions

It is impossible to summarize all the educational and social implications of the conditions we have so briefly described in this section. As we have mentioned, the majority of children under these headings can and do attend normal schools, and their conditions cause little or no stress to teachers and parents, provided all concerned have some knowledge of what is involved and are ready and willing to make a few concessions when necessary, e.g. excusing a child from too strenuous activity, giving extra help to make up for lost time due to hospitalization, etc.

Those children with conditions severe enough to warrant special educational provision do, of course, need more consideration, ranging from medical and nursing coverage, drugs and diets, therapy, long rest periods for some, to help with communication and mobility difficulties for those whose physical handicaps are similar to those we have described in our previous sections on children with cerebral palsy and spina bifida.

All the considerations concerning the psychology of handicap also apply, since any physical handicap is likely to mark certain children out as 'different' from ordinary children, and they are therefore at risk for being seen more in terms of the handicap than as a child first and foremost. Being demonstratively different in some respects from the ordinary population, they are apt to become victims of some of the prejudices and discriminations that confront most minority groups, based on ignorance, fear and stereotyped attitudes, mostly of a devaluing and depersonalizing kind. It is our job to dispel these prejudices.

ORGANIZATIONS

We have listed below only some of the organizations set up to help with the general and special problems which confront handicapped children and their families. A further list is obtainable from: The Voluntary Council for Handicapped Children, National Children's Bureau, 8 Wakley Street, London EC1V 7QE (Tel. 01-278 9441).

Action Research for the Crippled
 Child,
49 Victoria Street, London SW1
(01-222 5959 & 01-222 6006).

Association of Disabled Professionals,
General Secretary,
The Stables, 73 Pound Road,
Banstead,
Surrey SM7 2HU
(Burgh Heath 52366).

Disability Alliance,
5 Netherhall Gardens,
London NW3 5RN
(01-794 1536).
Pressure/Research federation on welfare rights; information.

Disabled Living Foundation,
346 Kensington High Street,
London W14 8NS
(01-602 2491).
Maintains an information service and standing exhibition of aids.

National Bureau for Handicapped
 Students,
Thomas Coram Foundation,
40 Brunswick Square,
London WC1N 1AZ
(01-278 3127).

National Fund for Research into
 Crippling Diseases,
Vincent House, 1 Springfield Road,
Horsham,
West Sussex RH12 2PN
(0403 64101).

National Society for Mentally
 Handicapped Children,
Pembridge Hall, 17 Pembridge
 Square,
London W2 4EP
(01-229 8941).

Royal Association for Disability and
 Rehabilitation,
25 Mortimer Street,
London W1N 8AB
(01-637 5400).
Formerly Central Council for the Disabled, and British Association for Rehabilitation of the Disabled.

REFERENCES

Abercrombie, M. J. L. (1964) Perceptual and visuo-motor disorders in cerebral palsy. *Little Club Clinics in Developmental Medicine*, No. 11. London: Spastics Society/Heinemann.

Anderson, E. M. & Spain, B. (1977) *The Child with Spina Bifida*. London: Methuen.

Asher, F. & Schonell, F. E. (1950) A survey of 400 cases of cerebral palsy in childhood. *Archives of Disease in Childhood*, **25**, 124, 360.

Bleackley, R. (Ed.) (1974) *Despite Disability*. Educational Enterprises Ltd.

Bleck, E. E. & Nagel, D. A. (Eds.) (1975) *Physically Handicapped Children, a Medical Atlas for Teachers*. New York: Grune & Stratton.

Blencowe, S. N. (Ed.) (1969) *Cerebral Palsy and the Young Child*. Edinburgh: Livingstone.

Bobath, K. (1966) The motor deficit in patients with cerebral palsy. *Little Club Clinics in Developmental Medicine*, No. 23. London: Spastics Society/ Heinemann.

Bowley, A. H. (1967a) Studying children from Cheyne. *Special Education incorporating Spastics Quarterly*, **56**, No. 1.

Bowley, A. H. (1967b) A follow-up study of 64 children with cerebral palsy. *Developmental Medicine and Child Neurology*, **9**, No. 2.

Brereton le Gay, B. & Sattler, J. (1975) *Cerebral Palsy: Basic Abilities*. Spastics Centre of New South Wales.

Bricker, W. A. & Bricker, D. D. (1973) Behaviour modification programmes. In *Assessment for Learning in Mentally Handicapped*. Ed. Mittler, P. IRMMH Symposium No. 5. Edinburgh: Churchill Livingstone.

Brimer, M. A. & Dunn, L. M. (1973) *English Picture Vocabulary Test. Full Range Version*. Bristol: Educational Evaluation Enterprises.

Burgemeister, B., Blum, L. H. & Lorge, L. (1972) *Columbia Mental Maturity Scale*. Revised edition. New York: World Book Company.

Collins, M. & Collins, D. (1976) *Kith and Kids: Self help for families of the handicapped*. London: Souvenir Press.

Cope, C. E. & Anderson, E. M. (1977) *Special Units for Ordinary Schools*. University of London Institute of Education/National Foundation for Educational Research.

Cotton, E. (1975) *Conductive Education and Cerebral Palsy*. London: The Spastics Society.

Cotton, E. & Parnell, M. (1967) From Hungary: the Peto method. *Special Education*, **56**, No. 4.

Crothers, B. & Paine, R. S. (1959) *The Natural History of Cerebral Palsy*. Cambridge: Harvard University Press.

Cruickshank, W. M. (1961) *A Teaching Method for Brain Injured and Hyperactive Children*. New York: Syracuse University Press.

Cruickshank, W. M. (1966) *Cerebral Palsy: its Implications and Community Problems*. New York: Syracuse University Press.

Cruickshank, W. M. & Hallahan, D. P. (1973) *Psychoeducational Foundations of Learning Disabilities*. New York: Prentice Hall.

Cunningham, C. C. & Jeffree, D. M. (1974) *The Organization and Structure of Workshops for Parents of Mentally Handicapped Children*. Hester Adrian Research Centre, University of Manchester.

Davies, P. A. & Tizard, J. P. M. (1975) Very low birthweight and subsequent neurological defects. *Developmental Medicine and Child Neurology*, **17**, 3.

Department of Education and Science (1970) *Diagnostic and Assessment Units for Young Handicapped Children*. Education Survey 9. London: HMSO.

Doll, E. A. (1947) *Vineland Social Maturity Scale*. Nashville: American Guidance Service Inc.

Dorner, S. (1975) The relationship of physical handicap to stress in families with an adolescent with spina bifida. *Developmental Medicine and Child Neurology*, **17** (6).

Douglas, A. A. (1961) Opthalmological aspects. In *Cerebral Palsy in Childhood and Adolescence*. Ed. Henderson, J. L. Edinburgh: Livingstone.

Elliott, C. D., Murrey, D. J. & Pearson, L. S. (1978) *The British Abilities Scales*. Windsor: National Foundation for Educational Research.

Fields, A. (1970) *The Challenge of Spina Bifida*. London: Heinemann.

Finnie, N. R. (1974) *Handling the Young Cerebral Palsied Child at Home*. London: Heinemann.

Fisch, L. (1957) Hearing impairment and cerebral palsy. *Speech*, **21**, 43.

Frostig, M. (1968) Testing as a basis for educational therapy. In *Assessment of the Cerebral Palsied Child for Education*. Ed. Loring, J. London: Spastics Society/Heinemann.

Frostig, M. *et al.* (1964) *The Marianne Frostig Developmental Test of Visual Perception*. Palo Alto, California: Consulting Psychologists Press.

Frostig, M. & Maslow, P. (1973) *Learning Problems in the Classroom*. New York: Grune & Stratton.

Gardner, L. (1969) Planning for planned dependence. *Special Education*, **58**, No. 1.

Gardner, L. (1970a) Handicapped children in ordinary schools. *Teachers' World*, No. 3141.

Gardner, L. (1970b) Assessment and outcome. *Special Education*, **59**, No. 4.

Gardner, L. & Johnson, J. (1964) The long-term assessment and experimental education of retarded cerebral palsied children. *Developmental Medicine and Child Neurology*, **6**, 250.

Gorman, P. & Paget, G. (1970) *A Systematic Sign Language*. London: Association for Experiment in Oral Education.

Greaves, M. (1969) *Work and Disability*. London: British Council for Rehabilitation of the Disabled.

Gunzburg, H. C. (1966) *Progress Assessment Charts*. London: National Association for Mental Health.

Hagberg, B. (1978) The epidemiologic panorama of major neuropaediatric handicaps in Sweden. In *Care of the Handicapped Child*. Ed. Apley, J. London: Spastics International Publications/Heinemann.

Hellings, D. A. (1964) *Spastic School Leavers*. London: The Spastics Society.

Henderson, J. L. (1961) *Cerebral Palsy in Childhood and Adolescence*. Edinburgh: Livingstone.

Hewett, S. (1970) *The Family and the Handicapped Child*. London: Allen & Unwin.

HMSO (1978) *Special Educational Needs: Report of Committee of Enquiry*, headed by H. M. Warnock. London: HMSO.

Holt, K. S. (1965) *Assessment of Cerebral Palsy*, Vol. I. London: Lloyd-Luke.

Holt, K. S. & Reynell, J. K. (1967) *Assessment of Cerebral Palsy*, Vol. II. London: Lloyd-Luke.

Hopkins, T. *et al.* (1954) *Evaluation and Education of the Cerebral Palsied Child*. Washington D.C.: International Council for Exceptional Children.

Ingram, T. T. S., Jameson, S., Errington, J. & Mitchell, R. G. (1964) Living with cerebral palsy. *Little Club Clinics in Developmental Medicine*, No. 14. London: Spastics Society Medical Education and Information Unit/Heinemann.

Jackson, S. (1972) *A Teachers' Guide to Tests and Testing*. London: Longman.

Jeffree, D. M. & McConkey, R. (1976a) *Let Me Speak*. London: Souvenir Press.

Jeffree, D. M. & McConkey, R. (1976b) *Parental Involvement Project Development Charts*. London: Hodder & Stoughton.

Jeffree, D. M., McConkey, R. & Hewson, S. (1977) *Teaching the Handicapped Child*. London: Hodder & Stoughton.

Jernqvist, L. (1978) *My Head is in the Middle*. Bulletin of International Cerebral Palsy Society, London.

Jones, M. (1976) *The use of cued social reinforcement to increase the 'on task' behaviour of a distractible multi-handicapped boy in the classroom*. Meldreth Occasional Papers, Meldreth Manor School, near Royston, Hertfordshire.

Jones, M. (1977) *An application of observation techniques to explore interaction patterns of teachers in the classroom*. Meldreth Occasional Papers, Meldreth Manor School, near Royston, Hertfordshire.

Jones, M. & Ketteridge, K. (1977) *Meldreth Electronic Aids Book No. 1 and the Meldreth A4 Tutor*. Meldreth Occasional Papers, Meldreth Manor School, near Royston, Hertfordshire.

Kephart, N. C. (1961) *The Slow Learner in the Classroom*. Columbus, Ohio: Merrill.

Kiernan, C. & Jones, M. (1977) *Behaviour Assessment Battery*. Windsor: National Foundation for Educational Research.

Kiernan, C., Jordan, R. & Saunders, C. (1978) *Starting Off*. London: Souvenir Press.

Kirk, S. A. & McCarthy, J. J. (1961) *Illinois Test of Psycholinguistic Abilities*. Institute for Research on Exceptional Children.

Kushlick, A. & Blunden, R. (1974) The epidemiology of mental subnormality. In *Mental Deficiency*. Ed. Clarke, A. M. & Clarke, A. D. B. London: Methuen.

Levitt, S. (1977) *Treatment of Cerebral Palsy and Motor Delay*. Oxford: Blackwell.

Levin, M. L., Brightman, I. J. & Burtt, E. J. (1949) The problem of cerebral palsy. *New York Journal of Medicine*, **49,** 2793.

Lindon, R. L. (1963) The pultibec system for the medical assessment of handicapped children. *Developmental Medicine and Child Neurology*, **5,** No. 2.

Lorber, J. (1977) Spina bifida cystica. In *Neuro-development Problems in Early Childhood*. Ed. Drillien, C. M. & Drummond, M. B. Oxford: Blackwell.

Loring, J. A. (1965) The contribution of a voluntary society to special education. In *Teaching the Cerebral Palsied Child*. Ed. Loring, J. A. London: Spastics Society/Heinemann.

Loring, J. A. (Ed.) (1968) *Assessment of the Cerebral Palsied Child for Education*. London: Spastics Society/Heinemann.

Luria, A. R. (1961) *The Role of Speech in the Regulation of Normal and Abnormal Behaviour*. Ed. Tizard, J. Oxford: Pergamon Press.

Margulec, I. (Ed.) (1966) *Cerebral Palsy in Adolescence and Adulthood: a rehabilitation study*. Jerusalem: Academic Press.

Mittler, P. (1974) *A Rationale for Parent Partnership*. Hester Adrian Research Centre, University of Manchester.

Morgan, M. R. (1966) Predictions, provision and progress. In *The Spastic School Child and the Outside World*. Ed. Loring, J. & Mason, A. London: Spastics Society/Heinemann.

Muthard, J. E. & Hutchison, J. (1968) *Cerebral Palsied College Students: their Education and Employment*. Gainesville: University of Florida.

Newton, M. & Thomson, M. (1977) *The Aston Index*. Wisbech, Cambs: Learning Development Aids.

Nielsen, H. H. (1966) *A Psychological Study of Cerebral Palsied Children*. Copenhagen: Munksgaard.

Oswin, M. (1967) *Behaviour Problems amongst Children with Cerebral Palsy*. Bristol: Wright.

Patterson, G. R. & Gullion, M. E. (1968) *Living with Children: new methods for parents and teachers*. Illinois: Research Press.

Piaget, J. & Inhelder, B. (1956) *The Child's Conception of Space*. London: Routledge & Kegan Paul.

Pre-school Playgroups Association (1978) *Guidelines for Playgroups with a Handicapped Child*. London: P.P.A.

Reynell, J. (1977) *Reynell Developmental Language Scales, Revised Manual and Test Material*. Windsor: National Foundation for Educational Research.

Rutter, M., Graham, P. & Yule, W. (1970) A neuropsychiatric study in childhood. *Little Club Clinics in Developmental Medicine*, Nos 35 and 36. London: Spastics International Medical Publications/Heinemann.

Spain, B. (1974) Verbal and performance ability in pre-school children with spina bifida. *Developmental Medicine and Child Neurology*, **16**, (6) 773–780.

Tansley, A. E. (1967) *Reading and Remedial Reading*. London: Routledge & Kegan Paul.

Tew, B. J. & Laurence, K. M. (1975) The effects of hydrocephalus on intelligence, visual perception and school attainments. *Developmental Medicine and Child Neurology*, **17**, No. 6, Suppl. 35.

Thompson, D. A. & Johnson, J. (1971) The touch-tutor at Hawksworth Hall. *Special Education*, **60**, No. 1. (pages 11, 12).

Tizard, J. (1964) *Community Services for the Mentally Handicapped*. London: Oxford University Press.

Wedell, K. (1973) *Learning and Perceptuo-motor Disabilities in Children*. New York: Wiley.

Wilshere, E. R. (Ed.) (1975) *Communication. Equipment for the Disabled Series*. Oxford Regional Health Authority.

Wolfe, J. M. (Ed.) (1969) *The Results of Treatment in Cerebral Palsy*. Springfield, Ill.: Thomas.

Woodburn, M. (1973) *Social Implications of Spina Bifida—a Study in South East Scotland*. Edinburgh: Eastern Scottish Spina Bifida Association.

Woods, G. E. (1957) *Cerebral Palsy in Childhood*. Bristol: Wright.

Wynn, M. & Wynn, A. 1977) *The Prevention of Pre-term Birth*. London: Foundation for Research in Child Bearing.

Younghusband, E., Birchall, D., Davie, R. & Pringle, M. L. K. (Eds.) (1970) *Living with Handicap*. London: National Children's Bureau.

3

The child with minimal cerebral dysfunction

GENERAL OVERVIEW

Children with minimal cerebral dysfunction are a very intriguing and heterogeneous group whose special learning and behaviour difficulties have become much better understood in recent years. What sort of learning and behaviour difficulties do we mean? Parents' and teachers' descriptions often include the following features: 'He is restless, fidgety, difficult to manage; has no self-control, is undisciplined and cannot stand frustration; she breaks things impulsively and has lots of accidents; she is bird-witted, inattentive, distractible, always on the move; he is clumsy and hopeless at school work in spite of high intelligence; she can talk the hind leg off a donkey, but cannot put anything down on paper.'

Many of these features can be applied to almost every child at one time or another: normal children at certain ages and in certain situations are expected to show some of these features: emotionally disturbed children show many and so do some children brought up in socially and culturally deprived areas. But do particular, long-standing combinations of some of these features suggest a category of handicap—that of minimal cerebral dysfunctioning or brain damage?* It is likely that they do, although there are many ambiguities in this field.

We have briefly discussed brain-damaged children in other sections of this book, such as the spastic and hydrocephalic children whose brain damage has well-recognized physical accompaniments, such as lack of motor control. Readers will be familiar with brain damage in adults, such as those due to head injuries, leading

* The term 'brain damage' is unsatisfactory because it suggests that some agency has physically damaged a brain which was originally intact. Though this may be an accurate description for some children, it does not include those whose brains have failed to develop normally because of, for example, a biochemical disorder, which might be inborn and have nothing to do with externally caused damage. For the sake of convenience, however, we shall use the term in this Chapter.

to a temporary loss of speech (aphasia) and strokes leading to some loss of control of one side of the body (hemiplegia). With newborn and young children, who may have no definite physical signs, the concept of brain damage is on a much less firm foundation. We are not yet clear exactly what is involved concerning the neurological causes of their condition, the effects on the learning and behaviour of the child, and their remediation.

It was Strauss and Lehtinen (1947) who in the 1940s crystallized many of the ideas about brain damage and its effects on behaviour that were intriguing neurologists, psychologists and educators around that time. Looking at children whose learning was retarded, Strauss considered that most cases could be classified into two major groups (with some overlap):

1. *The endogenous group:* those whose retardation was caused by familial or genetic factors (such as mongol children whom we now know to have a chromosome defect).
2. *The exogenous group:* those whose retardation 'came from without' as it were, due to some damaging agent often during pregnancy or around the time of birth which had impaired an immature brain that would have otherwise developed normally. For example, a virus infection to the mother during the early months of pregnancy, such as rubella, is believed to be one cause of brain damage.

Strauss' major interest, however, was not so much in the causes of brain damage, but in its effect on the behaviour and learning capacity of these children. He believed that the brain-damaged group showed certain patterns of behaviour and learning, notably involving hyperactivity and distractibility, linked with perceptual and behaviour difficulties, that fall into a recognized pattern, and could not be explained or understood by reference to other explanatory concepts. In other words such children could not be regarded as generally mentally subnormal, emotionally disturbed as a result of poor parental attitudes, or affected by social deprivation or by physical and sensory handicaps such as visual and hearing difficulties. The explanations instead were along neurological lines, to the effect that the higher nervous system had suffered some kind of damage and that this resulted in odd, patchy, uneven behaviour and learning.

Subsequent research suggests that Strauss overstated his case. The evidence for any definite patterns of behaviour is tenuous: although some children show some characteristics, the link with neurological causes is even more tenuous. However, Strauss' ideas are a valuable starting point in this field. Let us briefly consider a case history.

Graham was referred to the Schools' Psychological Service for 'backwardness and emotional disturbance' at aged seven. Psychological interview showed normal general intelligence (Binet I.Q. approximately 100) but with many odd and uneven features. Graham was noted to be particularly poor at copying and creating drawings: on purely practical tests of his performance abilities, severe visual motor and visual perceptual difficulties were shown (Wechsler Performance I.Q. approximately 60 compared to a verbal I.Q. of over 100).

His educational attainments were also uneven: his reading was almost normal whilst his writing and arithmetic were practically nil. He could count a little by rote but had no knowledge of number concepts.

His major problems were in his behaviour: his distractibility and restlessness were extreme. In the individual interview he showed considerable 'forced responsiveness', was easily distracted by slight visual and auditory cues, and quite unable to stick to the point in conversation. Linked with this was his excessive motor disinhibition—he seemed compelled to touch things and could rarely sit and contemplate anything. He also showed occasional perseveration, repeating questions, drawings and odd movements, such as obsessionally patting his head. His speech was telegraphic.

His general behaviour was even worse. He was generally hyperactive, restless and unconforming in the classroom, wandering around, failing to join in group activities, lying on the floor when he felt inclined or under the teacher's desk, showing many odd movements, talking to himself. He was such an interference with the work and behaviour of other children that he was offered only part-time infant schooling after the age of 5½ and excluded completely from school at the age of seven. The school noted his vivid imagination, but apart from his keenness on animals, they could find nothing positive to say about him and tended to regard him as sub-normal.

The medical history was suggestive but not very definite. He had been diagnosed at the age of three as a case of mild hypotonia and clumsiness. His e.e.g. showed nothing strongly abnormal. His early history showed some difficulties at birth. His mother was unwell throughout the pregnancy with a threatened abortion, and he was jaundiced on the second day and seemed sleepy and did not suck very well for some time. Developmental milestones were rather slow; he walked at 17 months but fell easily. He was treated for 'knock knees'.

His family is of professional class and there are two younger normal siblings. His mother was a very sensible, warm person and was becoming very despondent about Graham's behaviour both at home and at school. The parents were at a loss to account for his behaviour and at odds with the school authorities.

This brief picture of Graham's history and behaviour is typical of many children who are designated as brain injured. His difficulties cannot be explained by reference to general subnormality or to parental handling—which had been excellent; he had no obvious physical or sensory handicaps, nor was he deprived of experience. Let us see what light other studies can throw on these sorts of problems, first dealing with the question of the incidence and causes of brain damage.

Incidence and causes

The incidence of brain-damaged children amongst those attending normal schools is estimated to be quite high, varying between 1 and 7 per cent of the general school population, which means that most age groups in most schools might have one or two such children. Estimates of the numbers are bound to vary because of the vagueness of the definition, once we leave the relatively well-defined groups of brain-injured children, such as spastics who show definite neurological signs. In a large-scale study of 810 children aged eight to nine years attending normal schools in the Cambridge region, Brenner (1966) suggested that nearly 7 per cent show difficulties on visual perceptual and visual motor tests that are commonly used to assess brain damage. In a study which involved the screening of over 2000 junior school children, one of the present writers (Bowley, 1969) produced a more realistic figure of 1·5 per cent and we will consider this study in more detail later.

The medical background of such children usually shows some suggestive features such as a history of birth difficulties, including signs of asphyxia, jaundice, or either a too rapid or too prolonged delivery, but these are rarely conclusive, for many children for whom birth difficulties are reported show quite normal development later on. At any age, e.e.g. studies are also apt to be inconclusive, for as Schulman (1965) points out, many normal children show abnormal e.e.g. recordings and some very abnormal children show no abnormal e.e.g. records. Objective techniques for detecting the presence of brain damage are still in their early stages. The recently developed EMI scanner, giving complete X-ray views of the brain (harmlessly since the exposures are so brief), may eventually help in this respect.

The causes of brain damage are many and varied and can occur either during pregnancy or at birth or after birth and at any time in later life due to illness such as encephalitis. During pregnancy, as we have mentioned, virus infections can occasionally cause damage and so might excessive drug taking or excessive exposure to radiation. During birth anything that might interfere with the fetal oxygen supply to the brain might be suspect. Rhesus incompatibility can occasionally cause brain damage, but modern preventive measures in the case of this problem are nearly always effective. After birth, rare diseases such as meningitis can occasionally lead to brain damage, as, of course, can serious head injuries.

Our concern in this Chapter is mainly with the behaviour and learning difficulties that often accompany brain damage. As Birch (1964) has pointed out, our knowledge of the causes of brain damage is very sketchy: there are many kinds of brain damage ranging from minimal, hardly detectable states to severe and obvious conditions. We will not find a single cause and every individual case may show some unique features. The efforts of psychologists, therapists, educationalists and social workers should centre on the description and understanding of the behaviour, and the educational and social needs of these children—a difficult task when present knowledge of the neurological background is so sketchy, but a task which cannot be ignored. Children such as Graham simply cannot be ignored.

The behaviour and learning of children with minimal cerebral dysfunction

The most frequently reported behaviour and learning difficulties in 'brain-damaged' children were listed by Clements (1962, 1966) in the following order:

1. Hyperactivity and restlessness.
2. Perceptual motor impairments, such as poor drawing and constructional skills.
3. Erratic emotional behaviour, such as sudden emotional outbursts without obvious causes.
4. Clumsiness and poor motor co-ordination.
5. Attention disorders, such as distractibility and perseveration.

Most clinicians working in this field would feel that a child showing several of these features over a lengthy period might be brain-damaged and that such an explanation is more plausible than alternative explanations, such as mental deficiency, and environmentally caused emotional disturbance or physical or sensory handicaps—assuming of course that these other causes have been excluded. The terms 'minimal cerebral dysfunction' and 'brain damage', as we have said, are both unsatisfactory, but if they have been carefully considered and applied to a particular child then this implies that the other causes have been excluded. The important question is, can we find out more about these diffi-

culties and do something about them? Let us describe the difficulties in more detail and comment on some of the experimental
treatment and remedial work that has been carried out.

Hyperactivity and restlessness

Hyperactivity is often mentioned in reports on brain-damaged
children, partly because of its nuisance value, as is implied in terms
often used: 'restless', 'disruptive', 'disorganized', etc. Cruickshank (1961, 1966, 1975) laid much emphasis on hyperactivity and
its control, the theory being that, in the normal brain, one of the
functions of the cortex is to *inhibit* immediate motor reactions to
a stimulus—partly to give us time to think about what we are
doing. In the brain-damaged child this inhibitory function of the
cortex is presumed to be much reduced, and he seems almost compelled to make immediate physical response to what he sees and
hears. His parents complain 'He grabs at anything at the table as
soon as it appears' and teachers complain 'He leaves his desk and
darts to the window whenever he hears a distant fire-engine'. With
ordinary children there is usually a process of thought or feeling,
however brief, that intervenes, between the perception of the
stimulus on the one hand, and their motor response on the other
(except of course in the case of reflex actions, such as blinking
to a very loud sound). With the brain-damaged child this interven-
ing thought or feeling seems very reduced at times, and his behaviour is impulsive and overactive.

Research studies on hyperactivity have not been very clear cut.
Indeed, some research casts doubts on the very existence of
hyperactivity. For example, Schulman (1965) carried out some
very objective measurements, using an actometer, in the form of
a modified self-winding watch strapped to the child's wrist and
ankle, the total day activity levels of 35 boys of roughly ESN intelligence were recorded: no significant differences were found
between those designated as brain-damaged and those who were
not. Other researchers, however, using different methods of
measurement, have shown different results, e.g. the Hutts (1963,
1964) used a special playroom to observe the child's movements:
starting with the room quite bare, the child's movements were
plotted on numbered squares on the floor space, and objective
measurements of levels and directions of activities were recorded,
in response to various controlled conditions in the room, for
example the presence of a box of bricks, the presence of a passive
adult, an active adult, etc. The use of this technique in measuring
a reduction in a child's hyperactivity following certain drug

treatments has been demonstrated. These studies show the importance of accurate measurements in helping us to reach an understanding of complex behaviour such as hyperactivity. The activity level of the child depends a great deal on what kind of situation he is placed in, and what adults are expecting him to do. It is perhaps the relative *aimlessness* of the brain-damaged child's behaviour, in the eyes of the adult observer, that is troublesome, rather than the actual amount of activity.

As for the treatment of hyperactivity, this work is still in its experimental stages: some alleviation through drug treatment has been reported, but medical opinion is divided on this matter, for though it may be possible to damp down the activity levels of some children, the side effects of massive sedation are not always acceptable.

Educationalists such as Cruickshank have tried to manage hyperactivity by arranging for a type of education that encourages plenty of motor response within a controlled setting, e.g. making great use of peg boards in simple number work, so that the child can enjoy plenty of 'motor expression', at least in the early stages. Parents' handling of the hyperactive child at home must of course include a firm framework of discipline. For example, there must be times and places in which the child must be persuaded, gently but firmly, that he must show control, such as in his bedroom in the evening, with the knowledge that he will be able to 'let off steam' at some other time and place, such as in the garden. Excessive punishment or permissiveness is unlikely to help such a child to gradually gain more control of his impulsive movements— movements which of course may often appear to a parent to be a kind of deliberate disobedience, when in fact this is not the case with most of the behaviour of neurologically impaired children. Hyperactivity is related to another difficult feature of brain-damaged children—that of attention disorders.

Attention disorders
These are more subtle than hyperactivity. Very active children are bound to be inattentive, such as certain youngsters who have had a serious attack of meningitis, and whose behaviour at least for some months after their illness can only be described as 'highly acrobatic': they rarely sit or stand still long enough to attend sufficiently to learn very much about a particular toy or object in the room. But attention disorders also occur in children who are not overactive: as we mentioned in our chapter on the cerebral palsied child, some children are highly distractible, showing great diffi-

culty in controlling or focusing their attention. It would be wrong to call them inattentive: in a sense they are overattentive—but to too many stimuli. They seem to be unable to refrain from responding to stimuli that most children would regard as irrelevant, e.g. in the classroom, things that most children might find only slightly distracting, such as an ink blot on a page, the brain-injured child is apt to find very distracting. Furthermore, his distractibility is not confined to the visual sphere: auditory and tactile stimulation can be equally distracting.

Objective measures of distractibility have not yet been satisfactorily carried out. Cruickshank and his co-workers attached great importance to distractibility, considering it to be a major factor, together with hyperactivity, in the behaviour and learning difficulties of brain-damaged children: he used various means of measuring distractibility, including various figure/background tests, such as marble boards in which patterns had to be copied, and briefly exposed pictures of objects, all against a confusing background. In his very thorough 1957 study (revised 1965) on 325 brain-damaged (cerebral palsied) children, great difficulties in these tests were revealed, compared to the performance of ordinary children, and these difficulties were largely thought to be due to distractibility—the theory being that the distractible child was unable to refrain from irrelevant 'background' stimuli, which diverted the child's attention from the main 'figure' to which he should be attending.

Educational implications of distractibility have been carefully studied by Cruickshank and he advocated, like Strauss, radical educational measures, such as setting up 'distraction-free' classrooms, which were relatively bare, silent, small cubicles, providing a visually neutral background, against which the work material could be thrown into relief. The design of the work material itself followed the same reasoning, e.g. in a typical reading book the words are brightly coloured, against a perfectly plain background.

The effectiveness of this type of education has not yet been convincingly demonstrated and it has not gained widespread support in the UK. This is partly because distractibility is not simply a matter of a distracting environment: it 'comes from within' and although a distractible child can probably be helped a little by having an environment that does not contain too many diversions, his difficulties cannot necessarily be solved in this way. In Brown's studies (1966, 1967), for example using formboard errors as a measure of distractibility amongst 28 severely subnormal children attending an ESN school, no differences were noted between the child's scores in their usual highly decorated, nursery-type class-room, and their scores within a bare experimental room. Brown also differs from Cruickshank about the origin of some distracti-bility, pointing out that in some children it might be caused by poor environmental experience, such as prolonged hospitalization accompanied by lack of stimulation, rather than brain damage. Brown's studies, however, are no more conclusive than Cruick-shank's.

One cannot help feeling that some aspects of modern infant and junior schooling, with their emphasis on 'activity' methods, in-volving multi-sensory stimulation, and a great deal of practical activities, could aggravate the distractibility of some brain-injured children—and the latter are likely to respond better to somewhat sheltered conditions, at least during the early educational years.

Distractibility does not occur only within one sensory system, such as the visual system: as Abercrombie (1968) points out, several sensory systems are involved in even simple activities, such as copying a diamond shape. The child's successful performance depends not only on visual information but on the sense of touch and movement as he guides the pencil: messages are fed back to the child through several senses about the correctness or otherwise about what he has done; since the child cannot attend to several at once, they compete for his attention, and the brain-damaged child finds this particularly confusing.

Our educational measures must allow for these types of diffi-culties, and this calls for a careful consideration of what processes are actually involved in learning a particular task, and how these processes can be simplified. Our present understanding of distrac-tibility is too patchy to point to any definite educational measures: in any case no single factor in the complex learning and behaviour problems of brain-damaged children can be divorced from the other difficulties that are present. Some educationalists have con-centrated on motor incoordination as a very important factor of brain-damaged children and suggest that measures to improve co-ordination may have a generalized effect on the whole learning of children with neurological impairments.

Clumsiness and motor incoordination
Clumsiness and motor incoordination are obvious in most cases of severe brain damage and the question arises whether slight clumsiness and incoordination might, by analogy, indicate the condition of minimal brain damage. According to many workers (Walton, 1962; Stott, 1966) this seems likely in the case of many

children. Traditional neurological investigations have always included the study of both gross motor movements, such as balance and symmetry, and fine motor control, such as of hand and facial muscles, as possible indicators of dysfunctioning in certain parts of the brain. These clinical investigations, however, are rarely fine enough to detect minimal cases of motor incoordination and clumsiness, especially in younger children: therefore efforts have been made in recent years to develop finer, standardized scales of 'motor proficiency' based on 'norms' that are applicable for children at various ages, including large numbers of children attending normal schools. In addition to versions of Oseretzky's original scale a new test of 'motor competence' is being finalized, for use with British children (Stott, 1972). In a study of 9- to 10-year-old school children in the Isle of Wight, Rutter, Graham and Yule (1970) used a shortened, twelve-item version of the Sloan scale of motor proficiency and showed a high percentage (12 per cent) of 'severely clumsy' children amongst poor readers compared to ordinary readers. Another motor proficiency test developed by the same team is 'motor impersistence', which refers to the inability to sustain a voluntary act, such as closing eyes, protruding one's tongue, for a period of 20 seconds: failures on this test showed a considerable correlation with clumsiness.

Since minor impairments show some link with educational difficulties, the question arises, that if the motor impairments can be improved, is it possible that there will be an accompanying improvement in educational and other skills? This approach underlies several educational and therapeutic programmes, and we have already mentioned some in Chapter 2, such as the Peto method of conductive education. Kephart in the United States and Tansley in England have developed educational programmes designed to help 'clumsy' children. These pay great attention in the early stages to improving motor responses, as a basis for more complex perceptual motor learning later. The carefully graduated programme of motor training, for example, in Kephart's work starts with:

1. *General posture and balance:* these determine a child's 'point of reference' as far as his observations of objects in the external world and their position relative to him (left, right, up, down, diagonal, etc.) are concerned.
2. *Locomotion,* including creeping, crawling, running, walking, hopping, skipping and jumping, by which a child explores the space around him.

3. *Contact,* including the manipulation of objects with the hand, reaching, grasping, releasing; an impairment in any of these processes could reduce the information a child gains through manipulation.

4. *Receipt and propulsion:* these include the child's relationship to moving objects, such as catching a ball and similar activities which involve a complex sequence of perceptual and motor actions.

Kephart has described his basic motor training programme in detail (1960, 1968), and Tansley (1967) working mostly with slow-learning children in Birmingham, many of whom were considered to have minimal brain damage, has done valuable work in suggesting how such basic motor training can be linked later with perceptual training that, in turn, may help to improve reading skills.

Studies of a more theoretical kind, furthering our understanding of the complex processes by which motor and perceptual skills develop in humans and other primates, can be found in the work of Connolly (1973) based on his findings in the Spastics Society's 'Motor Development Research Unit' at Sheffield. It is through a combination of perceptual and motor skills, as Piaget (1956) has shown, that so much of the foundations of learning, in the child's early life, are laid down and the results of the work we have described in training and conditioning some aspects of motor skills, particularly at an early age, are awaited with great interest.

Perceptual and motor impairments
Perceptual motor impairments can best be illustrated by a brief case study:

Sally, now age 15, has minimal brain damage, with an accompanying mild degree of spasticity largely affecting her legs so that she walks unsteadily, whilst her hand control is almost normal, e.g. she can trace a complex pattern very well. Her speech development is excellent, and she scores a verbal I.Q. of 125 on the Wechsler Verbal Scale, yet in certain other respects her performance is almost unbelievably poor: in maths the simplest division sum will confuse her; in art her drawings are reported to be like those 'of a rather odd seven-year-old', and her domestic science teacher comments, 'she can rarely get a pie in the oven'.

It is understandable that this 'unevenness' in her performance in different spheres, causes tension—within Sally, her parents and her teachers and therapists. We normally expect a more even and consistent level of performance, unless of course the person concerned has an obvious physical, emotional or cultural handicap. Sally's real handicaps are quite subtle, and her difficulty is one of perceptual motor disorders.

Here are her attempts at copying a diamond, which most seven-year-olds can manage (Fig. 16). Sally was 12 at the time.

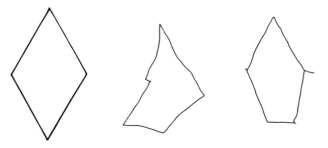

Fig. 16 A 12-year-old girl's (spastic diplegia, verbal I.Q. 125) attempts to copy a diamond.

Even a simple act, such as putting a pie in an oven, involves many components and we usually take their intactness for granted, including the following:

1. The use of sensory information, vision, hearing and smell.
2. The use of motor control such as in touching objects (with care in the case of a hot oven).
3. The process of organizing sensory impressions to form a perception—such as the completeness or otherwise of the object that we call a pie.
4. The organization of movements—up, down, left, right, backwards, forwards, their speed and duration and what to do about obstacles (such as other objects that might be in the oven).
5. The feedback of information about the effectiveness or otherwise of the movements that we make, and our response to this feedback in altering our performance.
6. Our attention, memory and motivation, any of which will affect our performance.
7. Most important, the process of intersensory integration—all these components must to some extent be *integrated* and somehow ordered into a coherent *sequence*. For example vision and touch may have to work together and in our simple example, Sally should first use vision to judge whether there is enough space in the oven, and if she considers there is, she should then confirm this by her action. Sally would usually act first, tending

to use force when things did not seem to work out: her visual perception, and the process of linking it with her movements, are so poor that she rarely tried to judge space and form in a normal way. She is undoubtedly impaired in several of the components we have mentioned and in the links between them, and her practical skills both in everyday life and in classroom activities were very weak. Yet she is highly competent in many other directions, especially in her language and social skills and her general knowledge, and she is very likely to be successful in several academic examinations.

Psychological studies of groups of children showing similar impairments have been carried out by Wedell (1973, 1975), Abercrombie (1964), Abercrombie *et al.* (1964) and Francis-Williams (1974) and these brought out the essential unevenness in the intellectual and educational performance of brain-damaged children. For example, Wedell's 1960 study, using very carefully devised tests on 73 brain-damaged (cerebral palsied) children and 40 controls, showed the difficulty the former had in tests involving matching of figures, copying patterns of bricks, assembling jigsaws, etc. (Fig. 17). In these tasks, low scores were recorded on 25 per cent of the brain-damaged children compared to less than 3 per cent of the controls. The tests were specially designed so that the child's motor control was not an important consideration.

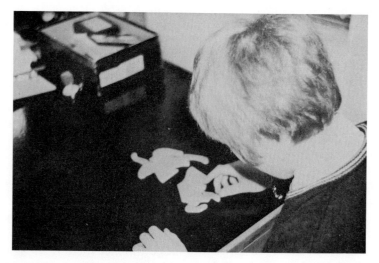

Fig. 17 Perceptual motor difficulties: a boy aged nine years with normal intelligence, who has great difficulty in putting together a jigsaw of a horse.

Abercrombie *et al.* (1964) confirmed that there was a high incidence of perceptual motor disorders amongst cerebral palsied children in their extensive study of thirty-nine cases and eleven controls, using the Wechsler Scales, the Frostig Developmental Test of Visual Perception and various matching tasks, both through visual and tactile means. The degree to which the children had sensory or motor handicaps was carefully assessed so that the influence of these could be allowed for. 75 per cent of the cases showed specific perceptual motor difficulties on one or more of the tests, which could not be attributed to motor or sensory handicaps: children with equal degrees of motor handicap, but who were not brain-damaged (e.g. cases of poliomyelitis), did not show such difficulties. Birch, in the USA (1964, 1965), and his co-workers have made considerable contributions to understanding the many puzzling features: they have shown that some brain-damaged children have quite good visual perceptual skills (e.g. they can match picture to picture and shape to shape fairly normally), but they cannot *construct* patterns, either through making patterns with coloured bricks, or attempting to draw them. Their difficulties were not due to perceptual disorders themselves but lay somewhere in the process of translating a perception into action. Birch's work also shows the enormous difficulties that brain-injured children have in intersensory integration. In his 1964 study he showed that some brain-damaged children could match geometric shapes visually as well as ordinary children, but when visual information was reduced, for example one of the geometrical shapes in a pair being screened from view, and the children were asked to use their sense of touch and movement (tracking the outline with a stylus) to compare this with the visually presented geometrical pattern, large errors were recorded amongst the brain-damaged children. They were unable to link the information they obtained visually, with the information they obtained through their sense of touch and movement. Although these results are tentative, they suggest at least considerable delay in the development of intersensory integration in brain-damaged children, which could seriously limit the use they make of information from various channels, and so lead to confusion and educational retardation. Reading, for example, involves information from several senses.

A great deal has been learned from such studies of perceptual motor disorders in cerebral palsied children and, more recently, in children with spina bifida (Anderson and Spain, 1977). Work with non-cerebral palsied children, although subject to the difficulties of diagnosis that we have already mentioned, is important in that it offers some explanation of learning difficulties that may be applicable to very large groups of children, including those attending normal schools.

In 1966 Brenner reported on the application of a battery of visual motor tests (including parts of the Bender Gestalt, Goodenough Draw a Man, Benton), and rated nearly 7 per cent of 810 normal school children aged eight to nine as showing visual perceptual and visual motor difficulties. Bowley (1969) using a large battery of similar tests, including the Frostig, reported an incidence of 1·5 per cent, designated as showing 'minimal cerebral dysfunctioning', out of a total sample of over 2000 children who had been roughly screened. Cruickshank (1967) mentions incidence figures of between 1 and 7 per cent of the general population showing learning difficulties of a comparable kind.

Several workers in this field, following the lead in studies of brain-damaged adults, have attempted to use Wechsler's Intelligence Scale as an indication of brain damage, notably studying discrepancies between the person's verbal I.Q. and his performance I.Q. on this scale. This has led to some exaggerated claims about incidence of brain damage amongst the general population. For example, Clements and Peters (1962) considered that a discrepancy of 10 to 15 points between the verbal and the performance scores might indicate brain damage but, according to Field's (1960) studies of the Wechsler Scale and its norms, this amount of discrepancy would be found in about 25 per cent of the general population—clearly a vast over-estimate. A useful discussion of these points is to be found in Rutter, Graham and Yule (1970) which concludes that large discrepancies, in the order of 25 points, did appear to show some association with the presence of brain damage, as measured by other criteria.

Many workers have stressed the importance of the early detection of special learning difficulties in order that remedial work might be planned at a very early stage and so prevent a child from going from bad to worse, and to help reduce parental anxiety and confusion, which would otherwise affect the child's learning. Studies of perceptual motor difficulties in under fives are difficult to make, since the performance of young children is variable and erratic at the best of times, and this calls for very careful assessment of what types of behaviour in young children might be considered abnormal and might, in turn, be indicative of brain damage. Francis-Williams (1974) is one of the few workers in this country to have attempted such studies. She selected 44 cases out of a total of 3000, who had been noted to show 'minor neurological dysfunctioning' at birth, but who had no major birth difficulties and no major neurological signs in very early years—in other words there were no frank cases of spasticity, blindness or deafness or similar, well-recognized conditions. Over half the 44 children turned out to be of normal intelligence, and two-thirds of these showed impairments on certain tests, which were largely based on Frances Graham's work (1963) on the perceptual motor development of young children, and Joan Reynell's language tests. Her book also contains a useful general description of psychological assessment and educational techniques, including those for older children, and the work of Albetreccia, Strauss, Cruickshank and Frostig is well documented. Valuable suggestions are made, not only in ways of identifying early learning difficulties in young children but in suggestions about educational and therapeutic techniques.

Educational provision

Educational provision and techniques designed to help brain-damaged children have been largely centred on the perceptual motor disorders. In the USA, the growth of special educational facilities has been rapid in the past decade: we have mentioned the early work by Strauss and Kephart (1955) at the Cove School for brain-injured children, Wisconsin, and we have also mentioned the educational work of Cruickshank (1975) with its emphasis on providing a distraction-free environment. Marianne Frostig (1968, 1973) at the Centre for Educational Therapy, Los Angeles, has followed up her diagnostic test of visual perceptual development, with a remedial programme that is designed to provide training in any of the specific weaknesses denoted by her tests, such as in figure ground confusion, perceptual constancy, etc. Her work is also concerned with language development and she places great emphasis on all developmental areas, based on very comprehensive assessments. Gallacher (1960) reported on a first-rate study of ways of tutoring brain-injured children: although he modestly admitted the educational gains were small, he considered that the individual one hour per day tutoring might be much more effective than group work for such children and that it might be possible to use peripatetic tutors within the ordinary school system as a result of this. Vellutino (1977) on the other hand considers that the concept of 'perceptual deficit' as a major factor in reading retardation has been greatly over-emphasized, and that instead of devoting too much time to diagnostic techniques in this area and the search for underlying causes, we should return to a more direct, trial-and-error approach to the teaching of reading—which is as much a verbal skill as a perceptual one.

In the UK very little specific provision has been made, it being generally considered that most brain-damaged children could, on the whole, be adequately catered for in existing remedial groups in special schools. This situation, however, is not very satisfactory and a more concentrated effort could give rise to more expertise in helping such children. We have noted the work of Tansley (1967), with its emphasis on Kephart's educational programme. In addition, a few studies of Frostig's remedial methods have emerged, such as those by Tyson (1963) and Thompson (1972) on small groups of cerebral palsied children, and Lansdown's (1970) and Horn's (1970) studies of small groups of non-cerebral palsied children who showed perceptual motor difficulties. On the whole, such work has tended to produce slight improvements, in terms of increased scores on the Frostig perceptual tests, but not necessarily in the educational attainments so far. This kind of work needs expanding, and it is likely that some highly trained teachers would produce more favourable results. More sophisticated techniques, including the use of operant conditioning and a variety of electronic aids such as the Touch-Tutor (Thompson, 1971), are showing promise and there is a need for more intensive studies of the effectiveness of various educational methods. These must be based on a much more thorough understanding of the precise nature of the learning disorders than we have at present.

Emotional instability
There is a rough parallel between hyperactivity, distractibility, motor incoordination and perceptual confusion that we have so far described, and a comparable kind of fluctuation in the child's emotional life. For example, brain-damaged children have been described as 'over-excitable, uninhibited, explosive and over-reactive', and minor changes of routine are seen to provoke great outbursts of rage or grief. Objective studies of these characteristics are difficult to carry out, since we still need to develop reliable techniques of measurement, but clinical observation and our case studies leave no doubt about the high 'emotionality' of certain brain-damaged children. These are partly the result of their neurological condition, such as a basic weakness in controlling their feelings under certain conditions of stress, and indirectly through the frustrations that are caused by their other difficulties, e.g. the confusion that arises from motor clumsiness in an otherwise bright child, and the reactions of adults to these difficulties

which, in turn, impinge on the child. The admonishment to 'Look more carefully and watch what you are doing' may be a fair one for normal children, but it is not necessarily fair to a brain-damaged child. He may be trying to look carefully, but finds it impossible to perceive accurately, so that his mistakes may appear to the adult to be sheer carelessness or even wilful disobedience, with resulting anger on the part of the adult, and consternation on the part of the child.

This sort of situation can be considerably relieved when the parents and teachers fully understand that a child's excessive emotionality may be a direct outcome of his neurological difficulties and that he is not simply being 'bloody-minded' or attention-seeking. An attitude of calm acceptance can also be helpful.

Birch and his co-workers have provided many useful concepts and much sound advice about the handling of children with differing 'temperaments' or deeply characteristic ways of reacting to their environment, such as we see in brain-damaged children. We never observe brain damage directly, but only its consequences, such as the child's behaviour. The latter is rarely determined by brain damage alone: it is a product of many factors, not only his neurological condition, but his relationship with his environment and the people within it, including family reactions, community attitudes and such factors as whether his neurological impairment has led to a delayed entry to school, and to frequent hospitalizations, etc. In other words, when a child has a handicap, it is very likely that the environment that surrounds him will deviate from normal. Therefore he has to contend with two factors. Birch's work helps us to understand the ramifications of this. For example, different parents react differently to children who might be, at least initially, showing the same patterns of behaviour, such as distractibility or emotional lability. In a fascinating longitudinal study (Thomas and Birch, 1968) of differences in the behaviour of very young babies, Birch shows the possibilities of rating levels of activity, rhythmiticity, adaptability, sensitivity, distractibility and general mood, resulting in rough classifications ranging between 'intensively reactive' to 'placid and easy'. Given such behavioural characteristics, the question then arises: are the parents' reactions matched or mismatched, in relation to these? In other words, their child-rearing methods may either be harmonious or dissonant in respect of a particular child's 'early temperament'. For example, an intensively reactive child confronted by an intensely reactive adult, who meets temper tantrums with temper tantrums, is likely to have his difficulties severely aggravated.

Birch's work is still in its experimental stages but is proving useful in reminding us to consider children's behaviour as a closely linked process involving both environmental and organic factors. In work directed at helping handicapped children, the exact assessment of the role of organic factors and their influence on the child's behaviour and learning is crucial.

LANGUAGE DISORDERS: APHASIA AND SPECIFIC READING DIFFICULTIES (DYSLEXIA)

So far we have concentrated on children showing perceptual motor and other impairments, whose language development has, by contrast, been relatively good. Some children show discrepancies in the other direction. Their perceptual motor skills are relatively high, whilst their language development is relatively low. Do discrepancies in this direction suggest some kind of brain damage, perhaps of a different kind? This is not so in every case. Language development is dependent on a whole host of environmental factors as well as on basic neurological and physical factors. Normal language development depends particularly on 'social imitation' and the desire to communicate through speech, on the intactness of the child's physical and sensory state, notably his control of breathing and tongue movements, and, of course, on his general intelligence. There is a very small group of children who appear to have all the necessary environmental, physical and sensory facilities (including good hearing) for speech and language development, yet fail to develop the latter normally, for reasons which might well be linked with 'minimal cerebral dysfunctioning'.

Receptive and expressive aphasia

Ann: normal birth, weight $7\frac{1}{2}$ lb, healthy, walked at 13 months, used words at 12 months, phrases at two years, and all development reported normal until aged $3\frac{1}{2}$, when she had a very feverish illness diagnosed as a form of 'measles encephalitis'. Ann was very ill and feeble for several weeks, then started to show gradual physical recovery and became alert once again and able to play with toys constructively, etc. However, her speech did not recover at this stage: she used very few words and tended instead to point and gesture: furthermore she did not appear to hear spoken instructions.

At age 3 years, 9 months, audiology assessment showed puzzling features. She did not respond to spoken instructions even at a maximum loudness although she responded very quickly to gesture and was generally co-operative and helpful and sociable: she stared at faces a great deal.

Her responses to non-speech sounds such as music boxes, rattles, animal noises, etc., were erratic but occasionally quite good: response to pure tones, very poor, but after enormous encouragement she responded to conditioning tests, at about 50 decibels above threshold for most frequencies.

A moderate hearing loss was suspected but not enough to account for her developing language failure. But subsequent assessments a few weeks later proved that her hearing for pure tones and various other sounds was virtually normal. Yet there was still no sign of a return of her language skills.

She was noted in interview and at home to be a cooperative, sociable girl, responding well to gestured instructions. Normal intelligence was confirmed on non-verbal tests (Merrill-Palmer Scale I.Q. approximately 110), and the diagnosis of receptive and expressive aphasia, due to encephalitis at age $3\frac{1}{2}$, was made.

Her subsequent progress confirmed this: and soon after age five she was admitted to a special residential school for children with speech and language difficulties. Her general development was satisfactory and she learned to read at a simple level at age $7\frac{1}{2}$ years, and was soon able to follow simple written instructions, e.g. she was able to learn some language through visual but not through auditory-comprehension channels and her language development remained virtually nil. She learned to identify a few animal noises and would occasionally use a word, but on the whole she was unable to attach meaning to sounds.

Children with severe and definite receptive language difficulties, such as Ann, are very rare: they represent an extreme example of very selective brain damage, following a feverish illness, which had, by peculiar chance, virtually destroyed her language function, although her other abilities were almost intact. She showed none of the other behavioural and learning symptoms of brain damage, such as hyperactivity, distractibility, perceptual motor difficulties and emotional lability. Mild forms of partial aphasia are more common, but these are difficult to disentangle from all the other causes of language failure, including social, emotional and cultural deprivation, and severe subnormality. See Mittler (1970) for an excellent review of work in the field of language disorders. For more specialized work on aphasia, see Eisenson (1972).

Central deafness is a term referring to a similar condition. The work of Taylor (1964) has shown the existence of a few children, some of whom had attended deaf schools for some years, whose language development is extremely limited and who gave every impression of not being able to hear, but when subjected to very specialized audiology techniques, including e.e.g. audiometry, proved to have normal or at least considerable hearing; the difficulty of these children is very similar to that we mentioned in connection with aphasic conditions, namely a failure to interpret the sounds that they hear.

Combinations of ordinary hearing losses, such as peripheral nerve deafness, either mild, partial or severe, with some degree of central deafness or aphasia have also occasionally been observed, and possibly account for the fact that some deaf children make very little progress in spite of long-term educational help. However, such combinations are the exception rather than the rule and not much is known about their treatment prospects.

Educational approaches, partly based on work with aphasic adults, such as those who have lost their language skills following a severe head injury, are best exemplified by the work of McGinnis (1963). These are based on 'association techniques', e.g. initially an attempt is made to teach several dozen nouns by gradually building up individual sounds which are then synthesized to form the words: short phrases are then gradually introduced, through repetitive drill, and the complexity of the language stimulation gradually increased, taking great care not to overload the child with too much language that he simply cannot comprehend or execute.

Specific reading difficulty

Language comes in many forms, spoken and gestured, etc., and an important form is our response to written language. Failure to read competently has serious consequences for a child, affecting not only writing and spelling but most other school subjects, even including mathematics in that the pupil cannot handle written problems.

Reading failure is common amongst school children: Morris (1966) found that, at aged eight, almost 14 per cent of Kent schoolchildren were reading either not at all or extremely poorly in comparison with their peers. However, some of these reading difficulties could be accounted for by generally low mental age or intelligence: intensive studies by Rutter, Tizard and Whitmore (1970), in which the factors of mental age and intelligence were controlled, suggest that specific retardation, defined as reading ages more than two years below mental age, occurred in nearly 4 per cent of the children.

Clearly with reading and other educational difficulties we are concerned with a very complex situation and there are many explanations to be considered, including emotional disturbance and cultural deprivation, as well as subtle neurological factors. *Dyslexia* is a term sometimes used in connection with reading retardation. It is popular amongst medical experts but is not generally favoured by educationalists. This disagreement over terms is not purely semantic; it reflects a difference in outlook between the two professions, as well as differences in the child populations 'sampled' by each. For instance, an experienced teacher or educational psychologist will encounter a whole spectrum of learning problems involving a wide variety of home backgrounds and schools; and, significantly, they will have witnessed the successful outcome of skilled teaching using very varied teaching methods. A medical specialist is likely, on the other hand, mainly to see cases with a long-standing history of reading failure; and his training, being based upon an 'illness model', will lead him to view the failure as a 'symptom' of some underlying disorder, namely dyslexia.

'Specific dyslexia' has in the past been thought to be due to a malfunction of one particular part of the brain or to a failure to establish cerebral dominance. More recently, it has come to be considered as a type of developmental delay, affecting certain specific perceptual functions and possibly to some extent inherited. (There is a tendency for reading/spelling difficulty to run in families.) Educationalists, on the other hand, generally avoid the word 'dyslexia', feeling that the use of a Greek term (which means literally 'disability in language') has little explanatory value and may encourage a fatalistic approach in teachers and lend an air of scientific certainty where none as yet exists.

Remedial specialists and psychologists look upon reading as a complex learning process, depending on a great number of interlocking factors, any one of which might cause failure. For example, Stott (1978) has made a systematic attempt to delineate the various factors that affect learning, and his book *Helping Children with Learning Difficulties* exemplifies this multi-faceted approach.

Stott emphasizes the need for careful observation of the pupil in the classroom performing a variety of tasks, pointing out that the child's temperament, confidence and speed of response need to be taken into account, as crucial aspects of learning. He postulates that lack of progress in reading skills may be due to *faulty learning styles*: a child may fail because his approach is over-hasty, diffident or discouraged and not primarily because he lacks the necessary perceptual skills. Stott designed a programme of group activities to encourage more effective learning strategies, and has devised a schedule for teachers to sharpen and systematize their observation of pupils.

In their day-to-day contact with a child, teachers are very much aware that emotional factors influence how effectively a child learns. Health or relationship problems within the family may be observed to have a striking, though temporary, effect on the pupil's ability to concentrate. It is also true to say that children with generally poor self-esteem, or with a perfectionist streak in their nature, may find any complex task quite daunting: they cannot take small mistakes in their stride, hesitate to read aloud and may tear up their attempts at written work. These extremely self-critical children can come to view the process of learning to read and write as a journey full of stumbling blocks, and often become disheartened and despondent.

A thought-provoking, small-scale study by Lawrence (1973) in Wiltshire highlights this view that it is often the child's confidence and emotional resilience that limits the pace of learning, rather than more neurological factors such as perception and memory. Lawrence offered weekly counselling sessions to retarded readers, and noticed that their reading skills improved as much as those of pupils who were given remedial lessons; he explained this in terms of a probable improvement in the child's attitude towards himself and his ability to cope with the challenge that mastering a skill such as reading presents. This explanation corresponds closely to the views we expressed in Chapter 1, stressing the importance of 'self-image' and its effects on performance.

Recently, there has been a good deal of questioning of the widely held belief that reading delay is associated with some type of perceptual deficit. For instance, Vellutino and his colleagues in America compared 'average' with 'retarded' readers, as far as their competence in writing down briefly glimpsed nonsense words was concerned. They found, rather surprisingly, that although unable to pronounce the words correctly, the poor readers were able to write down short, three- or four-letter words just as efficiently as the average readers. Vellutino considers that children who confuse WAS and SAW, for example, perceive the words correctly but 'mis-label' them; in other words the weakness lies more in the verbal than in the visual sphere. Clearly further studies along these lines are needed.

After many years of research there is still little agreement among investigators about the causes of severe specific reading difficulty, and it is becoming apparent that there are no 'ready answers', no combination of deficiencies common to all retarded readers. Disillusionment with the 'perceptual deficit hypothesis' has led to a switching of emphasis amongst educationalists to a more pragmatic approach. Attempts are being made to tackle the problem of how best to help those children who seem likely to encounter reading difficulties before failure sets in. The approach is from two directions:

1. By looking at the early developmental history of children with long-standing reading problems.
2. By large-scale screening devices of all pupils in their first year of school.

1. Developmental History

In connection with the first point, we can describe some recent work by Bowley, which contains a detailed study of the early life of 40 children with reading/spelling difficulties who were of at least average intelligence. Careful histories were taken and individual testing and tuition were undertaken with each child. According to the parents' account, rather more than two-thirds of the children had shown delayed speech development or minor hearing loss in their early years, and half were described as having a particularly worrying or abnormal birth history. Of the parents themselves, quite a proportion complained of still having a pronounced difficulty with the spelling of irregular words.

On individual testing, Bowley found that over half of the pupils showed crossed laterality or poor sequential memory, and over a quarter had poor co-ordination (see Table 4 for details).

Table 4 Summary of study of 40 children with reading/spelling difficulties

		%
History of:	Abnormal birth, prematurity, very low or high birth-weight	55
	Delayed speech/early hearing loss	72
	Parental difficulties with reading/spelling	22
On individual testing:	Clumsiness and poor co-ordination	27
	Poor sequential memory	50
	Crossed laterality (L-handed and R-eyed)	55

Many displayed bizarre and confused spelling, with persistence of letter reversals in writing (see Figs. 18 and 19 on pages 122–23).

Other researchers have noted an association between speech and reading delay; for instance, as many as a third of a series of children with severe reading difficulty studied by Critchley (1970) were reported to have had delayed speech development.

Looking at it from another angle, the National Child Birth Study followed up the 124 pupils in ordinary schools who had

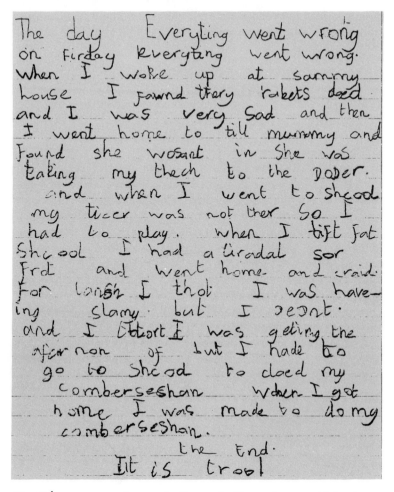

Fig. 18 Spontaneous written work of a very intelligent nine-year-old showing left–right confusion and sequencing problems.

demonstrated marked speech defects at age seven (Sheridan and Peckham, 1975). By the end of their junior school years (age 11) 12 per cent were rated by their teachers as poor or non-readers, and nearly 60 per cent as below average readers (control group figures 2 per cent and 20 per cent).

Although the reasons for this link between coordination, hearing or speech difficulties and reading delay are not entirely clear, the results from these studies should alert school doctors, teachers and speech therapists to the possibility of learning problems in this particular group of children. If there are additional features of poor co-ordination and crossed laterality, then careful monitoring of progress and opportunities for extra help are essential.

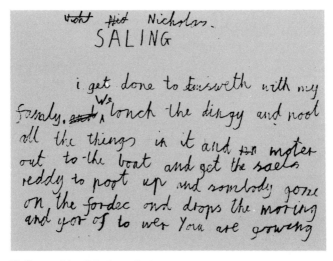

Fig. 19 Composition 'My favourite hobby' by intelligent 11-year-old with severe spelling difficulties. Errors suggest poor visual memory plus misapplication of English spelling rules (e.g. poot, reddy, gowing).

2. *Large-scale screening devices*

So that help can be offered at an early stage (before failure has had a disheartening effect) it is clearly necessary to find some simple means of monitoring progress. Large-scale screening devices have been set up by many education authorities (as recommended in the Bullock Report, 1975) in order to pick out especially vulnerable pupils in their first year of schooling. The checklists devised by Wolfendale in Croydon (Fig. 20) and by Tansley in Birmingham are good examples. Both are described by Wedell and Raybould (1976) in an Education Review Occasional Publication. These and many other education authorities provide guidelines for teachers in the form of booklets and special workshops in which appropriate remedial measures are outlined.

To quote from the Bullock Report: 'Information (from screening procedures) would alert teachers to preventive action and indicate the need for further investigation in specific cases. Screening procedures would be applied at the beginning of the child's school life, before his growing involvement with the process of learning to read gives him an experience of failure. In other words, it identifies the child "at risk" in the sense that though failure is to some extent predictable in his case, he has not yet encountered it.'

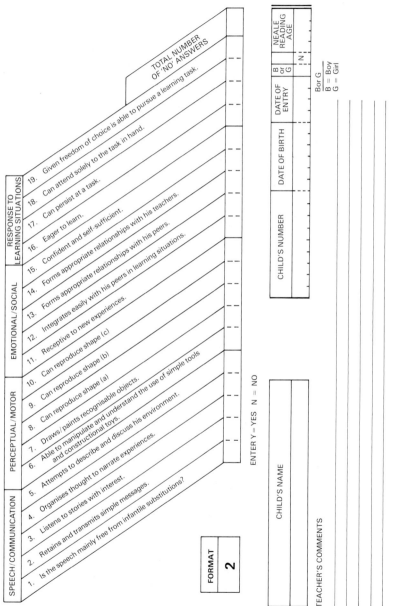

SPEECH/COMMUNICATION					PERCEPTUAL/MOTOR					EMOTIONAL/SOCIAL					RESPONSE TO LEARNING SITUATIONS				

1. Is the speech mainly free from infantile substitutions?
2. Retains and transmits simple messages.
3. Listens to stories with interest.
4. Organises thought to narrate experiences.
5. Attempts to describe and discuss his environment.
6. Able to manipulate and understand the use of simple tools and constructional toys.
7. Draws/paints recognisable objects.
8. Can reproduce shape (a)
9. Can reproduce shape (b)
10. Can reproduce shape (c)
11. Receptive to new experiences.
12. Integrates easily with his peers in learning situations.
13. Forms appropriate relationships with his peers.
14. Forms appropriate relationships with his teachers.
15. Confident and self-sufficient.
16. Eager to learn.
17. Can persist at a task.
18. Can attend solely to the task in hand.
19. Given freedom of choice is able to pursue a learning task.

TOTAL NUMBER OF 'NO' ANSWERS

FORMAT 2

ENTER Y = YES   N = NO

CHILD'S NAME		CHILD'S NUMBER	DATE OF BIRTH	DATE OF ENTRY	B or G	NEALE READING AGE
					N	

B or G
B = Boy
G = Girl

TEACHER'S COMMENTS

Fig. 20 Screening for special educational needs: London Borough of Croydon—checklist score sheet.

A pilot study of assessment and educational work with children with minimal cerebral dysfunctioning*

A survey of a section of the primary school population of a London borough was carried out, in which teachers in 7 primary schools, representing a primary-school-age population of 1634, were asked to identify children showing signs of restlessness, clumsiness and poor verbal and reading ability by means of a questionnaire. A total of 24 children were selected (i.e. 1·46 per cent) showing this syndrome with marked reading retardation despite normal intelligence. Including the schools in the pilot study the total was 34 out of 2280, i.e. 1·49 per cent.

Most of these children were then given a detailed neurological assessment, an electroencephalogram and a psychological assessment. The following neurological evaluation was made of the group:

1. *Motor.* Inability to hop or stand on one leg; ataxia in heel/toe walking; choreiform jerks; slowness of movement; dysarthria; physical immaturity; abnormal e.e.g. in some cases.
2. *Dyspraxic.* Involving voluntary or schematic movements of limbs, face or eye, or construction in two dimensions or drawing or writing.
3. *Perceptual.* Visual, tactile and possibly auditory agnosias and specific reading difficulties.
4. *Language.* Developmental dysphasia and word poverty.
5. *Psychological.* Restlessness and short attention span.

All of these children showed one or more of these characteristics. The psychological assessment was planned to be a fairly comprehensive survey of the child's intellectual, perceptual and linguistic skills and disabilities, usually requiring two interviews. It included the Wechsler performance scale, tests of vocabulary, reading and arithmetic, the Illinois test of psycho-linguistic abilities, the Frostig perception test and the Bender Gestalt designs. By this means an attempt was made to explore the child's strengths and weaknesses, with a view to planning remedial measures.

The following were considered to be the factors contributing to the child's learning difficulties:

1. *Language immaturity.* Slow onset of speech and growth of vocabulary; a low language age on the I.T.P.A. was common (though verbal comprehension was good), coupled with poor

* Many of the characteristic behaviour and learning problems discussed in this Chapter are exemplified in a pilot study by Bowley (1969).

Fig. 21 Drawing of a horse and rider by a nine-year-old boy with minimal cerebral dysfunction and reading retardation. Note the limited visual recall, sense of proportion and hand control.

auditory or visual memory and sequencing ability. This last was found in almost all the children.

2. *Visual-spatial disabilities*. Difficulty in copying shapes or recalling designs, difficulty in some figure-ground and spatial relationships tests and a tendency to reverse letters and words.

Fig. 22 Drawing of himself by a timid 10-year-old boy of average verbal ability with severe co-ordination and learning problems.

3. *Distractibility and poor attention* were very evident both during
   testing and teaching periods and were frequently reported from
   school.

As a result of this study, a remedial class was set up for a small
group of children showing these difficulties between the ages of
eight and ten years and with I.Q.s above 90. A carefully structured
programme was planned to meet their special needs. This included
perceptual training using Frostig techniques and other devices by
the occupational therapist, speech therapy using the Language
Master and other methods by the speech therapist, and remedial
reading using visual aids, practical material, drawing, reading
games and carefully chosen books to suit the child's stage of progress by the teacher and psychologist. These specialists worked
as a team with the group of six children and so a great deal of
individual attention was ensured during the session, which took
up one morning a week. The rest of the time was spent in their
ordinary schools. Each child received a great deal of praise, and
encouragement and the atmosphere of the class was accepting,
tolerant and stimulating. None of the children showed serious
emotional problems but many had become discouraged and unco-
operative at school and some had played truant. They were
regarded by their teachers as dullards or trouble-makers, as lazy,
inattentive and unresponsive. They flourished on the special
treatment they received by the centre and in many cases made
quite remarkable progress.

A brief case study will illustrate the variety of problems involved.

K at the age of eight had a reading age assessed at the $4\frac{1}{2}$-year level.
His spelling was chaotic and his writing unintelligible. He was restless, distractible and moody in school. When he was reprimanded he would often
abscond from school and slip off home. His parents were simple but very
concerned people and K was especially devoted to his mother. Methods
of upbringing had been rather permissive. K's older brother had similar
learning and behaviour problems.

Neurological assessment noted odd choreiform movements of shoulders
and lips, slight ataxia of the lower limbs, dyslalic speech and the e.e.g.
record was suggestive of epilepsy though he had never had any fits. Sensa-
tion was normal. Minimally abnormal neurological signs were recorded.

Psychological assessment showed a W.I.S.C. Performance I.Q. of 90,
a language age of only 6·2 years (I.T.P.A.) with very poor results on
memory and sequencing tests. His arithmetic was at about a six-year level,
but he could only read some five words on the Burt reading test. Frostig
perception test results were good, but he did badly on the Bender Gestalt

copying designs test. His teacher assessed his score on the Bristol adjustment guide as 32, indicating quite severe maladjustment.

K became a faithful member of the group. He never truanted on the day he was due to come to the Centre, but he was often moody, restless and distractible. Very short lesson periods were given at first, frequently changing the type of occupation. He did a lot of colourful drawings of which he was very proud. He enjoyed dexterity and perception games and self-corrective reading games involving matching and word discrimination. Phonics were gradually introduced and he soon got interested in the Pirate books and the Micky Mix-Up* series. He had a lively sense of humour, always enjoyed a practical joke, could tell a good story or riddle and became quite a popular member of the group. He attended for six terms, once a week, and his reading age rose from a $4\frac{1}{2}$-year level to $7\frac{1}{2}$ in that time. He became really keen on reading for its own sake and improved in attentivity, motor skills and general stability. At school he won medals for swimming, became a school prefect and no longer absconded. At 10 years of age he was discharged from the Centre with flying colours. Progress has been maintained.

This type of child cannot make much progress in a large class full of distractions, movements and noise. Such children cannot learn well by global methods and need special techniques and a carefully structured form of teaching. They usually cannot work on their own and need far more individual attention than an ordinary teacher can give them. They tend to drift into day-dreaming or undisciplined behaviour, and severe maladjustment may be the end result. Our progress rate in the remedial class has been high and this intensive work has proved therapeutic in the widest sense, for general stability, attitude to work and educational achievement have greatly improved. Increased physical maturity has helped and we have found it is best to start with children at the early stage of their junior school career, at seven, eight or nine years of age, when time is on our side and a sense of defeat not too firmly entrenched.

EPILEPSY

Although epilepsy, being a sign of brain disturbance, does occur in conjunction with cerebral palsy and severe mental retardation, we shall concentrate here on the adjustment of pupils with epilepsy to the ordinary school system. (To avoid constant qualification,

---

* *The Three Pirates.* S. K. McCullagh. Griffin Readers. Arnold; *Micky Mix-Up.* D. H. Stott. Holmes, Glasgow.

the shorthand term 'epileptic' will be used to refer to those children who have suffered seizures, who are under medical supervision and who have at some time received drug therapy.)

Convulsions take different forms and not all are epileptic in character. In infancy, quite a few children have a form of mild fit associated with a high temperature. Although as many as 2 per cent of babies may have febrile convulsions, as they are called, very few go on to have true epileptic fits, at a later age. Although these feverish convulsions are worrying to parents who witness them, several studies have shown that they do not usually affect the growing brain and that all but a tiny proportion of these babies go on to develop quite normally.

Very little is known as to why some people have fits while most of us, in normal circumstances, do not. (In abnormal conditions, everyone would have a convulsion, for instance following a severe electric shock.) Fits or convulsions are the result of sudden abnormal electrical activity in the brain. It is not generally realized that our brains send out minute electrical discharges all the time, and it is only when there is a sudden increase of electrical activity that a physical effect is apparent, which takes the form of a convulsion.

There are various medical classifications of epilepsy, according to the type of fit produced or the location in the brain. For simplicity we will describe only the three main categories, according to the type of convulsion produced.

Grand mal. 50 per cent of epilepsy is of this type. Before losing consciousness, the individual is often aware of distinct sensations, of taste and smell for instance (the aura), there is a rigid contraction of muscles followed by jerking of the jaw and limbs; this may last for only a few seconds or for many minutes. After this phase passes, the subject will often fall into a deep sleep or experience some degree of headache or a feeling of confusion for a brief period.

Petit mal. On the other hand, this consists of such a brief lapse of consciousness that it may sometimes pass unnoticed by the subject or the casual onlooker. There may be a faltering in conversation or a flickering of the eyelids, the child will momentarily stop what he is doing or turn his head to one side. Petit mal, on its own, is a relatively rare condition, and is most frequently seen in conjunction with other types of epilepsy.

Psycho-motor epilepsy. This is more difficult to define and differentiate. There is no loss of consciousness, but the individual experiences some alteration in awareness; for instance, he may be acutely aware of sensations of taste, or vividly recall a past scene. To the onlooker there are only rather vague signs that a fit is occurring; the subject may stare into space, stroke his hair in a repetitive fashion, or turn his head momentarily to one side; this may last a few seconds or minutes.

Fortunately, modern anti-convulsant drugs have made it possible to control fits in most people with epilepsy, and it is quite likely that a child known to have epilepsy would not actually have any fits during the school day. If a child should have a fit at school there is not a great deal that needs to be done by the teacher, she should merely see that the child is lying on his side, preferably on the floor (so that he cannot fall) and away from objects against which he could hurt himself, such as electric fires. Any tight clothing round the neck should be loosened so that the child can breathe easily. Although the child needs to be watched over, for his own safety, there is usually no need to call a doctor or an ambulance when a fit occurs. The main requirement for the teacher is to remain calm and encourage the rest of the class to continue their normal activities. As one adolescent said, 'I don't mind the fits, they just give me a bit of a headache afterwards, the worst thing is to be surrounded by a sea of open-mouthed faces, when I come round.'

Present-day medical advice suggests that there is no need to restrict ordinary youthful activities, except those that present a hazard if the child overbalances, for instance cycling or climbing trees. Swimming is not discouraged as long as there is close adult supervision. The child's best interests are served if there is opportunity for discussion between the school doctor, teachers, family doctor and parents regarding the treatment needed in each particular case.

Incidence of epilepsy

In the UK three surveys have been carried out which tell us something of the incidence and associated problems of children with epilepsy. The first two surveys are mentioned elsewhere in this book:

1. The Isle of Wight Cross Sectional Study of all children between the ages of 9 and 12. In this survey, pupils with neurological impairments, including epilepsy, were tested in greater

detail with regard to their educational attainments and behaviour.

2. The massive National Child Development Study, which is following the development of all 17 000 children born in one particular week in 1958.
3. A study of children with epilepsy in an area of rural Bedfordshire, carried out by a doctor and an educationalist (Holdsworth and Whitmore, 1974).

Thanks to improvements in the general health of the population during this century and to more effective medication, the number of pupils thought to be epileptic who are attending ordinary schools has decreased dramatically. Recent figures show that numbers are continuing to fall and, for instance, between the years 1951 and 1973, despite a general rise in the school population, the number of pupils in ordinary schools who were suffering from epilepsy had dropped by nearly half.

Estimates of the incidence of epilepsy in childhood vary, depending on the sampling techniques and the exactitude of the definition, but it does seem that about four or five in every 1000 pupils attending ordinary schools could be classed as 'epileptic'. Although most of these pupils' fits would be relatively well controlled by medication, we could expect about two in every 1000 to experience a fit during their early teens.

For some years, it has been official policy that pupils with epilepsy should be educated in the ordinary school system, on the assumption that they can be treated like any other child. However, several recent studies have indicated that some pupils do experience difficulty in adapting to school. There is no evidence to suggest that these educational problems are connected with lack of all-round intelligence. For instance, the Isle of Wight study, pupils with epilepsy were found to be of average intelligence. In looking at possible explanations for the difficulties in adapting to school life, we must consider the general public's attitude. In talking to epileptics themselves, and to their parents, it is apparent that a great deal of anxiety still surrounds the label 'epileptic'. The idea of a seizure seems to cause anxiety for two reasons, firstly, there is *fear of the unexpected*, and secondly, *fear of the unknown*.

The *unpredictability* of the timing of seizures is said by patients to be the most worrying aspect of their illness. No matter how many seizures they have had, not knowing when and where the next fit might occur causes them to feel insecure and uncertain and sometimes to avoid participating in activities outside the home or making plans for the future.

The second worrying aspect of epilepsy is fear of *loss of conscious control*. For the epileptic this is particularly frightening, especially in Western society, which is imbued with an ethic of rationality and self-control. For the peers and associates of epileptics the disorder is equally disturbing, and in the past this led to epileptics being regarded as 'possessed of spirits' and different from other people. This naturally tended to their being ostracized from normal society and nurtured the belief in an 'epileptic personality'.

The idea of an epileptic personality as such is no longer credited; but nevertheless research indicates that a relatively large proportion of affected children do have difficulty in adjusting to school life and are subject to behavioural problems. In the Isle of Wight and Bedfordshire surveys, as many as 25 per cent of children with epilepsy were reported by their teachers to show problem behaviour in school (compared to about 7 per cent among non-epileptic pupils).

Some children with epilepsy were described as aggressive and attention-seeking, some as rather withdrawn, listless and inattentive. It is of particular interest to note that most of the pupils with behaviour difficulties, in the Bedfordshire survey, were either at the beginning (nursery/reception class) or nearing the end of their school life. Without more evidence we can only speculate about the reason for this: it could be that after a settling-in period, when child and teacher get to know each other, all goes reasonably well, until adolescence. Then during the last two years at school, self-doubt and apprehensiveness about ability to cope in the adult world could have a disturbing effect, resulting in the excitable attention-seeking behaviour noted by their teachers.

Again, because of concern about emotional difficulties, a quarter of the children with epilepsy followed up in the National Child Development Study had been referred, by the age of 11, for psychiatric consultation.

Taking the evidence from various sources it does appear that pupils with epilepsy, although educated within the normal school system, experience more than usual difficulty in adapting to class routines and peer-group relationships.

In order to find ways of helping these pupils to make a better adjustment to school we need to know more about the sort of situations in which problems arise (e.g. level of noise/distractions/time of day, etc.) and whether there is any connection with the type of epilepsy the child suffers from.

Stores (1978) and his colleagues in Oxford have completed a number of small-scale studies exploring the characteristics thought to be associated with epilepsy; looking separately at such factors as attentiveness, overactivity and dependency, in pupils with, for instance, focal and generalized fits. Measures of distractibility and perseverance were obtained for each child and rating scales of behaviour were completed by class teachers.

Although numbers tested were small, the results obtained so far indicate that boys whose focus of epileptic disturbance is in the left side of the brain show more signs of anxiety, inattentiveness and overactivity than their normal class-mates. Apart from this finding, there were fewer differences on individual testing than might have been expected from the teachers' reports. Teachers on the whole rated boys with epilepsy as more disturbed and overactive; epileptic girls on the other hand were indistinguishable, in these matters, from their class-mates.

This preliminary finding, that girls who suffer convulsions show no more than normal behavioural difficulties, does suggest that social expectations play a predominant role in a child's capacity to cope with the demands and discipline of school life.

Regarding the educational attainments of epileptic pupils, there is some discrepancy between the results of the various studies. As part of a series of investigations in Oxford, children with generalized epilepsy, tested individually by a psychologist, displayed reading skills commensurate with their intellectual level. However, in other surveys, quite serious retardation in reading ability has been reported. For instance, in the Isle of Wight study, nearly a fifth of the 9- to 10-year-olds with epilepsy were two or more years retarded in their reading.

It will be clear, from this brief account, that there are many unanswered questions, concerning the causes of epilepsy, its control by medication, the effects of such medication on the child's behaviour and attention and the reasons for the difficulties that some epileptic subjects experience in school. Although some behaviours, such as inattentiveness or overactivity are most likely to be the result of some electrical disturbance in the brain cells, the finding that girls with epilepsy have no more problems than the normal run of girls suggests that we should look more closely at general social factors. Parental anxiety and overprotection, and the pockets of prejudice that still exist amongst the public might be expected to have an adverse effect on a child's evaluation of himself as a worthwhile person. Through general education of the public and through improved information and counselling services, for parents and children alike, we can be hopeful that the emotional problems will lessen.

Although the investigations cited here are concerned to discover the areas of difficulty that these children experience, it is true to say that the majority of pupils with epilepsy in the normal educational system do make a satisfactory adaptation and do integrate well into the life of school.

Those who wish to read more about this condition will find a clear exposition in Scott (1973).

Future work with children with minimal cerebral dysfunction

The next decade should bring consolidation of many of the tentative ideas we have expressed in this Chapter concerning the causes, the incidence, the learning and behaviour problems and the educational and other treatment of these children. Although our present knowledge is sketchy, the ideas we have described represent a useful addition to our knowledge of certain children's difficulties, that cannot be explained by other means. The terms 'brain damage' and 'minimal cerebral dysfunction' are, as we have already stated, unsatisfactory: few writers can avoid using them, but a more satisfactory one might be 'specific learning difficulties' as used by Francis-Williams (1974) in her survey of this field. Much finer diagnostic and assessment techniques need to be developed by neurologists and psychologists and, of course, many more experiments in educational techniques need to be pursued.

Organizations

In this country, compared to the United States, there are no fully recognized national organizations that produce literature and guidance specifically for brain-damaged children, it being generally felt in official quarters that their needs can be met by existing hospital and local education authorities and schools psychological services. Advice can be obtained from various voluntary societies.

The Spastics Society,
12 Park Crescent,
London W1N 4EQ.
Largely concerned with children whose brain damage is accompanied by physical difficulties.

The Invalid Children's Aid
  Association,
126 Buckingham Palace Road,
London SW1.

This association is concerned with children with language and reading difficulties and has set up two very specialized residential schools for children with severe language disorders, Moor House and John Horniman School.

The National Society for Mentally
    Handicapped Children,
Pembridge Hall, 17 Pembridge
    Square,
London W2 4EP.

This society also provides services
relevant to the problems of many
children with minimal cerebral
dysfunctioning.

Organizations for more specific conditions:

British Dyslexia Association,
18 The Circus,
Bath.

The Dyslexia Institute,
133 Gresham Road,
Staines.

These organizations publish useful pamphlets on specific reading difficulties.

The following provide a practical approach to helping children with reading difficulties:

Hornsby, B. & Shear, F. (1975) *From Alpha to Omega.* London: Heinemann.
Miles, T. R. (1970) *On Helping the Dyslectic Child.* London: Methuen
    Educational.
Miles, T. R. & Miles, E. (1975) *More Help for Dyslexic Children.* London:
    Methuen Educational.
Stott, D. H. (1974). *The Parent as Teacher.* University of London Press.
Webster, J. (1965) *Practical Reading.* London: Evans.

REFERENCES

Abercrombie, M. L. J. (1964) Perceptual and visuomotor disorders in cerebral
    palsy. *Little Club Clinics in Developmental Medicine*, No. 11. London: Spastics
    Society/Heinemann.
Abercrombie, M. L. J. *et al.* (1964) Visual perceptual and visuomotor
    impairments in physically handicapped children. *Perceptual and Motor Skills,
    Monographs*, Suppl. 3, **V**, No. 18.
Abercrombie, M. L. J. (1965) On drawing a diamond. Article in *Penguin Science
    Survey* B.
Abercrombie, M. L. J. (1968) Some notes on spatial disability: movement,
    intelligence quotient and attentiveness. *Developmental Medicine and Child
    Neurology*, **10**, No. 2.
Anderson, E. M. & Spain, B. (1977) *The Child with Spina Bifida.* London:
    Methuen.
Birch, H. G. (1964) *Brain Damage in Children. The Biological and Social Aspects.*
    Baltimore: Williams & Wilkins.
Birch, H. G. (1965) Auditory visual integration, intelligence and reading ability
    in school children. *Perceptual and Motor Skills, Monographs*, **20.**
Bortner, M. (Ed.) (1968) *Evaluation and Education of Children with Brain
    Damage.* Illinois: Thomas.
Bowley, A. H. (1969) Reading difficulty with minor neurological dysfunctioning.
    Developmental Medicine and Child Neurology, **11** (4), 493–503.
Brenner, M. W. & Gillman, S. (1966) Visual motor ability in schoolchildren: a
    survey. *Developmental Medicine and Child Neurology*, **8** (6), 686.
Brown, R. I. (1966) The effects of varied environmental stimuli on the
    performance of subnormal children. *Journal of Child Psychology and
    Psychiatry*, **7**, 251–61.
Brown, R. I. & Semple, L. (1970) Effects of unfamiliarity on the overt
    verbalization and perceptual motor behaviour of nursery school children.
    British Journal of Educational Psychology, **40** (3), 291–8.

Clements, S. D. (1966) *Minimal Brain Dysfunction in Children*. Phase one of a three phase project, US National Institute of Neurologic Diseases and Stroke. Monogr. No. 3, US Dept. of Health, Education and Welfare.

Clements, S. D. & Peters, J. F. (1962) Minimal brain dysfunction in school age children. *Archives of General Psychiatry*, **6**, 185.

Connolly, K. & Bruner, J. S. (Eds.) (1973) *The Growth of Competence*. New York: Academic Press.

Critchley, M. (1970) *Developmental Dyslexia*. London: Heinemann Medical Books.

Cruickshank, W. M. *et al.* (1961) *A Teaching Method for Brain Injured and Hyperactive Children*. New York: Syracuse University Press.

Cruickshank, W. M., Bice H. V. & Wallen, N. R. (1965) *Perception in Cerebral Palsy, a Study in Figure Background Relationship*. New York: Syracuse University Press.

Cruickshank, W. M. (Ed.) (1966) *The Teacher of Brain Injured Children: a Discussion of the Bases for Competency*. New York: Syracuse University Press.

Cruickshank, W. M. & Hallahan, D. P. (Eds.) (1975) *Perceptual and Learning Difficulties in Children*. New York: Syracuse University Press.

Field, J. G. (1960) Two types of tables for use with Wechsler's intelligence scales. *Journal of Clinical Psychology*, **16**, 6.

Francis-Williams, J. (1974) *Children with Specific Learning Difficulties*. Oxford: Pergamon.

Frostig. M. (1964) *The Marianne Frostig Developmental Test of Visual Perception*. Palo Alto, California: Consulting Psychologists Press.

Frostig, M. (1968) Testing as a basis for educational therapy. In *Assessment of the Cerebral Palsied Child for Education*. Ed. Loring, J. London: Spastics Society/Heinemann.

Frostig, M. & Maslow, P. (1973) *Learning Problems in the Classroom*. New York: Grune & Stratton.

Gallacher, J. J. (1960) *The Tutoring of Brain Injured Mentally Retarded Children* Illinois: Thomas.

Graham, F. K. *et al.* (1963) Brain injury in the preschool child, some developmental considerations. *Psychological Monographs*, 77 (10).

Holdsworth, L. & Whitmore, K. (1974) A study of children with epilepsy attending ordinary school. *Developmental Medicine and Child Neurology*, **16,**

Horn, J. & Quarmby, D. (1970). The problems of older non-readers. *Special Education*, 59 (3), 23–5.

Hutt, C. *et al.* (1964) Arousal and childhood autism. *Nature*, **204.**

Hutt, S. J. Hutt, C. & Ounsted, C. (1963) A Method of studying children's behaviour. *Developmental Medicine and Child Neurology*, 5 (3), 233–45.

Hutt, S. J. & Hutt, C. (1964) Hyperactivity in a group of epileptic (and some non-epileptic) brain damaged children. *Epilepsia*, **5,** 334–51.

Hutt, S. J. & Hutt, C. (Eds.) (1970) *Behaviour Studies in Psychiatry*. Oxford: Pergamon.

Johnson, D. D. & Myklebust, H. R. (1967) *Learning Disabilities: Educational Principles and Practice*. New York: Grune & Stratton.

Kephart, N. C. (1960) *The Slow Learner in the Classroom*. Columbus, Ohio: Merrill.

Kephart, N. C. (1968) Chapter in Bortner (q.v.).

Lansdown, R. (1970) *A Study of the Frostig Programme for the Development of Visual Perception used in the Ordinary Primary School*. London Borough of Waltham Forest.

Lawrence, D. (1973) *Improved Reading through Counselling*. London: Ward Lock.

McGinnis, M. (1963) *Aphasic Children*. Washington. Alexander Graham Bell Association for the Deaf.

Mittler, P. (1970) *The Psychological Assessment of Mental and Physical Handicaps*. London: Methuen.

Morris, J. M. (1966) *Standards and Progress in Reading*. Slough, Bucks.: N.F.E.R.

Newton, M. (1971) *A Guide for Teachers and Parents*. Birmingham: University of Aston Press.

Piaget, J. & Inhelder, B. (1956) *The Child's Conception of Space*. London: Routledge & Kegan Paul.

Ravenette, A. T. (1968) *Dimensions of Reading Difficulties*. Oxford: Pergamon.

Reynell, J. (1969) *Infant and Young Children's Language Scales, Manual and Test Material*. Windsor: National Foundation for Educational Research.

Rutter, M., Graham, P. & Yule, W. (1970) A neuropsychiatric study in childhood. *Little Club Clinics in Developmental Medicine*, Nos. 35 and 36. Spastics Society/Heinemann.

Rutter, M., Tizard, J. & Whitmore, K. (1970) *Education, Health and Behaviour*. London: Longman.

Schulman, J. L. Kaspar, J. C. & Thorne, F. M. (1965) *Brain Damage and Behaviour*. Springfield, Illinois: Thomas.

Scott, D. (1973) *About Epilepsy*. London: Duckworth.

Sheridan, M. D. & Peckham, C. (1975) Follow up at eleven years of children with marked speech defects at seven years. *Child: Care, Health and Development, Vol. 1, No. 3 Page 157–66.*

Stores, G. & Hart, J. (1976) Reading skills in children with generalized or focal epilepsy. *Developmental Medicine and Child Neurology*, **18,** (6), 705–16.

Stores, G. (1978) School children with epilepsy at risk for learning and behavioural problems. *Developmental Medicine and Child Neurology*, **20** (6), 502–8.

Stott, D. H. (1966) A general test of motor impairment for children. *Developmental Medicine and Child Neurology*, **8** (5), 523–31.

Stott, D. H. (1978) *Helping Children with Learning Difficulties*. London: Ward Lock.

Stott, D. H., Moyes, F. & Henderson, S. (1972) *Test of Motor Impairment*. Windsor: National Foundation for Educational Research.

Strauss, A. A. & Kephart, N. C. (1955) *Psychopathology and Education of the Brain-injured Child*, Vol. 2. New York: Grune & Stratton.

Strauss, A. A. & Lehtinen, L. E. (1947) *Psychopathology and Education of the Brain-injured Child*, Vol. 1, New York: Grune & Stratton.

Tansley, A. E. (1967) *Reading and Remedial Reading*. London: Routledge & Kegan Paul.

Taylor, I. G. (1964) *Neurological Mechanisms of Hearing and Speech in Children*. London: Manchester University Press.

Thomas, A., Chess, S. & Birch, H. G. (1968) *Temperament and Behaviour Disorders in Children*. New York: University Press.

Thompson, D. A. & Johnson, J. D. (1971) Teaching machines for the very handicapped: the Touch-Tutor at Hawksworth Hall. *Special Education*, **60** (1), 9–11.

Thompson, D. Kearslake, C. C. Pearce, B. (1972) Do perceptual handicaps matter? *Special Education*, **61**(3), 15–18.

Tyson, M. (1963) Pilot study of remedial visuomotor training. *Special Education*, **52** (4), 27–33.

Vellutino, F. R. *et al.* (1977) Has the perceptual deficit hypothesis led us astray? *Journal of Learning Disabilities*, **10,** 375–385.

Walton, J. N., Ellis, E. & Court, S. D. (1962) Clumsy children, a study of developmental apraxia and agnosia. *Brain*, **85,** 603.

Wedell, K. (1960) The visual perception of cerebral palsied children. *Journal of Child Psychology and Psychiatry*, **1,** 217–27.

Wedell, K. (1973) *Learning and Perceptuo-Motor Disabilities in Children*. New York: Wiley.

Wedell, K. (Ed.) (1975) Chapter on 'Specific learning difficulties'. In *Orientations in Special Education*. New York: Wiley.

Wedell, K. & Rambould, E. C. (Eds.) (1976) The early identification of educationally 'at risk' children. *Educational Review Occasional Publication* No. 6. University of Birmingham.

Wolfendale, S. & Bryans, T. (1979) *Identification of Learning Difficulties*. National Association for Remedial Education U.K. Stafford.

4

The child with hearing loss

The need for understanding

A serious handicap such as deafness tends to isolate a child from normal life, unless steps are taken to prevent such isolation. A handicap makes special demands on the child: he is cut off from many of the experiences and opportunities for learning that ordinary children enjoy, and has to make constant and considerable efforts to achieve things that come relatively easily to ordinary children. For example, ordinary children learn speech and language, more or less naturally and spontaneously in their early years, as a result of certain inborn abilities, coupled with an environment that includes speech stimulation, from adults and other children. Ordinary children learn language almost 'incidentally'. But for severely deaf children, it must be taught, gradually and skilfully.

A severe handicap also makes special demands of the parents: to understand exactly what the handicap means to the child, how it impinges on his life, and then to work out ways of lessening its effects and promoting the child's learning in as many directions as possible. The crucial part the parents play in their child's early years of learning cannot be too strongly emphasized, and it follows that the help that experts can give must be directed as much to the parents as to the handicapped child himself. Most of the growing numbers of doctors, teachers, psychologists, therapists, health visitors and social workers who have specialized in helping handicapped children and their families now realize that the best form of help consists not in occasional visits to experts for treatment, but in advising parents of the best way that they can help their young child within the natural setting of his home.

We must also mention that a serious handicap makes demands not only on the child and his family, but on the wider community, including the neighbours, shopkeepers, the man in the street, and so on, most of whom will have had little or no contact with seriously handicapped children. In the past, the majority of blind, deaf and spastic children tended to remain isolated in hospitals, remote boarding schools and other institutions. However, this picture has changed in recent years as we move towards less isolation and more 'integration' for the handicapped within the normal community. The general public's attitudes to the handicapped are improving, but there is much work still to be done in promoting true understanding and acceptance.

People with a hearing loss are often misunderstood because their handicap is less obvious than that of the blind and the spastic. Deafness fails to evoke the immediate sympathy that a more obviously dependent spastic or blind child can evoke: yet the handicap of deafness is a formidable one, when it is realized that the untrained, seriously deaf child is cut off not merely from sounds, but from speech, and is therefore drastically cut off from so many kinds of social contact and opportunities for learning. The major efforts of the parents of young deaf children must therefore centre on fostering the child's ability to communicate. There are many ways in which a mother communicates to her child: by her facial expressions, her gestures, by touching him, by picking him up, by cuddling him, and so on: the young severely deaf child can understand these, but he is almost completely cut off from the most commonly used, most precise, easily remembered and far-reaching way that a mother communicates to her child, namely, that of speech. He cannot hear the prohibiting 'No' every time he goes near the electric fire; he cannot hear the encouraging 'Good' when he first succeeds in building a tower of bricks. He cannot hear the compromise, 'Have Teddy instead', or 'In a minute', or the reassuring 'See you in the morning'. It is not only the words that he misses, but many of the *concepts*, the ideas, the ways of thinking, that lie behind the words: for example, the *ideas* of postponing or compromising on his wishes are difficult for the deaf child to grasp, since he is denied the use of words in having such ideas explained to him. Furthermore it is not only the words and the concepts that he misses, but the guidance, comfort and reassurance that follow from the words, and it is not surprising that he is often bewildered and frustrated.

If we can gain an understanding of the difficulties that follow from the fact that a child is deaf, we can go far in overcoming these difficulties and reducing the frustrations and can begin to work out a positive plan for his care and training and education, so that when he is older he is both willing and able to communicate as much as possible with hearing people and thereby take his place in the community.

Before continuing with these topics let us first consider how many deaf children there are and, briefly, the question of why they are deaf and what different kinds of deafness there are.

The incidence and types of deafness

Hearing losses can be of any degree, from very slight to very severe, and even total deafness is occasionally found. Many children's hearing losses are temporary, such as those caused by blockages and infections: these are known as conductive hearing losses, they impair the hearing of at least 5 per cent of children for short periods of time and nearly always respond quickly to medical treatment.

In this book, we are largely concerned with the type of hearing loss known as 'nerve' or 'perceptive' deafness, which is not medically treatable, but can be treated through training at home and through therapy and education. There are four degrees of hearing and language impairment:

1. *Mild hearing loss*, sometimes described as 'hard of hearing', which interferes very little with the child's language development and requires very little specialized help, other than assuring people's *awareness* of the mild loss so that they do not confuse it with backwardness or inattentiveness.

2. *Partial hearing loss*, leading to difficulties in hearing an ordinary conversational voice, requiring a hearing aid in most cases, and training at home in how to make good use of the considerable hearing that remains and combine this with lip-reading, if the child is to avoid difficulties not only in hearing other people's speech, but in developing his own speech. Given ample language stimulation at home during the early years, it has been found that many such children can attend ordinary schools at age five, with occasional supervision from a visiting teacher of the partially hearing (Ewing, 1961). Others can attend a special unit for the partially hearing attached to an ordinary school.

3. *Severe hearing loss:* failing to hear a conversation unless very loud and at close range, and even then frequently failing to understand what is heard because of lack of experience: requiring intensive and regular training at home as early as possible, in making some use of a hearing aid but relying a great deal on lip-reading. A few children with serious hearing losses develop enough language to attend ordinary schools, but the majority attend special units, more and more of which have

the advantage of being attached to ordinary schools, so that the child remains in contact with the ordinary community.

4. *Profoundly deaf:* again requiring intensive training at home as early as possible, able in some cases to hear just a few sounds through a powerful hearing aid, but nothing which sounds like speech, and relying almost entirely on lip-reading and of course requiring intensive and specialized help both at home and within a special school for very deaf children when older, where many of the children eventually develop some speech and understanding of speech. Some experts, however, are dissatisfied with the amount of language that current 'oral' methods of education are giving to very deaf children, and are advocating some return to earlier 'manual' methods of education, including the use of gesture and signs and finger spelling. We will discuss this controversy later.

Many studies have indicated that just under two in every thousand children have a sufficient loss to warrant the use of a hearing aid. In England and Wales in 1967, approximately 6500 children were attending deaf and partially hearing schools and units (Dept of Education and Science, 1968). The exact numbers of partially hearing children with hearing aids attending ordinary classes in ordinary schools is not accurately known but probably in excess of 6000. This total of approximately 12 500 school children known to have sufficient hearing loss to require a hearing aid gives an incidence of 1·7 per thousand, to which must be added many hundreds of children outside the formal school system, such as children with multiple handicaps in hospitals and other units. The incidence of children requiring a hearing aid was very similar in the Isle of Wight studies (Rutter *et al.*, 1970). Although the number of deaf children is large enough to give rise to the development of excellent audiology and educational services, voluntary associations and clubs, it is not large enough for the general public to have encountered personally the problems of severe deafness in children, and parents will find it necessary to explain very fully to friends and neighbours what is involved.

Causes of hearing loss

There are many different causes of deafness: the ear is a very complicated organ and may be affected in a variety of ways, so producing various types of deafness.

Some children are born deaf, either due to some inherited defect in the ear and its nerve connections to the brain, to the illness of the mother during pregnancy, or to difficulties during the birth process. A great deal has been learned about the effects on the unborn child of certain infections of the mother during pregnancy. Rubella (German measles) occurring during the early months of pregnancy has been found, for instance, to be a cause of deafness, a cause which is now being eliminated either by ensuring that women are exposed to rubella prior to pregnancy, or by injections. Blood group incompatibility between parents is another occasional cause of deafness at birth, which is gradually being eliminated, such as by prompt exchange transfusions. Children may also lose their hearing in infancy or childhood as a result of such illnesses as meningitis, scarlet fever and measles, and also, very occasionally, as a result of accidents.

Some deafness is caused by blockage or infection of the middle ear (which conducts the sound to the inner ear). Prompt medical treatment is often effective in improving this type of hearing loss.

The type of deafness that is our main concern in this Chapter is that which is due to the damage or disease of the *inner* ear or nerve fibres (see Fig. 23). This is termed 'nerve' or 'perceptive' deafness; it is different from 'conduction' deafness in that there

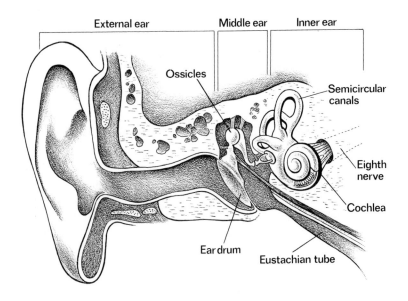

Auditory Mechanism

Fig. 23 Auditory mechanism, showing external, middle and inner ear.

is no treatment known at present that can bring back hearing to a person suffering from this type of deafness. In this case, when the inner ear itself is damaged, we have no means of providing a substitute for the delicate and intricate mechanism that transmits sounds to our brain. In many cases of nerve deafness there is an uneven loss of hearing over the different parts of the musical scale. For instance, the child may be unable to hear notes of a high pitch, but hears those of low pitch fairly normally. This particular type of deafness is termed 'high tone deafness'.

It must be emphasized that it is extremely important to make every effort to discover the causes of deafness and to seek specialized medical advice about any possibilities of treatment. When medical or surgical treatment proves impossible, as is the case at present with 'nerve deafness', it is still important for the parents to have as much knowledge as is available about the causes. The question 'Why is my child deaf?' is often uppermost in their minds when the deafness is first discovered, followed by concern about whether other children they may have will be affected, and whether their children's children may also be handicapped. In many cases, the cause of the deafness is known, such as rubella during the mother's early pregnancy, and carries no risk to subsequent children. Alternatively, in a few cases, there may be a strong history of deafness in the family and the risk to further children can be calculated. Since nearly 50 per cent of the children in Fraser's (1964) study of 2355 severely deaf children were considered to have a genetically determined type of deafness (usually due to a recessive gene in families with *no* known history of deafness) the importance of genetic counselling of parents about any risks to any future offspring must be emphasized. Given the facts (that, in the light of the particular family histories of the two parents, there is, say, a one in four chance of their next child having a hearing loss) the parents can then make their own decision. In other deaf children, at least 10 to 20 per cent, the causes are simply unknown. In all cases a thorough medical investigation and advice to parents about possible causes is essential. The deaf child himself will want to know when he is older. A comprehensive review of research, particularly into the causes of deafness, has been edited by Fisch (1964). More general books on causes and treatment are those of Davis and Silverman (1977) and Whetnall and Fry (1971). A strong plea for a new effort to discover methods of treating nerve deafness is to be found in Jack Ashley's article (1971).

The detection of hearing losses in young children

At what age can we tell whether or not a child has a hearing loss? Usually before the age of 12 months. This early detection is very important and in many areas valuable screening tests are carried out by health visitors and other local authority staff, who can then refer all babies who have failed the screening tests for more thorough examinations at specialized ENT and audiology units. Usually about a quarter of the children referred to audiology units turn out to have a hearing loss, and in these cases no time must be lost in advising parents who have a deaf child, giving them a clear indication of what his difficulties are and helping them to provide simple home training as soon as possible.

Distraction tests of hearing

The present-day clinical tests of hearing in a young child consist largely of skilled observations of his reactions to a wide variety of sounds, loud and soft, high and low pitched, within a quiet room and under carefully controlled conditions. For example, the baby's attention must not be too deeply engaged in any particular activity, and when the sounds are made, great care must be taken to ensure that he neither sees nor feels the examiner making the sounds. The ordinary baby under about five months of age is rarely mature enough to turn his head towards the sound, but usually shows some kind of response, such as a slight movement of his eyes, blinking, shifting his leg or hand, or interrupting his movements. Experienced personnel can observe these muscular responses to quite gentle sounds such as rattles, squeakers, rustling paper, etc., in babies under five months of age, and, combining these observations with a careful consideration of the parents' observations at home (e.g. is the baby easily awakened by sounds), can say whether the hearing is likely to be normal or not. Great importance must always be attached to the mother's views about her baby's hearing. If she is convinced that he cannot hear, she is usually right, and her testimony has even greater weight if she has other children with whom she can compare her baby's response to sounds at home.

After five months of age, the ordinary baby has enough muscular control and interest in his surroundings to turn his head to locate the source of the sounds visually, and the observations become more reliable. If, for example, the baby turns briskly and accurately both left and right to most of the gentle sounds, including high-pitched ones, and care has been taken not to let the baby see or feel our movements, there can be nothing seriously wrong with his hearing.

But what if the baby fails to show any signs of responding to these sounds? This does not necessarily mean that he is deaf and personnel engaged in screening tests in homes and clinics must be aware of this and not worry parents unnecessarily by jumping to conclusions about deafness on the basis of so little evidence. A small number of babies simply show little or no interest in sounds until after the age of six months and another group fail to respond to sounds because their development is slow in general. It is in such cases that the skilled observations of the audiology unit team, usually consisting of an otologist, a psychologist, a teacher of the deaf and an audiometrician, are essential. For example, if the child who fails to respond to sounds also fails to respond to visual stimuli, such as a moving light, and to touch, such as a puff of air on his cheek, then his difficulties may be more a matter of slow general development rather than of a hearing loss in particular. The audiology unit team look at the child as a whole before trying to pinpoint a particular difficulty such as deafness.

The tests we have described so far are known as *distraction* tests of hearing. Soon after the age of 12 months we can also use the most important test of all—the testing of the child's speech and understanding of speech.

Speech tests of hearing

At ages 12 to 18 months, many ordinary babies can say a few words and show some appreciation of their meaning, and follow simple spoken instructions such as 'Show me the ball' or 'Where's Mummy', and provided we have been careful in our testing, using a quiet voice and giving no visual or other help such as by gesturing or allowing lip-reading, such tests can prove considerable hearing to be present. Failure does not necessarily denote deafness, but combined with further distraction tests of hearing and observation of his general behaviour, such as alertness to visual and tactile (sense of touch) and social stimulation, these *speech tests* (Fig. 24) can provide very valuable information about the presence of a hearing loss. A monotonous flat tone of voice is also an indication.

By the age of two, a wide range of toys and pictures can be presented to the child, and even if he cannot name them, we can determine whether he can understand simple spoken instructions, such as can he point to the car, to the doll, to the ball, etc. Failures in such tests of the understanding of language at the age of two are usually significant, provided one is sure of the child's co-operation. More sophisticated speech tests after the age of three years include tests of understanding words which include high-frequency sounds, such as ship, foot, fish, which some children have particular difficulty in hearing compared to lower tone sounds (Reed, 1958).

Fig. 24 Speech tests of hearing: father tests son, in Urdu—with lips covered.

Conditioning tests
By the age of about $3\frac{1}{2}$ years a further kind of testing can be applied in addition to the distraction and speech tests and this is known as a 'conditioning' test. The child is engaged in play and is taught to put a peg in a hole or a brick into a box when he sees a drum being beaten and when we are sure that he is interested and understands the game, the drum is gradually taken out of sight so that he then has to rely on his hearing. Then sounds of varying loudness and pitch are given at various short intervals of time and a fairly accurate picture of the child's hearing can be obtained by experienced observers who understand children's behaviour, the effect of hearing loss and the nature of the sound stimuli. A valuable guide and set of equipment for distraction, speech and conditioning tests for young children is to be found in Mary Sheridan's (1968) 'Stycar' hearing tests.

By the age of four years, the majority of children can be reliably tested with headphones, through which sounds of precise loudness and pitch are fed by an audiometer, and provided the audiometrician can secure the child's full co-operation and attention so that he listens carefully to sounds which can only just be heard, a very accurate chart of the child's hearing can be obtained, for both ears. The following are two examples of children's responses to an audiometer. For simplicity, we have shown the responses of one ear only and will regard the hearing loss in the child's other ear as virtually the same.

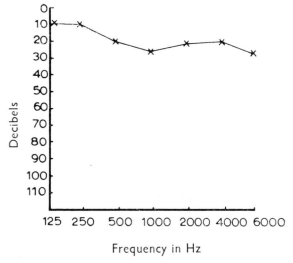

Fig. 25 Audiogram showing mild hearing loss.

Measuring the loudness of sounds

The loudness of sound is measured in decibels, shown on the vertical column of the audiogram. Quiet sounds, such as rustling leaves or a whisper, measure at about 40 decibels. An ordinary conversational voice in an ordinary room at three or four feet distance is at a level of about 60 to 70 decibels. A loud drum beaten at three feet is at a level of about 90 decibels. Sounds above the level of 100 decibels begin to feel unpleasant for both hearing and severely deaf children, such as the sound of a pneumatic drill at close range at about 110 decibels. A hearing loss of about 20 decibels, as shown in Figure 25, is a very slight one and it would be unlikely to cause the child any difficulties. A loss of 40 decibels would in many cases be enough to cause the child to miss a considerable proportion of ordinary conversation and might warrant the use of a hearing aid, but rarely specialized schooling. A loss of 60 to 70 decibels means that the child certainly cannot hear much of ordinary conversation, without the help of a hearing aid, and the supervision and expert help of a teacher of the deaf would be essential in most cases. A loss of 90 decibels, as shown in Figure 26, is a severe loss. Although the child with such a loss would derive

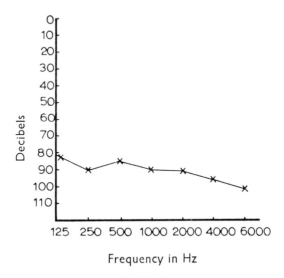

Fig. 26 Audiogram showing severe hearing loss.

considerable benefit from a hearing aid, he will not hear speech as we know it through the aid, and would need very specialized and intensive training in making the best use of his hearing, to develop skills in lip-reading, and would usually require specialized schooling when he is older. These degrees of hearing loss (see page 142) can be roughly summarized as follows:

1. Mild loss   15–30 decibels
2. Partial loss   30–65 decibels
3. Severe loss   65–95 decibels
4. Profound loss   95 decibels and above

Measuring the pitch of sounds

The audiometer also measures the child's hearing for various pitches or tones, ranging from low tones, such as middle C on the piano, at 256 cycles per second, to high notes, such as a high-pitched whistle at 4000 cycles per second. (The metric term for 'cycles per second' is Herz, and the abbreviation Hz will be used in future.) Speech sounds are made up of combinations of these tones and, as we have mentioned, some children have particular difficulty in hearing particular tones, such as the high ones. This distorts the speech that they hear and in turn distorts their own speech. Special, adjustable hearing aids such as those which amplify only the high notes can be provided. These children's hearing losses are often detected rather late because they appear to respond very well to ordinary sounds such as a faint tap. The first indication of what may be a high-tone hearing loss in such children is the fact that their own speech omits most of the high-tone consonants, such as f, sh, th, and s. Speech appears to them as a rumble of low-pitched sounds, making it difficult for them to understand and say words clearly. The audiogram in Figure 27 shows a typical high-tone loss.

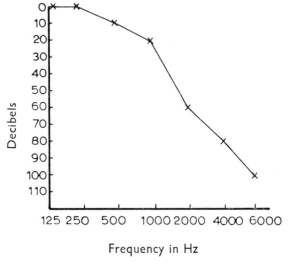

Frequency in Hz

Fig. 27 Audiogram showing severe high tone loss.

The early detection of hearing losses is of great importance and the hearing tests for young children that we have described, many of which were developed by the Ewings in Manchester (Ewing, 1961; 1971), should be given to all children who show even slight difficulties in hearing or speech. The results obtained are reliable in the majority of cases, even with babies who were formerly considered too young for hearing tests. The tests are not yet completely scientific or 'objective', but in the hands of personnel who are experienced in audiology work many accurate hearing tests can be carried out well before the baby is 12 months of age. Severe hearing loss in otherwise normal babies can usually be detected during the first few months of life. Indeed, interesting work is being carried out on the hearing responses of babies only a few days old (Turner and Macfarlane, 1978).

Hearing tests for the multiply handicapped

With the majority of young children, hearing tests can be carried out quite accurately by experienced personnel. Problems in testing arise, however, with the multiply handicapped, such as those children who are emotionally disturbed or who show autistic or hyperactive behaviour, those who show obscure language disorders, the cerebral palsied and certain rubella children who may also be blind as well as possibly deaf, and certain categories of subnormal children, who are sometimes too immature to attend to a stimulus with any reliability. In all these cases, the behaviour and language problems may or may not be aggravated by the presence of a hearing loss, and it is often difficult to be sure about the latter, in the midst of so many other handicaps.

This is where the skill and experience of the audiology team is really important. Their observations on the child's responses will be based on a close study of the responses of thousands of children, with one basic question in mind—is the child at least occasionally responding in any way to the sounds the examiner is making, to the sound and nothing but to the sound, and if so, what level of intensity of sound, at what frequencies, is required? The phrase 'at least occasionally' is important. Nobody expects children, or even adults, to respond regularly to a given sound. Boredom, for one thing, sets in after the novelty has worn off, and with many hyperactive, disturbed children, the audiologist expects him to ignore the sounds, usually because he is preoccupied with something else. And when such a child does respond, we expect him to be using his eyes and his sense of touch, as well as any hearing he may have. Indeed with difficult multiply handicapped children we deliberately give them massive cues, for example letting them see and feel as well as hear (if they can) the drum initially, rewarding their responses with tremendous praise and encouragement, in the conditioning tests that we have already described, where the child has to place a peg in a hole or knock a brick off the table in response to our massive signals. Then gradually the signals are reduced, the props are taken away, so that the child will no longer see the drum and the examiner's gestures, and instead has to start using his hearing, first for very loud signals and then gradually to softer ones—reverting to massive signals if and when his attention wanders, then returning again to discreet signals when he is again co-operative. Frequent changes in play material and types of signals are also important to avoid habituation or boredom. Such procedures usually take several sessions during which most of the child's responses will be quite useless as far as judging his hearing is concerned: but a certain percentage of his responses, much more than could occur by chance, will, to the skilled audiologist, show unequivocal responses (or failures to respond) to sounds, of more or less known intensity and pitch. These observations, in the context of the audiologist's clinical experience, are usually sufficient to detect whether a multiply handicapped child also has the burden of a hearing loss. In some cases, of course, his handicaps might be considerably aggravated by such a loss, for example the restless behaviour of children who have had meningitis is often aggravated by the fact that their hearing loss denies them the use of language in exploring and controlling their environment and modifying their behaviour.

From these descriptions of audiology work with difficult children, one can see the need to develop more efficient 'objective' tests, which will be less dependent on the co-operation of the child and on the clinical intuitions of the examiner. These objective tests are based on the theory that if and when a child hears a sound, there must, somewhere within his person, be an accompanying physical, electrical or chemical change, resulting from the fact that certain nerves are being stimulated. The task then is to discover and measure these accompanying changes, whether by electrical waves in the brain (known as e.e.g. or evoked response audiometry described by Taylor, 1964), by exact measurement in breathing or pulse rates or skin potential (known as psychogalvanic skin response, PGSR audiometry). In e.e.g. testing the child need hardly co-operate at all, since he can be put into a light sleep. Records of electrical and muscular activities can be carried out electronically and analysed by a computer, although observers do differ at present on the interpretation of some results. A more reliable, but elaborate, objective test of hearing is the electrochochleogram (Beagley, 1975). This involves a general anaesthetic and the insertion of a needle-type electrode through the child's eardrum and on to the auditory nerve. A series of sounds are then made, and the tiny electrical currents that are provoked in the nerve are summed up and analysed by a computer. According to some experts, the results are very reliable (for higher rather than lower tones) but not completely so. This type of testing is also too elaborate for routine use.

Objective tests tell us a great deal about the hearing in some children, but not in others; and these others tend to be precisely those children whom we have already described as difficult to test, such as hyperactive and multiply handicapped children. Objective hearing tests on these groups of children so far tend to produce a confusing picture, but work along these lines is promising and has been well documented (Gerber, 1977). The minute analysis of the characteristics of the cries of new-born babies is another experimental objective technique that may eventually prove helpful in early detection of handicaps such as deafness (Wasz-Höckert, 1968). In the next decade it is likely that a combination of several techniques, objective and subjective, will prove to be the most valuable approach in assessing the hearing of multiply handicapped children.

The psychological effects of deafness

When a child is found to have a serious disability, such as deafness, the psychological consequences can obviously be profound. The parents' first reactions on being told of their child's deafness is often one of shock and bewilderment, followed by a multitude of questions.

Some of these questions are deeply emotional, for example 'Why did it have to happen to my child?' or 'Why has it happened to me?' with an underlying feeling that in some mysterious way the parents feel responsible for the deafness and somehow caused it to happen. Such strong feelings of personal responsibility for the handicap are of course completely unwarranted—nearly all deafness is caused by factors completely outside anyone's control.

Other questions are more rational, such as 'Is it certain that he is deaf?', 'What caused the deafness?', 'Can it be cured?' or 'Will our child always be deaf?', 'Will he be able to manage ordinary school?', 'What sort of job will he do?', 'Will any grandchildren be deaf too?'

These are important questions, exploring the ramifications of the child's handicap now and in the future, and demanding careful and factual answers and frank confession of ignorance in cases where the facts are unclear, rather than vague reassurances that 'everything will be all right'. There is no point in denying that coming to terms with severe and permanent handicaps does make special demands on the courage and skill and understanding of the parents, and calls for considerable adjustment on their part, particularly in respect of their hopes and plans for their child's future. Parents are helped by the knowledge that the handicapped child's problems are the problems of all people and that society at large has become increasingly aware of its responsibilities in recent years. In other words, the parents are not alone and many individuals and organizations are available if and when they need help. See Bloom (1978) for an impressive account of parents' difficulties, and how personal and organized efforts can surmount many of them.

Parents are also helped by the knowledge that most of the handicapped children's difficulties are very similar to those of ordinary children, such as problems of temper tantrums, of disobedience, messy eating, so-called laziness, disappointments at school, and so on. Deaf children certainly have no monopoly on these problems and we must be careful not to assume that all their difficulties are necessarily due to their deafness. Deaf children vary as much in their behaviour as do ordinary children and on the whole they are helped or hindered to a large extent by the example that their parents set for them.

Parents are also helped to come to terms with the handicap when they realize how much they can do to minimize its effects: and this is particularly so in respect of the upbringing of deaf children compared to many other handicaps such as severe mental retardation.

Let us briefly consider the psychological effects of deafness now from the child's point of view, effects which parents must understand if they are to help overcome some of them. We can compare the start of the day for a young child of normal hearing and for a child who is severely deaf.

The young hearing child wakens from his sleep, perhaps because of a slight noise of a car or a bird. He gets out of bed, and goes to the window to look at the car. He thinks about its colour or shape and perhaps imitates the sound of its engine. He is reassured that breakfast will not be very long in coming by the sound of crockery in the kitchen and the murmur of parents' voices. Eventually he hears the sound of mother's footsteps approaching his bedroom, and he jumps back quickly into bed. She smiles, they talk, she finds his dressing-gown, and he is told to find his slippers and then go to the bathroom.

For the young, severely deaf child, who has had no training, the start of the day is very different.

He is awakened not by any sound, but perhaps by light. When he is awake he does not know whether his parents are out of bed. He cannot hear footsteps (but he might feel very slight vibrations of the floor). If he is hungry he hears no comforting sounds from the kitchen, and does not know whether the time for breakfast is near or far (but he might detect a smell). Crossing to the window he sees something outside. He has no name for what he sees, and his thinking about it is limited by the fact that he has no words (since he has never heard any words) in which to express his thoughts.

Suddenly the door opens. Things happen very suddenly for the deaf child. It is his mother coming into his room: he had no warning of her approach through the sound of her footsteps. Mother smiles and he returns her smile. Her lips move, her facial expression changes, and she hurriedly crosses to the cupboard, hunts for his dressing-gown, and quickly wraps it round him. He may not understand why mother does this and may even resist it; she thinks he is cold, but he may not feel in the least cold. They cannot explain to each other. Later at the breakfast table all is silent. Lips move but no sounds emerge. Mother suddenly darts out of the room. The young deaf child does not know that the door bell is ringing. He looks at father and tries to work out whether he will go to work or stay at home that day.

Comparing these two examples, we can bring out several points about the problems of deafness for the young child, and ways of minimizing the effects of handicaps, starting with a very general point about deafness.

The lack of auditory background noises and warnings
By this we mean that he does not hear those almost continual noises of everyday life that normally hearing people take for granted and hear only half-consciously, such as the distant noise of trains, voices, doors closing, and the wind in the trees. These are important psychologically. They mean for the normally hearing person that life is going on and that they are in contact with it. These half-heard noises add to our feeling of being alive and in touch with other living beings. Many of these noises, such as in our example the clink of crockery in the kitchen, are of a reassuring nature. The world of the severely deaf is silent, and this silence induces a sense of isolation.

The young deaf child does not get the warnings and promptings that help the hearing child to adjust to things. He frequently misses his cue, as in our example in which he did not hear his mother approaching his bedroom, and was not prepared emotionally for her arrival. His daily life is full of such surprises (since he lacks warnings through sound) which, however pleasant they turn out to be, are initially something of a shock.

Difficulties in participation in family life

The deaf child's participation in family life is limited to some extent by the difficulty in communication. The untrained severely deaf child lacks speech of his own and cannot understand the speech of others through lip-reading. This means that he is missing some aspects of the countless activities that a mother and child do together, such as dressing, bathing, eating, going out, learning what he can and cannot do, and later on, doing things with father and brother and sister.

Modern studies in psychology have emphasized that the child's personality is greatly influenced by these early activities, particularly those in which he participates with his mother during the first few years of life. The baby at birth is a helpless creature, dependent on his mother, not only for meeting his bodily needs, but his needs for affection and security which at this stage can come only from the mother. This stage of more or less complete dependence on mother slowly gives way to increasing independence after the child begins to walk in his second year of life. His desire to explore, and to gain some control of his surroundings and assert himself, becomes stronger and stronger, and his wishes come into conflict with his mother's wishes particularly in the second and third years.

Provided that the child feels fundamentally loved and secure, and has not been either rigidly over-controlled or his initiative and efforts at mastering things sapped by the fact that everything has been done for him, his self-assertion and defiance gradually diminish. He becomes reasonably independent, within a framework of co-operation, capable of some control over his wishes for the sake of the wishes of his parents and other people around him.

This process of child development, through participation in family life, takes place quite naturally in the great majority of families. It also takes place quite naturally in the families of the majority of deaf children, but some difficulties do occur and can be avoided. The deaf child is not born with a different personality from that of hearing children: personality develops largely as a result of his early participation in family life in just the same way as for a hearing child, but with some additional difficulties. We will consider some of these difficulties in the deaf child's emotional development, in his forming of habits, and in his social, intellectual and speech development.

The emotional development of the deaf child

All children need affection and security, and these needs are not so easily met in the case of the deaf child. For example, he cannot hear the voice of his mother, which reassures him when he is frightened. He often feels a little isolated and unsure of his mother's presence and her attention, since he cannot hear her footsteps close at hand. When she disappears from his sight she seems to him to disappear completely and suddenly. Since he cannot hear his mother, and is therefore cut off from this source of security, it is important that he should see her as much as possible. In the pram or cot, he should often be sat up so that he can see his mother in her daily activities. Light, too, is important to a deaf child, who depends a great deal on his vision, and he is therefore more readily frightened of the dark.

When he is older he may follow her around excessively, trying to keep her always within his sight. This cannot be overcome simply by thrusting him away. Independence does not develop in this way; it emerges slowly and naturally in children, provided they feel basically secure and are given opportunities to manage things without their mother's continual presence.

This business of managing things for themselves, of exploring the world around them, has some extra difficulties for the deaf child. His attempts at managing to drink from a cup, dressing himself and putting his toys away cannot be encouraged by speech as with a hearing child; and when he fails, as all children do when first attempting to master things for themselves, his sense of failure and possible show of temper cannot be so easily lessened by spoken reassurance or by a spoken suggestion of doing something else that is not so difficult.

He is, of course, helped by the gestures and reassuring smile of his mother, but only when he is looking at her. He cannot be both looking at mother and concentrating on a task such as trying to draw, in the same way as the hearing child can. It is important, therefore, that parents should not press upon him tasks that are too difficult. They must keep an eye on what tasks (such as buttoning his coat) he is ready and mature enough to accomplish and what tasks are obviously going to be difficult at his age. The difficult tasks must be shared between the parent and the child, or if impossible at his age, some easier task or activity substituted for it. Too many failures and resulting tantrums would cause the child to recoil from independence and cling excessively to his mother or become anxious and withdrawn.

Parents who are 'over-demanding' in relation to their handicapped child are less common than those at the other extreme, parents who are 'over-protective'. By this we mean the mother who does everything for the child, who 'over-protects' him from any challenge or difficulty, so that his learning to manage things himself is greatly impaired. A certain amount of protection, beyond that ordinarily given to children, is, of course, inevitable in bringing up a severely handicapped child, helping him with vital matters, such as adequate feeding, avoiding traffic dangers, dangerous stairs, etc. Protection becomes over-protection when it is carried to extremes and when every difficulty and need is foreseen by the parents and quickly met by them, and little or no effort is demanded on the part of the child. A vicious circle is soon set up in which the child comes to rely excessively on his parents, has no confidence in his own ability to cope, and goes through life expecting similar over-indulgence from other people. This can be as great a handicap as the deafness. In some cases over-protective parents may be the ones who feel in some way guilty about their children's handicaps and shower attention on him as if to try to make it up to him.

Successful emotional development lies in keeping a balance between doing too little for the child and over-pressing him, and doing too much and smothering him; in developing an attitude of realistic acceptance of the child, of his assets as well as of his handicaps, a real appreciation of his needs, and an overwhelming desire to encourage him to achieve as much independence as is possible within the context of his handicap.

Habits and their development
At the age of three or four the child's drive towards independence becomes strong, and both hearing and deaf children insist on doing forbidden things as if they were seeing how far they can go in challenging parents' rules.

The deaf child is likely to be particularly active in touching and moving things at this stage, since touching and close looking at things is a way in which he makes up for his lack of speech and the fact that he cannot have things explained to him. He should, of course, be allowed to explore things as much as possible, but must realize that there are limits to what he is allowed to do. From his parents' shaking their heads and from their gestures he will slowly realize this, provided the rules that he must follow (such as not touching the clock or turning the tap on) are applied consistently. He must not be allowed to throw his toys one day and forbidden the next. It is particularly difficult for him to grasp the exceptions to the rules, i.e. that he may throw a ball but not his toy bricks; patient demonstration of the difference must be made, otherwise he will not know where he stands.

Consistent rules and routines are a very important source of security for the deaf child, to some extent making up for his lack of hearing the spoken word and the sounds of everyday life. Routines are especially important in the development of habits such as resting, eating, and toilet training. These need not present any great difficulties. In learning to eat with a knife and fork he will take a little longer than the hearing child, and perhaps eat rather noisily, not being aware of the noise he is making. He can gradually be taught to eat with his mouth closed. In toilet training he may have more relapses after the age of two, especially if he has many frustrations and irritations in the day, causing a temporary breakdown in his control of his bowels and bladder. He will be helped by tolerance on the part of the parents, and fairly definite routines not only for his toilet needs but for the times of various daily activities such as meals, play, bed, etc.

Social development

By social development we mean the child's capacity to form friendships and generally for getting along with other children and adults. This development is greatly influenced by the early family life of the child, in which he first learns to give and take and share experiences in his relationship to his mother, and later in relation to other members of his family, and eventually, around the age of three, with persons outside his family circle. With the deaf child this social development presents some difficulty, since he can make only limited use of the speech and understanding of speech that are so important in social relationships. Unless helped he may be solitary, preferring to cling to his toys or to his mother instead of facing and overcoming the difficulties of communicating with hearing children. Seeing other children speak and act as a result of speech in their games, he may feel left out of things and withdrawn. This is particularly so after the age of five when children begin to play more in groups and have to follow rules in their games.

Speech, however, is not so important in children's play between the ages of three and five as are practical activities and skills. Many deaf children benefit in their social development by attending an ordinary day nursery for part of the day and it is important that deaf children should learn to enjoy the company of hearing children. This can be helped if the attitude of adults and children in the deaf child's neighbourhood is favourable. The child's parents should explain to the neighbours as fully and frankly as possible about the deafness and what follows from it, so that they gain some understanding of his difficulties, and some appreciation of his assets. The child's first contact with hearing children will be easier if at first one companion only is invited home to play and have tea, where mother can keep a watchful eye on the situation, in the background, and can, if the companion is old enough, explain a little about the deafness, in a matter-of-fact and certainly not a pitying manner.

Intellectual development

In the great majority of deaf children, there is no reason to suppose that the factors that impair their hearing have also impaired their basic intelligence. Many psychological studies (Murphy, 1957) have shown that on average the deaf children score the same intelligence quotient on tests that do not require speech or spoken instructions,* as do ordinary children. This does not mean that all deaf children are of average intelligence; there are some very dull deaf children (approximately 15 per cent) and a small percentage of very retarded ones, who usually have other handicaps such as cerebral palsy and blindness in addition to the deafness and these are known as children with multiple handicaps; and there are some very bright deaf children, again approximately 15 per cent and a small percentage of very gifted ones, who have shown their talents in writing books and achieving high academic degrees. The spread of intelligence on tests that do not involve language is about the same amongst deaf as amongst hearing persons. Their basic reasoning powers are intact, but severe hearing losses of course reduce the extent to which the basic intelligence can be developed

* The following tests are commonly used by psychologists in assessing learning abilities of children with hearing losses. They involve simple gestured instructions in place of spoken instructions and consist largely of attractive puzzles, in which the children have for example to match pictures and wooden shapes, sort and classify pictures, construct patterns of coloured bricks, complete drawings that have parts missing, complete jig-saw puzzles, and arrange pictures in a correct sequence so as to tell a story: many of the following tests have been well described by Reed (1970) and are obtainable from the National Foundation for Educational Research, Test Dept, Windsor.

For age $1\frac{1}{2}$–5 years	Merrill-Palmer Scale.
3 –11	Nebraska Test of Learning Aptitude.
$3\frac{1}{2}$–11	Columbia Mental Maturity Scale.
4 –16	Wechsler Intelligence Scale for Children and Wechsler Pre-school and Primary Scale of Intelligence (Performance Scales).
5–11	Raven's Coloured Progressive Matrices (1956).
7 -17	Starren Snijders–Oomen Scale.

and expressed through language. It is possible to think without words, and as Hans Furth (1966) has shown, severely deaf children can perform many intellectual tasks that used to be considered to be largely dependent on language, such as classifying objects, discovering similarities and other concepts amongst groups of objects and pictures, and remembering a long series of numbers (when presented visually), at a level often comparable to that of hearing children, provided they are given adequate, non-verbal instructions about the tasks that the examiner wishes them to perform. However, the quick and efficient communication of thoughts, particularly in the complex and changing world of today, depends a great deal on words: new ideas, concepts and points of view come at us from all angles and come to us largely through the medium of words. The average child as young as five years has a vocabulary of at least 2000 words (Watts, 1960). Some untrained deaf children know virtually no words at this age, which means their reception, storage, classification and expression of

Fig. 28 Stretching the limits of communication.

ideas are severely reduced, they lack experience, and cannot make full use of their intelligence, compared to ordinary children.

This is why we place so much importance on language training for the deaf at the earliest possible age: not simply to teach a young deaf child to say a few words, but first and foremost to encourage him to appreciate the usefulness of language, and to develop understanding of speech. We will deal with this language training in the following section. Parents can also help the child's intellectual development by ensuring that plenty of constructive play material is available, such as wooden bricks and building materials, constructional sets, plasticine, clay, paints and large pieces of paper, sand tray, and other equipment that can be used creatively and constructively and will help to develop the child's ideas of shape and colour, distance, position and movements of objects in space, without necessarily involving language. Colour, shape, smell, taste, and the feeling of movement and texture are obviously important to a child who can hear very little. Play is, of course, important not only to foster intellectual and language development, but to express emotions, to help the child develop confidence and, when playing with other children, to learn to co-operate and share activities.

Language development
Language has many uses. It is used, as we have already mentioned, to facilitate our thoughts and this can be termed our 'inner language', a sort of talking to ourselves, as when we sit and plan tomorrow's activities; to express our thoughts and feelings to other people through speech, and to interpret the thoughts and behaviour of other people through the understanding of their speech. Language also has its written as well as its 'inner' form and its expressive and receptive spoken forms. Now nearly all language comes to us through hearing. Language develops in a child of normal hearing through the imitation of the speech that he hears around him, and by his wish to use speech to gain further contact with, and control over, his surroundings.

In the first few months of life the deaf baby's vocal cries and gurgles, which are the spontaneous, primitive foundations of speech, sound the same as those of the hearing child, but they become a little repetitive and harsh in tone towards the end of the first year. He cannot hear his own babbling vocalizations (but can feel them) and does not receive the stimulus of hearing his own sounds; many deaf children tend to become relatively silent in their second year although their speech organs are normal. It is most important that parents should try to prevent this silence. This is particularly necessary in the case of children who have become deaf after they have learned speech, and tend to become silent. The help of a teacher of the deaf is essential here to conserve their speech.

Language training for the severely deaf
It must be emphasized that very few children indeed are totally deaf. Most profoundly deaf children have a residue of hearing, which means they can make some use of powerful hearing aids although they do not hear speech as we hear it. Instead they hear certain sounds, some of which may approximate blurred vowel sounds, and this at least helps the child's awareness of speech, and his appreciation of some of the rhythms of speech.

A severely deaf child's understanding of speech must chiefly be fostered through lip-reading, combined with the sounds he gets through the aid. Some children are amazingly adept and eager at this and attend very well to continuous training: others make slow progress. The basic idea is that the child is taught to use his vision, combined with his residue of hearing and to some extent his sense of touch, to compensate for his hearing loss. He must be encouraged to look at his parents' lips with the aim of learning that certain movements of the lips represent, what we know of as, a word. This lip-reading first of all demands that the parents' lips be visible in a good light, roughly on a level with and within a few feet of the child's eyes, and that there should not be too many other attractions such as gestures and movements of the body to draw the child's attention away from the lips.

No child will learn anything unless he is interested in what is going on. It is vital, therefore, to link the lip-reading with the child's natural interests and activities in the home, such as feeding, playing, preparing for walks and other routines that children enjoy in cooperation with their parents.

Early training in lip-reading must be regarded not as lessons but as play. The mother must encourage her child to become interested in speech connected with his daily activities, so that he learns to appreciate that speech exists and that it has its uses, although he can hear practically nothing. For example, let us consider the routine of preparing for a walk, the usual equipment being a coat, a hat and a ball. We aim to associate these objects with a certain movement of our lips. We show the child the ball, saying the word rather slowly and distinctly but naturally, when we are sure he is looking at our lips. The next day we say, 'Take the ball', looking

Fig. 29 The mother as well as the child learns from sessions with the teacher of the hearing-impaired.

at it, picking it up, handing it to the child, repeating the word 'ball'. After several repetitions we say 'ball' when the child is some distance away from the ball, without any gestures. If the child gets the ball, all well and good, but if not, no dismay or agitation should be shown, but the word 'ball' is accompanied by gesture and movement towards it as before.

Eventually after many repetitions of the game, he will learn to respond to the movement of the lips, grasping that they mean 'ball' with no aid from gestures but still with some clues from the general situation, that of preparing for a walk.

Our further aim is that he should respond to the word 'ball' in a new situation, such as whilst playing indoors. The method can be applied constantly to other things associated with preparing for a walk, but only one or two at a time at first, and, of course, to other pleasant activities in the child's life. In this way his appreciation of speech and its value, his understanding of words, and later of phrases, will slowly grow.

This training must not be forced. It must be carried out in a spirit of play and enjoyment. Sometimes the child will be so eager and active about, say, preparing for an outing that he simply will not look at his mother's lips. Mother must in these instances be tolerant and await her opportunity to catch his interest in her lip movements. There can be no forcing the pace. The most fruitful attitude to training is to view it as a natural procedure, as indeed it is, of a mother talking to her child. He will not hear her, but will gradually learn to read her lips as they engage in pleasant everyday activities together. Rigid and formal speech training will put up a barrier between the mother and child and unsettle him in general, and perhaps even cause him to dislike contact with people. One last warning about lip-reading is not to expect perfect results. Parents should try lip-reading themselves, and will realize that not every part of every word is visible: therefore some guess-work is necessary on the part of the child and considerable patience on the part of his parents. A list of useful booklets giving guidance to parents is to be found at the end of this Chapter.

Fig. 30 Getting the message through seeing, hearing and feeling.

The severely deaf child's production of his own voice and speech is a more difficult matter than lip-reading: parents must strive to prevent the dying away of the natural spontaneous sounds of infancy (unheard by him) by showing their great pleasure at every sound he makes and letting him feel the vibrations in the throat, especially in respect of those sounds which are pleasant in tone. In general they must show him their great interest in his sounds and respond quickly to them. The process of converting

these sounds into actual syllables and words is a highly skilled matter and the help of the teacher of the deaf will be essential. Most
children with a severe hearing loss will need regular and intensive
help from a teacher of the deaf and many excellent day schools
are available for them. Their early training, however, is very much
the concern of the parents and in most areas in this country a peripatetic teacher is available to give guidance and advice to the
parents in their very important task of laying the foundations to
the child's language development. Given these early foundations
nearly all children can develop some degree of inner language, of
speech, and understanding of speech. Their rates of progress vary
enormously in these respects, some children making excellent progress which enables them to communicate quite well with hearing
people under favourable conditions. Others develop language
much more slowly even after years of training and the reasons for
this are not always clear. In a few cases there may be some limitation in the child's intelligence: some appear to lack the necessary
attention and drive and eagerness to communicate and are generally over-active and restless. Others may be emotionally immature
and disturbed, perhaps as a result of the 'over-protective' attitudes
of some parents, which we have already mentioned. A very small
number of children have been shown to have considerable, and
in some cases normal hearing, but to be completely unable to
attach meaning to what they hear: this condition is described as
'central deafness' or 'receptive aphasia', and is extremely rare (see
p. 116). But in many cases the reasons for the poor progress are not
at all clear. Alternative means of communication, such as finger
spelling or signs, may be helpful at a later age if the oral methods
we have described are not fruitful after many years of experience.
The oral methods are successful for many severely deaf children
and we must bear in mind that even a small degree of language
development is of enormous benefit in allowing at least some communication between the deaf child and the hearing world.

Manual methods of communication
Manual methods of communication, such as by finger spelling and
systematic signs, have a long history and have been in use for centuries amongst deaf adults. In the present century, with the introduction of hearing aids and new ideas amongst educationalists,
manual methods have given way to the oral methods that we have
described above, largely with the aim of helping the deaf to communicate more easily with the hearing world—most members of
which know nothing about finger spelling and signs.

In recent years, however, some experts have been arguing the case for a partial return to manual methods. The manualists maintain that decades of oral methods in the education of the very deaf have simply not worked for the majority of children, who are alleged to leave deaf schools at the age of 16 with very limited language. Conrad (1976), for example, found that 50 per cent of the 15- and 16-year-olds in schools for the deaf and partially hearing who had hearing losses of more than 85 decibels had reading ages of below $7\frac{1}{2}$ years and only 10 per cent had easily comprehensible speech. The manualists maintain that the net result is not only very limited communication with the hearing world but little real communication between the deaf, whose oral education will have denied them any systematic training in the use of signs. It is further argued that oral methods are satisfactory only for a small proportion of bright and industrious deaf children. An excellent statement of the manualists' case is to be found in an article by Gilmour (1971): there is also some discussion of these problems in a D.E.S. report (1968).

The oralists maintain that their methods have led to miraculous results in some cases, and although it is admitted that too many very deaf children leave schools with limited language, this is considered to be due to the fact that many of these children were not properly taught, early in life—that their oral education has not been concentrated enough, has not made effective use of hearing aids and that many residential deaf schools are too isolated from hearing people, which has left them with little incentive to develop oral means of communication. Further, the oralists maintain that the introduction of manual methods in deaf schools might, as it were, drive out oral methods, which are known to be a slow, long-term process of learning.

There must be room for compromise on these opposing viewpoints. Some research, such as by Birch (1964), suggests that manual methods, if properly used as part of a wider programme of developing communication skills, may actually encourage oral skills. Perhaps a combined oral and manual approach should be instituted, at least for some very deaf children who are not responding to purely oral methods: such children could then use one or other method, depending on whether the child was communicating to a deaf or to a hearing person. We must await further studies before a definite opinion can be given on the possibilities of combining a manual with an oral approach for certain very deaf children, but it seems that more attention must be paid to the teaching of manual methods (see pp. 56 to 58), at least for the multiply handicapped children. Experiments at Meldreth Manor School for multiply handicapped subnormal spastics, using simple standard gestures, have shown promising results, including increased attempts to use speech, amongst a small group of very deaf children (Levett, 1971), and later experience with a simple version of Paget Gorman signs is proving useful.

Language training for the partially hearing
The partially hearing child develops language in a very different way from the severely deaf. The latter is very dependent on seeing and feeling speech, whilst the partially deaf can use hearing to a large extent if properly fitted with and instructed in the use of a hearing aid. Modern hearing aids are small and lightweight, and can be used with very young children, even before the age of six months. With such very young children, however, the aid must be used only for short intervals and under expert advice. Hearing aids have some limitations. They do not always bring the child's hearing up to normal standards. They amplify not only desirable sounds such as speech, but undesirable noises such as the rustle of the child's clothing and extraneous noises such as footsteps, which may irritate the child. The speech heard through them is often distorted to some extent, particularly where the child is more deaf to the high tones; the ordinary aid tends to over-amplify the low tones for such a child, and it is a fact that very loud sounds are almost as irritating and unpleasant to the deaf child as they are to the hearing child. If we amplify the sound too much it becomes painful: if we amplify too little, the sound is too faint for the child to understand the speech. Lastly, the aid does not enable the child to locate the direction from which the sound is coming.

In view of these limitations it is essential that the aid should be regarded as one part of the programme of language training, and not as an isolated, cure-all piece of apparatus. Its introduction to the child must be accompanied by pleasant activities such as listening to music, or playing a favourite game so that the sounds he hears through the aid will soon have real meaning to him.

It will help if the aid is used sparingly at first, with the volume control fairly low, especially in noisy situations such as in a busy street, so that no loud sounds frighten the child. Gradually he will be able to tolerate louder sounds.

Parents must always try to show him the source of the sound. When he hears a dog barking they must point out to him where the dog is. In this way the sounds he hears will begin to have real

Fig. 31 With a hearing aid, 'I can hear myself whistle.'

meaning for him, and he will be more able to tolerate loud sounds when he knows what they mean.

The only way of overcoming the difficulty that hearing aids simply do not provide anything like perfect hearing for many young partially deaf children is to encourage the child to use lip-reading in addition to the aid. This is most important, since it is the combination of lip-reading with a hearing aid that will provide the most effective means of communication. Some sounds, especially high tone sounds such as f, th, s, are too faint to be heard through the aid, but they are easy to lip-read. Other sounds, such as many of the vowels, cannot be seen on one's lips, but fortunately these are fairly loud sounds, well received through the aid. So the combination of aid with lip-reading is the best approach. There are occasions when one will want to separate the two, for some special training periods. The teacher of the deaf, for example, will show parents what is known as 'auditory training' in which the emphasis is on encouraging the child to listen very carefully so that he can discriminate between words which sound alike and during such periods of concentration on the qualities of sounds, of enhancing the child's appreciation of what he hears, visual stimulation such as lip-reading and gesture should be eliminated. But in the partially hearing child's everyday communication, both lip-reading and the sounds heard through the aid are used. Gestures and miming, however, must be used only occasionally. Parents and children are very tempted to use them. For example, the phone rings, the child does not hear it, so the parent is tempted either to point to the phone or to mime a dialling or lifting of the receiver motion with his hands, instead of gaining the child's attention to his face and clearly saying 'The telephone is ringing' so that eventually the child will learn these words after many repetitions. Too many gestures reduce the child's incentive to persist with true language training that can eventually be so much richer than mere gestures. Obviously it would be unnatural to try to eliminate all gesturing, but it should be reduced to a minimum.

When a child is first fitted with an aid, the speech that he hears through it will have little or no meaning for him, because he has most likely not heard it before. It will therefore be necessary to teach him the meaning of words, and if he has already learned to lip-read several words and phrases these will be a valuable basis upon which to build. This building-up must proceed in much the same way that we have outlined in the previous section on lip-reading for the severely deaf child. The rate of progress will be greater since he will be hearing a certain amount of speech through the aid as well as seeing speech on the lips. During the part of the day when, with a very young child, the aid is not being used, he can benefit by hearing his mother's voice very close to his ear. The partially hearing child's speech production will be very much more akin to ordinary speech than the speech of the severely deaf child.

In encouraging and training the partially deaf child's voice and understanding of speech (through lip-reading combined with the hearing aid) it is essential, as we saw in the section on the severely deaf child, to utilize the everyday natural activities of the child and his mother, maintaining his interest in speech and his desire to communicate. When he begins to appreciate the value of speech and find joy in verbal contact with people, he will then truly appreciate his hearing aid. But the child's desire to communicate must first be nourished by the parents. This desire will not be encouraged by over-pressing the child to respond to speech: too much shouting through his hearing aid is likely to make him 'keep himself to himself' and prefer restful silence.

The golden rule of language training is to take every opportunity to talk naturally about everyday activities and experiences and play. The parents should concentrate on a certain number of words and phrases at a time, repeating these until they are well known. It is vital to maintain the child's lively interest and give him continuous encouragement, emphasizing his successes rather than his failures, so that his confidence in his ability to communicate is gradually strengthened. Speech and comprehension of speech are developed in a partially hearing child largely by constant exposure to speech sounds, and these must reach his ears loud enough and often enough, in situations where their reference to the child's own world can be readily appreciated.

Electronic aids

As we have mentioned, equipment such as hearing aids must be regarded as part of a programme of language training for the young child. He must learn to make sense out of the sounds he hears. For the majority of children the Government-issued Medresco Aids are satisfactory instruments offering a considerable range of intensities and frequencies of sound, but some children need more versatile aids. For very severe hearing losses and losses affecting higher tones and for some children who have particular difficulties in tolerating loud sounds (a phenomenon known as recruitment), more expensive commercial types of aids are sometimes recommended. The very small aids (known as post-aural or head worn) that fit behind the ear are helpful for mild to moderate hearing losses, but are not powerful enough for the majority of severely deaf children.

Some experts recommend the provision of two aids, or two ear pieces fed by one aid in cases where the hearing loss is virtually the same in both ears, but opinions are divided on whether these techniques really help and we must await further studies. Aids in the form of a very compact radio transmitter and receiver, known as a 'Phonic Ear', are also available.

The loop system is a simpler way of getting better performance from a hearing aid in certain situations. It simply consists of a length of wire arranged round a living room and connected to a radio, T.V. or tape recorder loudspeaker output, and the electrical impulses in the wire can be picked up by a special coil inserted into the hearing aid, enabling the child to hear a high quality of sound anywhere in the room without the usual interference from surrounding noises. A leaflet on this subject has been published by the National Deaf Children's Society for the guidance of parents.

Auditory training apparatus is simply a large and very efficient type of amplifier, for providing carefully adjusted intensities of sound through headphones, and is a very useful adjunct to home training sessions (Fig. 32).

Fig. 32 Sessions with highly amplified speech help development.

Teachers of the deaf use all the above equipment in their school and home training work, and experiments are proceeding with more advanced electronic equipment such as in the field of 'visible speech', which presents to a severely deaf child a visual pattern of the sounds that he is attempting to produce, on a type of T.V. screen, so that he can be helped to attain speech sounds that more nearly approximate the normal pattern. With advances in electronics over the past decade, we can look forward to a wider variety of aids for many types of handicapped children. For example, there are experiments with 'speech machines' that can receive spoken language and transfer it into written form, so that a hearing person can communicate with a severely deaf and speechless one: the latter can type a message in return, which could be translated into a spoken form, to be heard by the other person. These are interesting experiments limited at present by the time factor— they produce slow communication compared to normal rates, but with increased computer assistance, such speech machines should eventually prove useful.

Schooling

The ordinary child goes to school for a variety of purposes, not only to acquire knowledge of school subjects, but to learn them in such a way that he develops his abilities to think for himself, to share experiences at work and play with other children, and contribute to the work and play of the group, and so learn more and more about the wider society and his possible place in it. A great deal of this learning takes place through the medium of language, both written and spoken, so we must ask to what extent can children whose hearing losses have impaired their language, participate in ordinary school life and share the life experiences of ordinary children?

The answer is an increasingly optimistic one. Many factors that we have described in this book, including the better facilities for the early detection of deafness leading to early and sustained home training, the increasing help available from visiting teachers of the deaf, and the provision of better hearing aids, have resulted in more deaf children being successfully 'integrated' with the normal school and community. An excellent description of the educational possibilities for deaf children is to be found in an article by Reed (1964).

Children with a mild hearing loss, of say less than 35 decibels, are likely to have so little impairment to their language development that they can cope with normal schooling without special help other than by sitting near to the teacher in the classroom. Staff should also be aware of the mild hearing loss so that they can occasionally make slight allowances for it.

Most children with a partial hearing loss develop enough language to profit by ordinary schooling, usually with the help of a hearing aid, especially if they have had the benefits of early training at home. At least occasional supervision by a visiting teacher of the deaf is essential, and in cases where the hearing loss is marked and the child's language development is noticeably below that of the other children, weekly training with a teacher of the deaf is essential. The teacher can also give valuable advice to the other staff about ways of providing opportunities for lip-reading, using the hearing aid effectively, and ensuring that the child's difficulties are understood by all the staff and the other children.

There is much to be said for giving the majority of children with a hearing loss a trial in an ordinary school, starting at the nursery stage, so that they have experience of mixing and communicating with the hearing world.

The trend from special schooling to ordinary schooling has been strong in the past decade and carries many advantages. Even some severely deaf children have successfully managed ordinary schooling. But not all partially hearing children and certainly not all severely deaf children can cope with ordinary schooling. Their language, for several reasons, remains several years below their age level so they are under a constant sense of strain in trying to keep up with the lessons and with the social life, particularly in the later stages of the junior school career where language in all its forms becomes very important.

The answer lies in a compromise: the partially hearing unit attached to an ordinary school. These units, which have developed since 1945, prior to which there was little or no official distinction between the partially hearing and the deaf, provide specialized teaching and a full range of aids to a small group of children, usually fewer than 10, who can share many of the activities within the normal school and, if their progress is good, can eventually join the ordinary school classes for the majority of their lessons. Provided the children have been carefully selected and their ordinary school teachers carefully advised about their needs, valuable work can be accomplished in these units. Three excellent Ministry

Fig. 33 Electronic clarinet through a powerful amplifier.

surveys highlight the strengths and weaknesses of various arrangements (D.E.S., 1963; 1967; 1968).

The very severely and profoundly deaf child will usually need
more specialized and intensive training than the partially hearing
unit can provide, since their very limited residues of hearing mean
that they can derive only a certain amount of help from powerful
hearing aids and other amplifying equipment, and their speech
and understanding of speech must be developed largely through
their vision and sense of touch. Progress through these means,
although remarkably good in some cases, is often not rapid
enough, although experiments are being made to form special
units for severely deaf children, attached to ordinary schools, as
described by Dale (1967, 1974).

Integration and segregation problems

Current training techniques and our present knowledge of deafness still make it necessary for the majority of very deaf children
to attend a special school for the deaf and this results in a certain
amount of 'segregation' from the ordinary community. The effect
of this segregation is less in a day school than in a residential
school, and many large towns have sufficient numbers to warrant
a special day school, which enables the children to remain in contact with the hearing community at least for a large part of the
week. The numbers, however, are too small to permit day schooling in all parts of the country and boarding schools are necessary
on these grounds. They are also necessary in some cases where
the family background is very unsettled or where the child has
handicaps in addition to deafness, such as cerebral palsy or visual
defects, which require very specialized teaching. The Spastics
Society, for example, has two units for partially hearing children
who are also cerebral palsied. Residential schooling is also available for other exceptional groups, such as deaf children and adolescents who are emotionally disturbed, those who are blind, and
for very intelligent and mature pupils requiring grammar school
or technical education. Schools are also available for slow learning
(educationally subnormal) pupils.

Opinions vary on the age at which young children should enter
boarding school. Some teachers of the deaf advocate early admission so that intensive training can be started during the early
formative years in the child's life, before he has developed fixed
habits of limited communication, such as simply by gesture. But
most teachers realize that there are risks in separating the young
child from his family and that the child may become emotionally

disturbed as a result of early separation, and this could outweigh the advantages of early training. It is now becoming increasingly rare to recommend children under the age of seven for residential schooling.

As more teachers of the deaf become available to organize more intensive home training and improve facilities within the ordinary school, it will be possible to reduce still further the number of deaf children who attend boarding schools wherein, in spite of the high standards of teaching and general skill and devotion of the staff, it is virtually impossible to overcome the disadvantages of separating children from their home and the normal community. These disadvantages become depressingly evident when the deaf child has reached the age of 16 and, after many years in a very specialized school environment, is suddenly expected to find his way in the normal hearing world of which he has had so little experience. Of course some boarding-school provision will always be necessary for some of the very specialized groups of children we have mentioned, and whatever type of school the child attends, whether it be an ordinary school, a partially hearing unit attached to an ordinary school, a special day or a special residential school, it is essential that the parents and the school should work in close co-operation, so that they share common aims and expectations about such matters as the child's rate of progress and the means of achieving this progress. As one example of gaining closer

Fig. 34 A modern, well-equipped classroom for deaf children.

contact between home and school, we can note the provision at one of the Spastics Society's residential partially hearing units in which facilities are offered to enable parents to come and stay at the school for certain periods. Weekly, Monday to Friday, boarding at a special school can also further the child's contact with home and the normal community, provided there is no great contrast between the style of life at school and that at home.

The child's future

What are our aims and expectations generally in respect of the young child with a hearing loss? What sort of adult do we hope will be fostered by the means we have briefly described in this book? We hope first and foremost that he will be socially mature, able to enjoy the company of both deaf and hearing people. In the past it had often been noted that the deaf mixed only with the deaf, leading to a kind of 'minority group' feeling that led to little contact with the life of the wider community. With the improvements in early assessment and home training, and increased education within the normal community, the child with partial hearing, and to some extent those who are severely deaf, now have a greater chance of a wider social life, not only because they are more accustomed to contact with hearing people, but because the latter are more accustomed to meeting those with hearing losses, or are at least gaining more understanding of them through the medium of books, plays and T.V.

Of great importance in achieving social integration is, of course, the ability to communicate effectively through speech and writing. Most partially hearing children achieve these adequately, but for some severely deaf children considerable difficulties persist into adult life. Although there are many examples, such as the studies by the Ewings (1961) which have shown the successes achieved by many severely deaf people, adequate communication with the normal hearing world does not come easily, as several moving autobiographies have testified. Frances Warfield (1948), who is partially hearing, described for example the tensions at adolescence that arose from her marginal position, as it were, on the periphery of the normal hearing community, struggling for some time to conceal her handicap: whilst David Wright (1969), who became totally deaf at age seven, describes in very moving terms his tremendous fight to achieve his ambition, a very high one for a deaf person, namely that of becoming a writer. Most of the published success stories of this kind are the result of a combination of exceptional talent and persistence and in most cases long-term help from parents and teachers. Since most deaf children are of average rather than exceptional ability, it follows that by no means all will achieve sufficient language to allow anything like normal integration within the community; and, as we have mentioned, alternative means of communication, such as 'manual' rather than 'oral' methods, are therefore necessary.

These manual methods have the advantage of facilitating communication between deaf people, but not between the deaf and the hearing—the latter would need someone to interpret the finger spelling. This kind of barrier to integration, which all severely handicapped people suffer in some form, has to be recognized; and, whilst continuing our efforts to reduce such barriers (e.g. by earlier assessment and training and better electronic aids), we must at present accept a goal of *partial* rather than full integration for some very handicapped persons. (An example of partial integration is seen in the recent formation of social clubs for both 'physically handicapped' and 'able-bodied' people, known as P.H.A.B. clubs.) Perhaps a measure of the wisdom and maturity of a community is the extent to which its members can adapt to quite deep *differences* between certain groups in its midst—whether the differences be those of colour, political outlook, intelligence or handicap—and yet retain an over-riding sense of unity and mutual respect. A pluralistic society does not expect all members to be cast

Fig. 35 Communication at all ages with the help of hearing aids.

ın the same mould. Integration in some form, is the ideal, and if the wider community can meet the deaf halfway, in coming to terms with the handicap, both the deaf and normally hearing person can enjoy a fuller life.

Finally, we hope that the adult will have maintained a reasonable level in his educational work, especially in reading and writing, so that the written word is always available to him and he will be able to take up employment in one of the many hundreds of occupations that do not demand a normal degree of speech and hearing, such as many branches of engineering, photography, woodwork, chemistry, and so on.

These aims of increased integration are being increasingly realized as we gain greater understanding of the handicap, and learn how to bring parents into partnership with experts, in our endeavours to overcome the difficulties. We are also learning how to bring home to the wider public the fact that handicapped persons, like all persons who appear different from the majority, are the proper concern of us all.

Organizations and literature

The two organizations concerned with the deaf which provide many valuable services are The National Deaf Children's Society, 31 Gloucester Place, London W1H 4EA, and The Royal National Institute for the Deaf, 105 Gower Street, London WC1E 6AH. These organizations provide many books and pamphlets on home training, and equipment including hearing aids, and issue on loan certain kinds of equipment such as auditory trainers. The N.D.C.S. produces a quarterly magazine entitled *Talk*; the R.N.I.D. a monthly entitled *Hearing*. General advice from a variety of experts—social workers, educationalists, ENT specialists, hearing-aid experts, club organizers and careers advisers— can usually be obtained through the R.N.I.D. and N.D.C.S. to supplement advice that is available from local clinics, schools and audiology units. The authors would like to thank the N.D.C.S. for several of the photographs in this Chapter.

Useful pamphlets for parents include the following:

A Guide for Parents of Very Young Deaf Children by D. H. Grossman (N.D.C.S.).
Suggestions to Parents of Deaf Children by D. M. C. Dale (N.D.C.S.).
Your Child's Hearing by Lady Irene and Sir Alexander Ewing (N.D.C.S.).
Notes on High Frequency Hearing Loss in Children by L. Fisch (Hearing Clinic, London Borough of Haringey).

Most of the following books and articles, referred to in this Chapter, can be borrowed from the R.N.I.D. library.

REFERENCES

Ashley, J. (1971) Deafness—personal viewpoints. *Hearing*, **26**, No. 4. London: R.N.I.D.

Beagley, H. A. (1975) Electrophysiological tests for hearing. *Proceedings of the Royal Society of Medicine*, **68**, 35–37.

Birch, J. W. & Stuckless, E. R. (1964) *Relationship between Early Manual Communication and Later Achievement of the Deaf*. Research Project No. 1269. US Department of Health, Education and Welfare.

Bloom, F. (1978) *Our Deaf Child: into the '80s*. Gresham Books/Unwin.

Conrad, R. (1976) *Towards a Definition of Oral Success:* paper at a meeting on the education of deaf children, Harrogate. R.N.I.D.

Dale, D. M. C. (1967a) Deaf education—a new approach. *Special Education, incorp. Spast. Q.*, **56**, No. 4, pp. 4–6.

Dale, D. M. C. (1967b) *Deaf Children at Home and at School*. University of London Press.

Dale, D. M. C. (1974) *Language Development in Deaf and Partially Deaf Children*. University of London Press.

Davis, H. & Silverman, R. (1977) *Hearing and Deafness*. New York: Holt, Rinehart & Winston.

Department of Education and Science (1963) *Survey of Deaf Children who have been transferred from Special Units to Ordinary Schools*. London: HMSO.

Department of Education and Science (1967) *Units for Partially Hearing Children*. Educational Survey 1. London: HMSO.

Department of Education and Science (1968) *The Education of Deaf Children*. London: HMSO.

Ewing, A. W. G. (Ed.) (1957) *Educational Guidance and the Deaf Child*. Manchester University Press.

Ewing, A. & Ewing, E. C. (1971) *Hearing-Impaired Children under Five. A Guide for Parents and Teachers*. Manchester University Press.

Ewing, I. R. & Ewing, A. W. G. (1961) *New Opportunities for Deaf Children*. University of London Press.

Fisch, L. (1964) *Research in Deafness in Children*. London: N.D.C.S./Blackwell.

Fraser, G. R. (1964) Causes of deafness in 2355 children in special schools. In *Research in Deafness in Children*. Ed. Fisch, L. London: N.D.C.S./Blackwell.

Furth, H. G. (1966) *Thinking Without Language: Psychological Implications of Deafness*. New York: The Free Press.

Gerber, S. E. (1977) *Audiometry in Infancy*. New York: Grune & Stratton.

Gilmour, A. J. (1971) Shades of grey. *Hearing*, **26**, No. 5. London: R.N.I.D.

Jerger, J. (1963) *Modern Developments in Audiology*. New York: Academic Press.

Levett, L. M. (1971) Discovering how mime can help. *Special Education, incorp. Spast. Q.*, **60**, No. 1.

Murphy, K. (1957) Psychological testing. In *Educational Guidance and the Deaf Child*. Ed. Ewing, A. W. G. Manchester University Press.

Myklebust, H. R. (1950) *Your Deaf Child: A Guide for Parents*. Springfield, Illinois: Thomas.

Myklebust, H. R. (1964) *Psychology of Deafness*. New York: Grune & Stratton.

Reed, M. (1958) *Hearing Test Cards*. The Royal National Institute for the Deaf, London.

Reed, M. (1964) Principles of education of deaf and partially deaf children. In *Clinics in Developmental Medicine*, No. 13. *The Child Who Does Not Talk*. Ed. Renfrew, C. & Murphy, K. London: Spastics Society/Heinemann.

Reed, M. (1970) Deaf and partially hearing children. In *The Psychological Assessment of Mental and Physical Handicaps*. Ed. Mittler, P. London: Methuen.

Rutter, M., Tizard, J. & Whitmore, K. (Eds.) (1970) *Education, Health, and Behaviour*. London: Longman.

Sheridan, M. D. (1968) *Stycar Hearing Test*. Windsor. Berks. National Foundation for Educational Research.

Taylor, I. G. (1964) *Neurological Mechanisms of Hearing and Speech in Children*. London: Manchester University Press.

Turner & Macfarlane, (1978) Localization of human speech by the newborn baby and the effects of Pethidine ('Meperidine'). *Developmental Medicine and Child Neurology*, **20**, No. 6. 727–34.

Warfield, F. (1948). *Cotton in my Ears*. New York: Viking Press.

Wasz-Höckert, O. *et al.* (1968) The infant cry, a spectographic and auditory analysis. *Little Club Clinics in Developmental Medicine*, No. 29. London: Spastics Society/Heinemann.

Watts, A. F. (1960) *Language and Mental Development of Children*. London: Harrap.

Whetnall, E. & Fry, D. B. (1971) *The Deaf Child*. London: Heinemann.

Wright, D. (1969) *Deafness, a Personal Account*. London: Penguin.

5

The child with visual handicaps

This Chapter is divided into two sections. The first part gives some idea of the needs and responses of very young children with visual impairments. The second, written by Heather Jones, Senior Education Adviser to the Royal National Institute for the Blind, deals with the wide range of care and educational support provided in the UK for children with visual handicaps.

Early care of the blind baby

Fortunately, the number of blind children in England is not very great. In 1977, for instance, only a few hundred children under five years were registered as blind but the incidence remains very high in several developing countries (see Ch. 8).

A serious handicap—such as blindness—in a baby places a great strain on parents, and they are often hesitant about their role. 'I don't know what to do for the best. I'm sure it's a job for the experts' is a comment heard frequently from them. But the blind baby, just as any other baby, needs his own mother more than anyone else in the world to care for him during his first years of life; his needs are the same, for affection, security and consistency of care. From the very beginning he needs to be made to feel that he is one of the family, and that the whole family unites in sharing the special opportunity and the special interest that his upbringing entails.

There are a few special things over and above all the usual consideration that any well cared for baby would receive. A blind baby needs rather more *demonstration of affection* by petting and cuddling because he cannot see the affectionate expression in his mother's face, although the tone of her voice will be an important indication of her feelings for him. He needs more *talking to*, and to hear more conversation and explanation about the objects and events in his world because his experience is so restricted by lack of visual information. He needs more *encouragement to be active*, more incentive to sit up, to crawl, to stand and to walk, because ordinary visual incentives do not exist for him, and because, since he cannot judge accurately the position of obstacles, he is fearful to adventure and explore on his own as a sighted child would do.

Parents of blind children often ask for advice on general management and care. The Royal National Institute for the Blind has drawn up a number of useful pamphlets on such subjects as feeding, toilet training and play materials. Meetings for parents are arranged so that they may discuss problems and exchange ideas.

Feeding. Many parents find particular difficulty in regard to the whole question of feeding. In general, feeding the blind baby should follow the same methods as those used for a sighted child. The physical contact with the mother during feeding is of special value to the blind baby, who cannot see her face but is aware of her feelings towards him by the tone of her voice and the touch of her hands and body. It is an experience of very real significance to the small child, and blind babies seem to resent weaning even more than sighted babies. Weaning needs to be gradual, and the baby needs to be accustomed to different tastes such as orange juice, sieved vegetables and cereals quite early. The usual routine should be followed, and as soon as the teeth begin to erupt, the child should be given something to bite, such as a rusk or biscuit. Blind babies seem more reluctant to accept solids than other babies. Possibly this is because they are more fearful of new experiences and tend to be more dependent and reluctant to leave babyhood behind.

Blind children may well take longer over the messy stage of learning to feed themselves than ordinary children. A spoon is difficult to manipulate if one cannot see the food on the plate and the easiest and most natural way to pick up the food is by the fingers. This latter method helps a child to find out about the food he is eating in the most effective way; and, what is more, the food does not get cold or unpalatable while he chases it vainly round his plate. The next stage is to put a spoon into his hand, and help him to find the food on his plate, which should have a turned-up rim like a puppy's plate, and guide the spoon to his mouth. It is a short step from this stage to independence in feeding matters. Three-year-olds can be quite skilful at feeding themselves if they are encouraged to do so, although they are naturally inclined to be untidy during the process. It is, of course, most important to avoid giving blind children food that is too hot, or containing bones or other unpalatable substances, though as they get older they learn to take the pips out of oranges or grapes most competently if carefully guided. It is a delight to watch young blind child-

Fig. 36 Encouraging self-help skills: 'the cereal is nearly up to my thumb'.

ren in nursery school eating ice cream or jelly, their skill almost equal to their enjoyment!

Toilet training. The process of toilet training may need to be rather more gradual than in the case of sighted children, but it is a mistake to prolong the wearing of napkins when it is clear that the child can indicate his needs. The child needs plenty of praise for success and only mild disapproval when accidents occur. Usually by the time he is two or three years old he will be fairly reliable, but if he is unwell, over-tired, over-excited or especially disturbed by anything, he is likely to relapse temporarily.

Bathing and dressing. Young blind children show great delight in playing with water, and bath-time provides a good opportunity for this. They become more relaxed muscularly; they enjoy vigorous play with boats and rubber toys, and it is a pity to rush and scurry through bathing when this can provide an outlet for energy and an occasion for experiment and discovery concerning the properties of water!

When washing a blind child it is helpful to talk to him about the objects he is feeling—the soap, face-cloth, nail-brush, rubber duck or any toy in which he is interested. Similarly, when dressing or undressing one naturally talks about the garments he is handling so that he comes to associate their texture and shape with their names. He likes to be told the colour of his clothes, and of other people's, and frequently asks about this as he gets older. If he is born blind he can have no conception of colour. His interest may be due to the fact that he hears sighted people talk about colour constantly, and feels this is something important and which he must know about also.

Gradually the child learns to wash, undress and dress himself, but these skills will naturally be difficult for him to acquire. Five- and six-year-old blind children are usually fairly competent, but may still need help with buckling sandals or tying laces. They will enjoy their independence in these matters if given proper encouragement.

Development of speech. The speech of a blind child will develop just as fast as that of a sighted child if he is given sufficient encouragement and if the adults around him take time and trouble to talk to him. Blind children ask a great many questions and enjoy using words a great deal. Sometimes they seem to talk just for the sake of talking, using words which they do not fully understand and concerning objects or events of which they have had no first-hand experience. This is known as 'verbalism'. In order to avoid this it is important to give the young blind child *as many and as varied experiences of everyday conditions as is possible.* One needs to talk about the objects he handles and the sounds he hears in terms that he can understand. 'Look! these are your new shoes I bought when I was out shopping. They are made of soft leather, and they have one button to do up which you will soon be able to manage yourself.' In the matter of sound, one might say: 'Yes, I can hear the milkman, too. His milk bottles make quite a clatter, and I can hear his van coming along the road.' One has to interpret the environment to the blind child constantly and help him to make his own observations and his own discoveries. A good game to play out of doors is to sit still and count all the different sounds you can hear—a distant train, a tractor ploughing, a cock crowing, a boy whistling, the wind in the fir wood and so on.

It is well to remember how a blind child learns about his en-vironment, and it is important to give plenty of opportunity to listen and to touch. In a vocabulary test his definitions show the way he comes to know about objects. An 'orange' is 'something you eat, has pips in it'; a 'puddle', 'to splash in'; a 'tap', 'you knock quietly like this'; an 'envelope', 'a square bag to put a letter in'; 'straw', 'to suck juice through'; 'scorch', 'to burn something when you're ironing'; and a 'hat' was once defined as 'a cylindrical object which fits exactly on your head'!

The golden rules are to tell the child about everything around him with reference to the real objects, to talk a great deal to him, to answer his questions fully, though sometimes turning them back to him with the request, 'You tell *me* this time', and above all to encourage him to make his own discoveries and report his own findings. If he can tell you about 'a lovely baby lamb at the farm, with thick curly hair and a very wet nose who keeps bleating and tries to suck my finger' you will know that this is from first-hand experience.

Blind children, just as other children, love to hear stories told or read to them, and will listen attentively usually much longer than sighted children. It is important to choose stories carefully. Stories that depend for effect on sound imagery are most appreciated. It is not much good reading a story which is profusely illustrated, which contains allusions to incidents and objects outside the blind child's experience and which need tedious and long explanations to make them intelligible.

Play and play material. The toys that a blind baby needs and will enjoy are not greatly different from those for a sighted child. They should be strong, 'bangable', suckable, washable and capable of withstanding tough baby-handling! Up to about six months of age the baby needs little more than a cuddly toy, a rattle with bells and a rubber toy that squeaks, but after six months he will appreciate a wider variety. He needs especially toys that will make noise, and he will be just as happy with the kitchen utensils— spoons, colanders, saucepan lids, empty tins (with no sharp edges, of course), as with the most expensive musical box or musical teddy-bear. When he begins to show signs of locomotion he needs toys which encourage movement and effort. A rubber ball with a bell inside, a pull-along toy with a bell attached interest him and help to give him the right direction when he is beginning to crawl or learning to walk. Blind children are hesitant about movement and timid about learning to walk because of the many unknown and unseen hazards they may encounter. They may need a good deal of patient encouragement and persuasion to try to get about on their own, and the baby's mother is the best person to give him the necessary confidence. Toddlers get a great deal of fun from pushing about an empty perambulator or a sturdy horse on wheels. They need toys which are heavy enough to resist them and which will give them sufficient support in the early stages of learning to walk.

Blind children, like sighted children, show great delight in water play. They will spend a great deal of time at the kitchen sink if

Fig. 37 Imaginative play.

allowed to turn the taps on and off, and make their own discoveries with toys which let the water through—funnels, sieves, rubber piping, old colanders, tin teapots and so on. They need a plastic apron to safeguard their clothes, of course. Sand is always an excellent play-fellow. If the seaside is not near at hand, a sand tray or pit in the garden is a good investment. Earth, water and clay are all natural and valuable materials for a child to use in his play activities, but for the younger child who still takes objects to his mouth to investigate their properties more fully, dough made from flour, water and salt is a good substitute.

Blind children develop great sensitivity of touch, but in the process of acquiring this they need to explore a great deal with their fingers. It is to be expected that very delicate, fragile materials easily become damaged, and it is a waste of money to present a blind three-year-old with a beautiful doll's house with elaborate fittings unable to stand up to explorations by eager fingers. Mechanical toys are of little real value to a blind child, except sometimes to urge him to movement, and last a very short time. Small cars and miniature wheel toys are enjoyed. Miniature animals are not of much interest because they have so little connection with the live animal. Their texture and their size are different, and they do not make the same noise. One has only to compare a painted

Fig. 38 Making a wedding cake.

wooden cow, whose colours the blind child cannot see, with the real cow in the field on the other side of the hedge to appreciate how little relationship exists between the two! Nevertheless, in order that the blind child does not feel greatly different from other children, it is probably best to give him much the same type of play material and let him put it to the use he prefers. He will enjoy fitting toy interlocking bricks. He likes to have dolls and teddy-bears, but does not play with them a great deal, although he may insist on taking one or several of his favourites to bed with him especially if away from his own home. Although partially sighted children will feed, wash, dress and push their dolls about in perambulators, blind children usually prefer other children for family play, and will push empty perambulators about quite contentedly because they can get no pleasure from seeing a doll dressed up in pretty clothes.

An important principle in the choice of play material, as in the case of ordinary children, is to make use of the natural material around you. Acorns, chestnuts, pebbles, sticks, different kinds of leaves and fruits, grasses, moss, shells and seaweed are of intrinsic interest to every small child. It is, of course, necessary to explain about poisonous fruits and toadstools, but children will learn this kind of thing very quickly. Continuously to forbid a blind child to touch for fear of getting dirty is tantamount to saying 'don't learn', 'don't grow'. Flowers grown indoors from bulbs fascinate blind children, but they are handled so frequently to measure their growth that their chance of survival is not very great!

Blind children tend to be rather passive and inactive because movement is obviously more hazardous and requires more effort for them. They, therefore, need more stimulation than sighted children and like to be played with. This does not mean that they need to be nursed a great deal or pushed in a swing or rocked on a horse or amused by record player or radio all the time. A blind child will enjoy a game of ball. He may like you to help him push his horse or pull his truck, or jump or climb or dig. When he has become familiar with his own house and garden he will be able to find his own way about and will not need to have his hand held all the time. If you call to him or clap your hands he will discover that it is quite safe and good fun to crawl or toddle across the grass out of doors. Later he will be running about freely and able to avoid obstacles with comparative ease. Of course, it is necessary to safeguard the child from obvious dangers such as steep stairs, open windows, unguarded fires, and open doors can cause unpleasant bumps if care is not taken.

Blind children usually learn to play with other children rather later than sighted children, but by about four years of age they will enjoy imaginative play with other children of their own age.

Family attitudes
The attitude of the family to the young blind child is a matter of great importance. It requires a great deal of courage to accept the fact that their baby is blind, and a considerable degree of maturity to plan realistically and constructively to provide the best possible care for him. Many parents find it very hard to face this issue and their distress in regard to the baby's disability deserves all the sympathy and understanding that relatives, friends and professional workers can give them.

It seems that there are two usual attitudes of parents to blindness in their children. The first arises out of their natural distress and an understandable but misguided desire to shield the blind child from any kind of harm. The child is smothered with mother love. He is protected from any kind of experience which might prove difficult for him. He is constantly sheltered from the hard, cold world and hedged round with reiterated admonitions—not to touch lest he hurt himself, lest he damage something. His every wish is anticipated and he receives very little encouragement to fend for himself. He is not encouraged to learn to crawl or to walk and may be kept amused by devoted and docile relatives, by radio and record-player. He thus lives a very passive kind of life. Both dangerous and interesting objects are kept well out of reach, and he is gently but firmly discouraged from experiments in self-help or from tentative efforts to find out about his environment for himself.

At the extreme, a child of three years of age may appear, at first sight, to be mentally defective. Usually he cannot walk, and he talks very little because his environment has been so restricted; he is afraid of strangers and strange places, and is very reluctant to leave his mother's side. Often such a child is still bottle-fed and is adamant in refusing to accept solid foods. He is seldom toilet trained. He is unwilling to explore a new environment or to handle new toys.

Such a degree of over-protection can thus only retard the development of a blind child and is certainly mistaken kindness. A normal blind child, unless handicapped by illness or long periods in hospital, will walk alone in a room with which he is familiar and enjoy climbing up and down stairs by about 18 months of age. By about two years he may well have acquired both bowel and bladder control if given patient and reasonable training. By three years often he can feed himself with a spoon if given a plate with a turned-up rim so that the food cannot slip off. Before he is five he can learn to ride a kiddy-car and even a tricycle. By the time he is six he can tell his left from his right hand, which is, of course, useful in giving him directions to find the toys he is looking for. To watch children in a nursery school climbing, scrambling, rolling down grassy slopes, steering prams or tricycles with unerring skill, and swinging high and fearlessly on an open swing is an education itself, and has proved so for many an over-anxious parent.

The second family attitude, which is not so common, fortunately, occurs in some cases when the mother has had special problems to meet in the bringing up of the family—economic stringency, marital difficulties, or constant ill health, for instance. The birth of a blind baby just tips the balance, and the mother feels unequal to the situation. She feels unable to show affection to the child, turns away from him and rejects him emotionally. She handles the child with distaste, and tends to ignore him. Lacking basic security and maternal love, and receiving none of the normal incentives from his own mother to grow and develop, the child may withdraw into himself and become remote and unresponsive to people generally. In such an instance both parents and child need help. The parents can gain relief in talking about their feelings of sorrow and disappointment with a social worker. Offers of practical help and relief care are usually welcomed by over-strained parents. The knowledge that such help will be available in times of family crisis is often sufficient to avoid the necessity of long-term residential placement in the early years.

In general the best place for the young blind child is his own home. Accepted and cherished by his whole family, he is made to feel that he belongs there, and that he, too, has a contribution to make towards family happiness. He needs to be loved, encouraged, and sometimes scolded by his own parents, just as any ordinary child, until such time as he appears ready to begin to form relationships and enjoy the company of other children, outside the family circle.

The readiness with which the child can adapt to nursery or school life will depend on the quality of these early relationships. If he feels secure and well loved by his family, he will be the more able to enjoy relationships both with adults and children outside his own home, and feel safe and able to learn in a new environment.

The following section by a Senior Education Adviser Heather Jones, of the R.N.I.B. describes the types of provision available for visually impaired children and young people in this country. She and her colleagues have also provided the illustrations in this Chapter.

Provision for the visually impaired.

Incidence of visual impairment

The number of children registered blind in England is small. In March 1977, there were 82 such children under two years of age, 265 between the ages of two and four years, and 1849 between 5 and 15 years. Half of the children attended special schools for the blind. Of the total of 2196 children registered as blind, 1013 had additional handicaps. As a proportion of the school-age children, the number of blind pupils is in the order of 1 : 10 000 of the total school population.

The number of children registered as partially sighted is only a little higher. At the same date, there were 180 partially sighted children under four years and 2455 between the ages of 5 and 15 years. Of the 2455 children of school age, 1074 attended special schools for the partially sighted. (These figures on blind and partially sighted children are taken from the D.H.S.S. Document A/F/77/7, *Registered Blind and Partially Sighted Persons, Year Ending 31st March 1977, England.*)

Causation

Visual handicap may be caused by a wide variety of factors. The specific patterns of visual handicap and blindness vary from country to country; trachoma, for example, is a very common cause of blindness in the third world, although rare in the UK. The specific causes of visual handicap have changed over the last few decades: ophthalmia neonatorum due to gonococcus is now relatively rare; retrolental fibroplasia caused by excess oxygen in premature babies is less common than it was, due to better care of the new-born. Many children with a visual handicap today have other sensory or motor handicaps—there are proportionately fewer 'able blind' children than previously, and probably many children with severe visual problems in mental handicap institutions who have never been registered. Genetic factors are of major importance in about 50 per cent of registered blind children.

Ocular defects, causing impairment, include cataracts, severe myopia, tumours of the retina, malformations of the eye, retrolental fibroplasia and a wide variety of retinal degenerations—some of infective origin and some genetic. Neurological causes of visual handicap, often associated with degeneration elsewhere in the nervous system, may affect the retina. The optic nerve may be damaged by infections or tumours; often retinal and optic nerve disease are associated. The occipital cortex, the light-sensitive area of the brain, may be damaged by lack of oxygen, trauma (e.g. at birth) or infection, and thus the brain cannot perceive light, though the eyes are normal. Nystagmus is an oscillating movement of the eyes, which may contribute to poor visual acuity or itself may be associated with other visual defects, as in albinism.

Care and provision: 0 to 2 years

During the last decade, in the UK, services for all young children with handicaps have been established or extended: by the Health Service nationally, by local authority departments in their respective areas and by voluntary agencies, locally and nationally. A child with a visual handicap is able to benefit from some of these services.

Early screening of babies has meant that handicaps have been identified more quickly than was previously the case. The number of children having a pattern of severe handicap, of which a visual limitation is part, appears to have increased in recent years. These children can be referred for paediatric examination, and then, if indicated, for ongoing assessment and help with their developmental needs from a specialist team of therapists and teachers at the child development centres of some hospitals. It can also be of particular benefit to some children who have little or no vision, but are otherwise normally able, to be moved through the natural sequence of motor development by the physiotherapist in the team.

The need for young children with a visual handicap to remain at home has long been understood. Help and guidance were available to parents of young children at the parents unit run by the Royal National Institute for the Blind from 1954 to 1973.

In 1970, the Birmingham Royal Institution for the Blind established a visiting service for young children and their parents. This extended nationally and is now the R.N.I.B. Advisory Service. Members of its team of advisers are available, on request, to help parents and care workers. They are ready to listen to parents, perhaps to help them understand what they have been told about their child and to advise on general management or on specific needs. The children are encouraged to explore and enjoy their world, first through people, later by means of appropriate play materials and then by finding ways of understanding the real world through their own experiences.

Helping some children 'learn to look' is of particular importance in the early years. For some with an ocular defect this may come quite readily, but for others, with perhaps cortical blindness, it may not. Careful observation when playing with a baby, followed by a programme using especially visually attractive materials, may help such children, who are often additionally handicapped, become sufficiently visually aware to establish the first important visually directed reaching to touch movements.

Education care and provision: 2 to 5 years

Over this period, a child may need wider opportunities to explore and learn than can be provided at home. Parents, too, may benefit from meeting other parents and people concerned with the needs of children generally or, at times, enjoy a short respite from the almost constant surveillance that some children require. Provision varies over the country. Nursery and playgroups will often take a visually handicapped child. In some areas, peripatetic specialist teachers can advise parents and nursing staff; in others there are nursery classes attached to schools for the visually handicapped.

The Research Centre for the Education of the Visually Handicapped at Birmingham University runs a playgroup and a toy library specially for visually handicapped children.

Health visitors organize play and opportunity groups in some places and one city has a parents advisory centre from which both children and parents may benefit. Child development units/paediatric assessment centres often have a nursery group or school as an integral part of the unit, while occupational therapy centres are available in some places.

Not every child can fit easily into the available nursery environment and particular consideration may need to be given to noise and lighting levels, speed of movement of able children, the presence of wheelchairs and walking frames and, above all, some quiet-area provision where a severely visually handicapped child may feel secure.

There are many toy libraries for children with special needs; information about them may be obtained from the Toy Libraries Association, Seabrook House, Wyllyotts Manor, Darkes Lane, Potters Bar, Hertfordshire. Apart from stories on tape, there are several excellent records of sounds and stories produced by the BBC, amongst others, that delight children in this age group.

The R.N.I.B. Sunshine House Nursery Schools have changed over the years to meet the special needs of present-day visually handicapped children and their parents. They provide a shared care service on a day- or weekly-boarding basis and, when needed, can offer short-term relief care or longer periods at school, according to the needs of the family. The staffing ratio is high, almost two to one, so that the individual needs and interests of each child can be provided for at all times. These needs may vary from learning the beginnings of self-care for some, to experiencing speed and movement, perhaps on a horse, for others. From finding out what is inside an eggshell to climbing a tower where they can experience something of the meaning of height by listening to the traffic below. From finding out

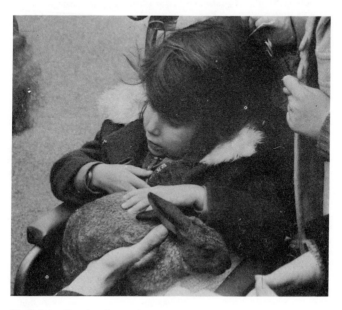

Fig. 39 Gaining first-hand experience.

the way a lamb feels, smells, eats and moves to sleeping in a tent listening to the sounds of the night.

The Nursery Schools have developed as *centres of information* for people con-cerned with helping visually handicapped children in other centres and for researchers and students, but particularly for parents anywhere whose children have visual and perhaps added difficulties. For those parents whose children attend the Nursery Schools regular information on progress and handling is exchanged. Meet-ings and workshops are arranged, particular use being made of film to highlight a child's responses and needs, which may then form the basis of discussion with parents, teachers and visiting experts. Children with dual handicaps, of hearing and sight, as well as those with some degree of emotional disturbance, are catered for in specialized units, the parents being encouraged to attend during the assessment period, so that the family as a whole may be helped.

Despite all the services detailed above there is not yet a nationwide service that adequately meets the needs of all children.

Education care and provision: 5 to 18 years

Schools for visually handicapped children have been founded over the years since the first school for the blind was established in Liverpool in 1791. Originally serving mostly the more able blind pupils, they now provide for a wide range of abilities.

For able children there are day and boarding schools, at primary and secondary level, and also facilities for students preparing for professional careers, as well as vocational assessment and career advisory services provided by the R.N.I.B.

Special schooling and residential units are provided for children and young people with additional handicaps of hearing, and of intellectual or emotional development.

The 1944 Education Act recommended that educationally blind pupils should be educated separately from pupils who were partially sighted. The emphasis is now much less on rigid categories, for teaching purposes, and it is the efficiency with which pupils are able to use their near vision (often with low-vision aids) that is taken into account when determining educational placement. Schools are now willing to take a wider range of visual ability and added handicap than they were previously.

Apart from those specialized schools for pupils with visual deficits, many children attend appropriate neighbourhood schools, with the supportive services of peripa-tetic teachers for the visually handicapped.

There is an unknown number of children who have a severe visual handicap in subnormality hospitals and many of them are not registered as blind or partially sighted. One hospital school that provides education appropriate to the needs of its visually handicapped pupils has 60 such children out of a school population of 250.

Aids to learning

Auxiliary aids to learning are being developed, and should greatly facilitate learning for visually handicapped students in both open and special education. Many are costly to buy but prove invaluable to their users. Examples of these are:

1. *The optacon* is a device for converting print into tactile form by electronic means.
2. *Talking calculators* are similar to ordinary calculators but have a synthetic speech output.
3. *Compressed speech.* Tape recorders are becoming available with this facility which increases the rate of speech reproduced without raising the pitch of the voice.
4. *Braille computer terminal outputs* are now in use.
5. *Thermoform machines* are used to duplicate braille and raised shapes on to plastic sheets from a braille master.
6. *Tape recorders* are in general use. Development is taking place of a tape recorder which runs at a very low speed, has four tracks and gives up to 12 hours' playing time.

7. *Braille writing and shorthand machines* are used generally, as well as typewriters for producing large print. Printing presses providing maps, diagrams and reading materials of a preferred size are installed in some schools.

8. *Closed-circuit television magnifiers* are proving invaluable to many pupils, especially those whose vision is so poor that they are unable to read ordinary print with comfort. There is a white on black facility which is especially helpful for some students.

Various electronic and other types of apparatus useful in school are detailed in the R.N.I.B. catalogue of apparatus and games. Talking books are available for children from the R.N.I.B. Talking Book Library and there are various tape libraries and tape copying services.

Low-vision aids. For a variety of reasons but especially following the work of Professor Barraga, *Increased Visual Behaviour in Low Vision Children* (1964), there has been increased use of print materials by children with poor vision. Low-vision aids (LVAs) have been in increasing demand, especially over the past eight years and there are LVA centres in most major cities. The 'Look and Think' Project, researched at the R.C.E.V.H. in Birmingham, has devised materials, with accompanying handbook, to encourage use of residual vision (available from the Schools Council).

Mobility training is available to pupils in many schools for the visually handicapped; teachers attend the National Mobility Centre for training. The Department of Psychology, Nottingham University, has a blind mobility unit which has given impetus to the production and use of mobility aids and tactile maps.

Fig. 40 Encouraging the mastery of a complex skill.

New developments

Integration of schooling
A programme of integrating visually handicapped pupils at the age of 12 years into the local comprehensive school was started at Tapton Mount Special School, Sheffield, in 1969. By 1979 there were 11 pupils in open education, 19 pupils having completed the course. Of the latter, several are now in professional employment or at various universities.

The school pupils have their own hostel where they can stay from Monday to Friday if the distance from their homes to school makes daily travel impracticable.

For efficiency, all equipment is duplicated. There are thermoform machines, typewriters, braille writing machines, tape recorders and other apparatus at both the comprehensive school and at the hostel.

The pupils are able and mobile, and have acquired the basic skills in learning and are able to produce work speedily and accurately. Braille text books, tactile maps and diagrams and other resource learning materials are prepared for each pupil, in advance of termly sessions. Marking of work and preparation for the needs of the following day are done by the two resource teachers with the pupils each evening. The resource teachers, who are experienced and qualified teachers of the visually handicapped, are employed by Tapton Mount School but work full time at the comprehensive school.

Regular discussions take place between parents, pupils and staff and when the time comes for placement at 12 years the decision is made by the family, who select appropriately from integrated provision, or more specialized secondary schooling.

Various other kinds of experiments in integrated education are proceeding.

Resource centres

Following recommendations in recent reports concerned with visually handicapped children, Lickey Grange School has become a resource centre for the Midland area. This centre provides a base for communication, offers advice and help, on request, to teachers and pupils at any school in the area, and provides materials, special aids and equipment. Assessment of pupils' needs can be made either at Lickey Grange (which continues as a regional school for the visually handicapped), or by specialist staff visiting local centres.

Similar kinds of arrangements are in existence elsewhere, e.g. at Shawgrove School, Manchester.

Fig. 41 Learning to use a braille typewriter.

A research centre for the education of the visually handicapped
This was established in Birmingham in 1970. Apart from carrying out research into the educational needs of the visually handicapped, the R.C.E.V.H. is acting as an information centre for everyone working in the field of visual handicap. The centre is able to undertake assessments at the request of local units; there is a variety of instruments for assessing the functioning of the visually handicapped, including the Williams Test, the Maxfield-Buchholz Scale and now the 'Look and Think' Checklist.

Training courses
The Diploma Course for Teachers of the Visually Handicapped, Birmingham University, is long established. From 1973 the B.Ed. Course has been available; a part-time course is planned to allow teachers to obtain their special qualification while teaching in schools for the visually handicapped.

   Child Care Staff Training Course in R.N.I.B. Schools. Recently, the R.N.I.B. began courses for in-service training for child care staff in its schools, so that a common standard can be maintained throughout the schools. The syllabus, based on one compiled by a D.E.S. Working Party, is designed to place greater emphasis on educational aspects than is usual in other courses for care staff.

The R.N.I.B. Education Advisory Service
This is an entirely free service provided by the R.N.I.B. to anyone concerned with a visually handicapped child. It is not a teaching service, but the advisers will help and, where possible, give practical assistance with a child's management, development, training and educational placement. They visit on request and do not go anywhere without invitation. Some local authorities now have their own advisory or peripatetic teaching service so the R.N.I.B. advisers do not normally visit in these areas unless their specialized knowledge is requested.

   All the R.N.I.B. advisers are qualified and experienced teachers of visually handicapped children; some have added qualifications for teaching deaf/blind, physically handicapped and slow-learning children.

   The service is provided for any visually handicapped child, whether or not his name appears on the blind or partially sighted register, including children who have any additional handicap. The advisers will spend time talking to parents and other relatives, doctors and hospital staff, local authority officers, psychologists, teachers— in fact anyone connected with the visually handicapped child.

   Although the size of the problem of blindness in Western countries is small, due to a variety of medical and public health improvements during this century, the incidence is still very high in certain parts of the world. Many of the conditions that cause blindness are preventable, through the control of diseases such as smallpox and through the eradication of severe malnutrition. The building up of better preventive health measures, alongside the educational and care services for visually handicapped children, is clearly an urgent requirement.

   In addition to the services described above, the R.N.I.B. supplies pamphlets, records and equipment. Most of the books in the following list of suggested further reading are available in their library.

   The address is:

Royal National Institute for the Blind,
224 Great Portland Street,
London W1N 6AA.

SUGGESTIONS FOR FURTHER READING

American Foundation for the Blind (1977) *International Guide to Aids and Appliances for Blind and Visually Impaired Persons.* 2nd edition. Baltimore: Port City Press.

BBC (1977) *In Touch. A Comprehensive Guide to the Aids and Services Available to Blind People.* 2nd edition. London: BBC.

Barraga, N. C. (1976) *Visual Handicaps and Learning: A Developmental Approach.* Belmont (California): Wadsworth.

Bower, T. (1977) *The Perceptual World of the Child.* London: Open Books.

British Psychological Society (1978) Readings on the visually handicapped child. Division of Educational and Child Psychology. In *Occasional Papers,* **II.**

Chapman, E. K. (1978) *Visually Handicapped Children and Young People.* London: Routledge & Kegan Paul.

College of Teachers of the Blind (1970) *24 Selected Articles.* C.T.B.

Freeman, P. (1975) *Understanding the Deaf/Blind Child.* London: Heinemann.

Gray, P. & Todd, J. (1967) *Mobility and Reading Habits of the Blind.* London: Government Social Survey, H.M.S.O.

Gregory, R. L. (1966) *Eye and Brain: the Psychology of Seeing.* London: Weidenfeld & Nicolson.

HMSO (1968) *The Education of the Visually Handicapped.* London: HMSO.

HMSO (1978) *Special Education Needs: Report of the Committee of Enquiry into the Education of Handicapped Children and Young People,* London: HMSO.

Jamieson, M. *et al* (1977). *Towards Integration: a Study of Blind and Partially Sighted Children in Ordinary Schools.* Windsor : NFER.

Jensen, V. A. & Haller, D. W. (1979) *'What's That.' A Picture Book for Blind and Partially Sighted Preschool Children, as well as Sighted Children.* London: Collins.

Lear, R. (1977) *Play Helps: Toys and Activities for Handicapped Children.* London: Heinemann.

Lorimer, J. W. (1978) *Neale Analysis of Reading Ability Standardised for Use with Visually Handicapped Children.* Windsor: NFER.

Lowenfeld, B. (1971) *Our Blind Children—Growing and Learning with them.* Springfield (Illinois): Thomas.

Lowenfeld, B. (Ed.) (1974) *The Visually Handicapped Child in School.* London: Constable.

Marshall, G. H. (1977) *The Eyes and Vision.* Coventry: Exhall Grange School.

Myers, S. O. (1975) *Where Are They Now? A Follow-up Study of 314 Multi-Handicapped Blind People, Former Pupils of Condover Hall School.* London: R.N.I.B.

National Association for the Education of the Partially Sighted (1972) *Partially Sighted Children: A Summary of Their Needs and Existing Provisions.* London: NAEPS.

National Association for the Education of the Partially Sighted (1974) *List of Schools and Classes Engaged in Work with Partially Sighted Children.* The Partially Sighted Society.

Reynell, J. & Zinkin, P. (1975) New procedures for the developmental assessment of young children with severe visual handicaps. *Child: Care, Health and Development,* **1,** 61–69.

Reynell, J. (1978) Developmental patterns of visually handicapped children. *Child: Care, Health and Development,* **4** (5), 291–303.

Royal National Institute for the Blind (1978) *Guidelines for Parents and Teachers of Visually Handicapped Children with Additional Handicaps.* London: R.N.I.B. (Several other pamphlets are also available.)

Royal National Institute for the Blind (1978) *Illustrated Catalogue of Apparatus and Games.* London: R.N.I.B.

Scott, E. P. (1977) *Can't Your Child See?* Baltimore (Maryland): University Park Press.

Sheridan, M. D. (1973) *Children's Developmental Progress.* Windsor: NFER.

Silver, J. (1978) The use of low vision aids. *New Beacon,* **62** (739), 281–286. Reprinted from *Regional Review* (1978), **63,** 9–16.

Silver, J. & Fass, V. H. (1978) Closed circuit television as a low vision aid: development and application. *Visus*, 1 (3), 57–72.

Tobin, M. J. (1978) An introduction to the psychological and educational assessment of blind and partially sighted children. British Psychological Society, Division of Educational and Child Psychology. In *Occasional Papers*, **II**, 9–17.

Williams, M. (1956) *Williams Intelligence Test for Children with Defective Vision.* University of Birmingham Institute of Education.

Wills, D. M. (1965) Some observations on blind nursery school children's understanding of their world. *Psychoanalytic Study of the Child*, **20**, 344–64.

Wills, D. M. (1968) Problems of play and mastery in the blind child. *British Journal of Medical Psychology*, **41**, 213–222.

Wills, D. M. (1970) Vulnerable periods in the early development of blind children. *Psychoanalytic Study of the Child*, **25**, 461–80.

6

The child with autism

In this Chapter we are concerned with a small, but very intriguing group of children with a profound and disturbing handicap. In a word, they can be described as 'impersonal'—cut off from human contact. The problems of understanding the nature, causes and possible treatment of this 'autistic' condition are immense.

One of the first problems is in the diagnosis. By what criteria is a child to be regarded as autistic and how can his condition be differentiated from those who fail to learn normally or develop mature, social relationships because of mental retardation, emotional disturbance or some degree of hearing loss? Recent work has, therefore, centred on the study of the different behaviour patterns of children with conditions such as aphasia or intellectual retardation or emotional disturbance, making comparisons with those considered to be autistic.

In an attempt to clarify and describe the syndrome of childhood autism, a diagnostic criterion known as the 'nine points' was formulated by a committee under the chairmanship of Dr Mildred Creak (1961). This was based on the observations of a group of people who had had opportunity to study a number of such children, over a considerable period of time.

The 'nine points' can be summarized as follows:

1. Severe impairment in emotional relationships.
2. Apparent unawareness of his own personal identity.
3. Preoccupation with particular objects, and failure to use them in an appropriate way.
4. Marked resistance to change in his environment.
5. Abnormal perceptual responses including visual and auditory avoidance.
6. Acute and apparently illogical anxiety.
7. Failure to develop speech.
8. Mannerisms and bizarre movements.
9. General retardation with 'islands' of normal or exceptional intellectual ability or skill.

The purpose of drawing up these diagnostic criteria was to help to recognize children with a particular syndrome, and they have proved of considerable value. However, there has been some uncertainty as to whether all, or only a few, of the behaviours described above are necessary to justify a diagnosis of autism. The criteria have since been modified by O'Gorman (1967) and by Rutter and colleagues (1971). Rutter outlines four main points about which there is now fairly general agreement.

1. Failure to develop interpersonal relationships. For example, failure to cuddle, to seek comfort or to form a close attachment to the parents. Lack of eye-to-eye gaze and a general disinterest in people.
2. Delay in speech and language development.
3. Ritualistic and compulsive phenomena.
4. Onset before the age of $2\frac{1}{2}$ years.

All criteria must be met for a diagnosis of autism to be made.

Characteristic behaviour of children with autism

Superficially, the physical appearance of autistic children is usually quite normal. But on closer observation it becomes apparent that they make very limited contact with their environment and do not show normal curiosity. They are usually solitary, and appear dreamy and preoccupied. They make little effective contact with adults, but use them to serve their own purposes, by taking their hands to reach for what they want: to open cupboards, to put their coat on, or to obtain something to eat. Sometimes they show glimmerings of awareness of social relationships: by pushing another child away who has the attention of an adult, or pulling at a parent's hand who may be engaged in a lengthy conversation and ignoring the child.

Many autistic children use no speech before the age of five years. Some may use gestures or an occasional word or sound to convey meaning. They frequently show both visual and auditory avoidance, not looking at people, nor listening to adult requests, nor to conversation directed to them.

They accept an ordered routine and resent changes, often displaying a catastrophic reaction to going on holiday or moving house. They may be unwilling to go out for walks or on excursions to the shops, or even to play outside. They seem to need the familiar environment and familiar sequence of events to give them a feeling of safety. They appear desperately to be seeking an ordered world and a reality which they can control.

This seeking after an ordered world seems to tie up with their obsessive fixations on a certain style of play. Many observers have noted the autistic child's seemingly endless desire to place objects in straight lines or trace the already laid-down patterns in the wallpaper. Like some much younger toddlers, they often cling to a particular inanimate object (but not to a doll or teddy). This object can be anything from a toothbrush or a wire spring to a feather or bit of fluff. For weeks at a time they may refuse to be parted from their special object and panic if it is lost.

Autistic children do not play as ordinary children do. They may wander aimlessly in a playroom or garden, picking things up, examining them briefly and then relinquishing them. At other times they will investigate objects in unusual ways; for instance they may bite jigsaw pieces or plasticine, sniffing or licking any new object as if this was of more interest to them than looking at it. They are often fascinated by repetitive movements and will watch for hours the clothes going round in a washing machine, or records on a turntable. Often in their absorption with spinning objects, they will attempt to turn any wheeled vehicle, such as a truck or tricycle, on its side, in order to spin the wheels rather than propel it in the usual way.

Children with autism often spend long periods in active but repetitive play: bouncing on a trampoline, swinging on a rocking horse or swing, sliding down a slide. Constructive play with bricks or Lego is rarely seen, but if it does occur there is a strong repetitive element in the activity. For instance, one boy always made the outline shape of an aeroplane, with any materials to hand; this involved the same shape, whether he was using Lego, bricks, pegs, pencil and paper, or even the cutlery at mealtimes.

Many autistic children, like this boy, use play materials in unusual and repetitive ways.

Imaginative play, in particular the imitation of domestic activities, is usually non-existent. This is in striking contrast with the play of generally intellectually retarded children (see Wing, 1976). It is rare indeed for them to play co-operatively with another child.

Incidence

Owing to uncertainties about the diagnosis of this condition, it has been difficult to estimate the incidence. Now that diagnostic criteria have been more clearly formulated, it is proving easier to make more accurate estimates. In the past, some autistic children have been cared for in hospitals for the mentally retarded and mistakenly classified as 'severely subnormal'.

In a careful survey in Middlesex (Wing, O'Connor and Lotter, 1967), it was estimated that, in 1964, 4·5 per ten thousand had autistic symptoms in early childhood. It was more common in boys than girls, the ratio being 2·75 : 1. It was found that more autistic children had suffered from birth complications than their siblings and that one half had marked delay in motor milestones. Parents, in this survey, tended to be above average in intelligence, educational attainments and occupational levels.

Causal factors

When autism was first described there were considerable differences of opinion regarding the reasons for this tragic condition.

Emotional factors, particularly style of upbringing, were implicated by some observers as the main cause of the withdrawn, asocial behaviour of these children. Because a striking lack of reciprocal interaction was noted between child and mother, it was all too easily assumed that the mother herself was cold and inflexible and had produced this type of behaviour in her child.

Doubts have been cast on this rather simplistic view in the past. These earlier observers failed to realize the effects of an unresponsive child on the adults around him. For instance, the mother who finds that her overtures towards her baby have little effect will gradually cease to try and stimulate him. As one parent put it, 'It is most disconcerting and hurtful, when you are chatting away to your baby, to find that his gaze is fixed on a swaying branch or curtain, and not on your face.' The parent/child relationship is, above all, a reciprocal one and a withdrawn and uninterested child may well 'turn off' parental interest.

In looking at the characteristics of families of autistic children it has been noted that, firstly, the personalities of parents of autistic children are no different from those of any other parent. Secondly, siblings of autistic children are not themselves unusual (which would be anticipated if upbringing was all-important). Thirdly, the vast majority of children from extremely deprived backgrounds who experience quite inappropriate mothering do not become autistic (though they may be disturbed emotionally in other less idiosyncratic ways). Fourthly, there are several pointers to suggest that the condition—as with all the conditions described in this book—has an organic or physiological basis, probably congenital in the case of autism. Studies of twins support this theory. For example, Folstein and Rutter (1977) studied 21 pairs of twins in which at least one twin was diagnosed as autistic. Eleven of the twins were identical (monozygotic) and 10 were non-identical (dizygotic). Amongst the identical twins 36 per cent of their twin partners also showed autism, whereas amongst the non-identical twins, none of their twin partners showed autism. The groups were also tested for intellectual and language impairments: 82 per cent of the identical twins showed 'concordance' in these, compared to only 10 per cent of the non-identical twins.

Studies such as this underline the importance of congenital factors, although their precise nature is not yet clear.

Several other studies have drawn attention to a variety of organic factors associated with autism. For instance, 25 per cent have fits, at some time in their childhood, and about 30 per cent show signs of neurological dysfunction, such as abnormal e.e.g. records (see Wing, 1976).

Although it seems likely that there are organic factors that predispose a child to become autistic, the *degree* of autism, and its outcome in later years, is undoubtedly influenced by the parents' reactions and the general handling of the child.

Social and emotional development

As we have shown, autistic children tend to be solitary and withdrawn. Their faces show little expression, sometimes as if they were wearing a mask. They seldom show emotion overtly, yet occasionally show violent rage, prolonged tantrums if thwarted, panic states in an unfamiliar situation, or for no apparent reason at all. In an acute stage of the condition they retreat from all contact with people. Such children may creep into bed with their clothes on, and hide themselves under the bedclothes, or curl up on the floor and cover themselves with a rug. The world seems to them unpleasant, perhaps incomprehensible, uncontrollable and threatening. They seek to return to a state of warmth and comfort, a passive effortless state reminiscent of a pre-natal existence.

In a secure familiar environment, autistic children may gradually begin to show some fleeting interest in the adult who spends most time with them and may fix their interest on her dress, ornaments, her hair, occasionally making a detailed inspection of her face. They may show some pleasure when cuddled or picked up. They then become more demanding of exclusive adult attention and more discriminating in their relationships, one grown-up being the favoured one. This is a marked step forward, but the adult may then become the recipient of strong ambivalent feelings, and violent swings from affection to hostility may occur. A form of sibling jealousy may be shown towards the other children who have claims on the loved adult. Thus, from total aloofness or mere toleration of the presence of the other children, they progress to expression of hostility and rivalry. These outbursts have, of course, to be controlled, but they are a sign of returning emotional health. It is now possible for the child to show feeling openly. He no longer lives behind his own particular iron curtain. He may begin to play cooperatively as well as aggressively for short periods and to be aware of the feelings of both adults and children. He may show more capacity to tolerate delay or frustration and to share adult attention. Moreover, he will begin to take a more alert interest in the world around him, to show curiosity, to make points of contact, to attempt to communicate more effectively, and to begin to learn, even in a group situation. At this stage the autistic child is showing the beginnings of progress.

Fig. 42 Self-portrait by an autistic girl aged eight years.

Teaching and training techniques

In the course of making periodic psychological assessments of young autistic children and from observing them in small teaching groups, certain difficulties of learning become apparent.

It is evident that many of them remain at the sensori-motor stage of learning described by Piaget, and Woodward for a much longer period than is normal. Children of five and six years can, if persuaded to cooperate sufficiently, match colours, discriminate shape and size, complete simple jigsaws, and construct simple tri-dimensional models. Thus it may be possible to obtain a fairly satisfactory test result on the Merrill-Palmer Scale.* Often when the child is first seen, the assessment is inconclusive because no effective working relationship can be made with the child. When the child is settled in a special unit or nursery, familiar with the environment and the routine and slightly more responsive to the staff, an adequate relationship can be made with him by the teacher or the psychologist. Then the result on a non-verbal intelligence test can give some indication of intellectual potential.

Given the unusual problems of learning and behaviour presented by autistic children, it follows that considerable ingenuity is required in devising appropriate teaching and training techniques. We will mention some examples of experimental techniques, including those used at the Belmont Hospital Children's Unit with a number of non-communicating children. One approach, involving a combination of speech therapy and simple behaviour modification techniques designed to focus on the major deficits in 'communication' and 'motivation' that affect autistic children, is as follows. The first stage is to teach a complete repertoire of sounds, both vowel and consonant. In the therapy room all extraneous sounds are excluded and the child sits comfortably in a small cubicle in a darkened room facing a screen on which slides are projected. The therapist sits beside the child. The sounds to be learnt are magnified on a tape recorder and heard through earphones by the child. They are linked with visual clues, e.g. blowing at your finger for the sound P. If the child makes the correct sound he is immediately rewarded by a sweet or a sip of orange squash as well as a smile and words of approval. If he makes the incorrect sound this is followed by a frown and a 'no'. The aim is one of positive reinforcement for successful

---

* References to many of the tests mentioned in this section have been made in other Chapters and we will not repeat them here. Further information on tests can be found in the test catalogue from the National Foundation for Educational Research, Windsor, Berkshire.

achievement and negative reinforcement for unsuccessful. Tactual cues, by having the child feel the adult's lips or throat, can be helpful too.

The next stage is to teach the child words for familiar objects, parts of his body and names of familiar relatives and staff. The picture of the object or person is projected on the screen in front of the child at the same time as he hears the word through his earphones. He is rewarded if he repeats the word correctly. From single words the child should progress to saying simple phrases, e.g. 'cup and saucer', 'in the garden', 'up and down', and later to short sentences.

The rest of the staff are kept informed of the vocabulary the child has built up and are asked to use the same words frequently in the course of the day as the correct occasion arises, and expect the child gradually to do the same. Too much pressure is, of course, avoided and if the child shows resistance or anxiety in connection with the therapy sessions, which usually last about 45 minutes two or three times a week, they are discontinued.

This technique is based on the theory that the child has missed learning speech at the period of high cerebral sensitivity and has to learn from the earliest babyhood stages. It seems probable also that some of these children suffer from some perceptual defect which makes it especially difficult for them to link visual, auditory and tactual experiences, to codify them, and to associate words with objects. They appear to have great difficulty in understanding symbols. It seems basically an organic condition in which, as Lorna Wing has said, the maturation of the parts of the brain dealing with sensory information is delayed. The physical environment around the child may be unintelligible, unorganized and seemingly chaotic to him. He cannot organize his sensory input to make sense and hence his clinging to familiar objects which he has learnt to understand, his confusion in strange situations, and his tantrums due to frustration. Teaching techniques which aim to reinforce and build up links between visual, auditory, tactual and kinaesthetic experiences are of great value. Other workers are trying out less formal approaches in their attempt to encourage greater social interaction and responsiveness to speech in very young children. Parents are being encouraged and trained to act as co-therapists (Schopler, 1976). A home-visiting programme in which a therapist discussed and demonstrated to parents a behaviour modification approach was successful both in lessening ritualistic and negative behaviours, and in encouraging the beginnings of speech development (see Howlin et al., 1978).

Carefully planned teaching methods have been successful in many instances in helping autistic children to make contacts with people, and with the real world, to develop speech, to improve perception and gradually to gain some understanding of concepts, of symbols and of abstract ideas. There has been a gradual increase in specialized schools working out their own particular methods with small groups of autistic children.

Psychological and neurological workers have studied the factors which appear to underlie linguistic development, e.g. visual and auditory perception and memory, and the child's ability to deal with sequencing and symbols. For instance, it has been observed that rote memory (e.g. repeating a series of digits) is as well developed in the brighter autistic child, as it is in normal children.

Autistic children are characterized by their inability to attend selectively to the visual and auditory, tactile, kinaesthetic and olfactory stimuli which constantly impinge on them. They are highly distractible and assailed on all sides by such stimuli. Nor can many of them link visual, auditory and tactile stimuli together into a percept; they cannot attach a name to what they see, hear and feel. Others are so withdrawn and apparently so engrossed by their own state of feeling that they shut out all external stimuli and fail to register sense impressions or remember what is said to them. One approach to teaching these children is that of Joan Taylor (Taylor, 1976). She introduces the child to simple games consisting of matching, sorting, fitting and arranging coloured shapes. This is an activity usually enjoyed and enables the child to make some sort of order, some sort of pattern, and to reinforce his awareness of shape, size and colour. By these means a good working relationship is established and then the child can engage in a series of sense-training games which help to improve visual memory (hiding and finding objects) to match what he feels with a similar object presented visually which reinforces tactile and visual sensations, to grade sizes, to repeat a pattern and produce a sequence of different shaped beads or tiles or blocks, to deal with two concepts at once, e.g. to sort all the red and the square shapes into one pile and all the blue and round shapes into another. Attempts are also made to break into the child's obsessions and tendency to perseverate, by unhitching his attention from one task, forgetting it and tackling the next task. He is taught to attend and ignore distractions by helping him to focus attention on the immediate task, handing him the material and reminding him of each step. Gradually he can be taught to work for short periods on his own, but for a long time these children need virtually individual teaching. Number symbols can be introduced linked with concrete objects arranged in a pattern and counting introduced, using fingers, toes, eyes, ears and then bricks, shells, conkers, pennies, etc. The understanding of the number symbol comes very slowly. Patterns of letters can be built up to make words linked with pictures, and the letters can be copied under a picture of an object he has drawn, sounded to him and spoken as a name. Photographs or drawings of himself can be named and labelled. Very slowly the letter and word symbol becomes associated with the picture. But all this, which comes naturally to an intelligent pupil of six, has to be slowly built up in the autistic child's mind and repeated again and again.

All of these simple techniques appear to help the child organize his sense data, to reinforce links between sensory experiences, to reduce the muddle in his mind and find the world less puzzling and frustrating to him. He is beginning to communicate by drawing, speaking and word naming and writing. He is making contact with people and objects in his environment.

Case studies

The following three brief case studies involve children with severe communication deficits, at the Belmont Children's Unit. The first child illustrates some typical features of autism: the other two, form a contrast: their marked language delay being associated with emotional disturbance and aphasia.

1. L.T., now six years old, was an 8-lb baby at birth, seemed alert, walked before 12 months and understood simple commands before two years. He disliked being cuddled and tended to shun contact. He used no speech between two and five years and thereafter used dysarthric speech or pointed or took the adult's hand to obtain what he wanted. He ignored requests and instructions, frequently seeking to do forbidden acts and showed violent but short-lived tantrums, when frustrated in any way. He insists on rigid routines, and indulges in obsessional rituals. He ignores other children and prefers to be in the garden or playroom on his own, or with an adult at hand. He is hyperactive and hypotonic. Vision and hearing are normal, as is his intelligence on performance tests (I.Q. 107). His social maturity age is, however, assessed on the Vineland scale as $2\frac{1}{2}$ years. He is beginning to show interest in educational achievements, especially in number, linking this with his obsessional preoccupations in pattern and sequences. Verbal comprehension and vocabulary are slowly developing. Autistic traits are lessening.

The progress report of his teacher is fairly encouraging.

'This afternoon for the first time he occupied himself for 35 minutes—looking round—finding things to do and doing them. Put all the cars straight in the garage. Rolled large beads through holes in a wooden bridge. Matched pictures. Took all screws off stick and put them back on. Fitted shapes into board except triangle, which he threw across the room. Vocalized, pretend speech as he played, using car and train noises and an occasional shriek.'

Three months later:

'Found my box of "family at home". Named the people as he took them out: L., Daddy, Mummy, Baby (his family) and gave himself a cup of tea from a miniature teapot. I invited him into the classroom at the new unit and he accompanied me, a little nearer to the unfamiliar room each time, and then retreated to the swing. At the fourth invitation he came into the classroom, took a box of cars and lined them up on a chair. Put them back in the box, carried them into the sitting-room, lined them up on a ledge, took them out into the garden and lined them up on the rabbit hutch. (No doubt he was retreating to obsessional play as a safeguard in the new situation, where he as yet felt insecure.) He pointed to a picture I had drawn last week of his sore knee, and showed that it was better now. Showed interest in my jigsaw—naming things in it. Brought me a picture of a fire and wanted me to burn my fingers in it. This is one of our jokes. He will stand with his fingers on a picture of a fire until I show great concern and say "Oh don't do that, you'll burn your fingers".'

'Lined up the doll's house furniture. Said "table". Found a chair and said "red chair". Found some fitting cups—lined them up too. Asked me to name the things he had lined up—dressing table, stool, etc.—and said the names of some himself.

'Wandered about not settling to anything. All the other children were busy. I said he must find something to do. He did a simple jigsaw. I gave him the 100 board with cubes. He did this after some insistence, made each ten a different colour, counted them. Started throwing things, not violently, tipping things out and lining them up. I stopped him. He lay down on the floor, banging his head, thumping and shouting. I ignored him until he was quiet, then insisted that he should sit at a table and do an easy jigsaw. He did this, calmed down and then went out to play.'

2. A.C. at five years showed severe speech delay; he was very restless and distractible. He came from a disturbed home background, with much marital friction. He was found to be of average intelligence, but immature socially, hyperactive and difficult to teach on account of his limited attention span. He tended to cling to possessions and was disturbed if parted from a bag full of treasures which he carried around with him. However, after a brief period in a secure supportive school environment, his speech developed fast, from single words and phrases to sentences and the use of pronouns. After a period of assessment he was transferred to a school for

maladjusted children where he made good progress. The original query concerning possible autism was not confirmed.

3. M.A. was found to be of high intelligence. At four years eight months he had an I.Q. of 140 on the Merrill-Palmer Performance Scale and at five years a learning age of 6½ years on the Nebraska Scale. There was some instability in the family history and some difficulty in early family relationships. He had five changes of care before 12 months of age and was adopted at nine months. The relationship with the adoptive mother was not a warm or affectionate one and speech did not develop at all.

In the children's unit he showed good constructional ability and readiness to learn with practical material. His most effective means of communication was by elaborate and colourful drawings, depicting cars, trains, roads, people, houses, in great detail. Verbal comprehension and identification of toys and pictures, when named, improved. Speech slowly progressed and a simple vocabulary was built up. He is beginning to make more effective use of his good intelligence, and his obsessional fears and lack of communication are gradually reducing. His hearing is normal, but he is thought to be aphasic.

Some extracts from his teacher's records are interesting:

'Another child, C., had been at the seaside and decided to make a seaside scene in the sand tray. M. drew pictures of a house, a boy, a car and a caravan as his contribution to add to the scene. This is the first time he has voluntarily joined in a common interest and contributed something to the general endeavour.

'C. found Mrs. G.'s name and said she was ill. We talked about this and I wrote up for C. what he was telling me. M. drew spontaneously Mrs. G. in bed, the door, the floor, a mat beside the door. This is the first time he has shown that he is aware of talk between me and other children.

'He found some long narrow strips of paper and they seemed to symbolize roads to him. He put these end to end with one as a side road branching off and ran his lorry along it ... He can use plasticine quite well, and usually makes a railway line and a signal and a train on the line ... He murmurs with pretend speech as he plays.

'He saw a picture of a house with a woman and a boy waving at the window. He made a long babble, pointing out of the window, perhaps showing that it reminded him of his mother with him at home.

'With five other children M. was very happily busy all the morning, constructing a complete scene on the sand tray—a long trough into which he poured water, a bridge made of large blocks with a lorry on, sheds, animals and a block road with cars on it—a combination of zoo and the seaside. He guarded his creation and marched round the room for a few minutes, keeping his eye on it.

'It is evident that M. is gradually learning to represent his environment by means of play activity, especially by drawing and creative play, and

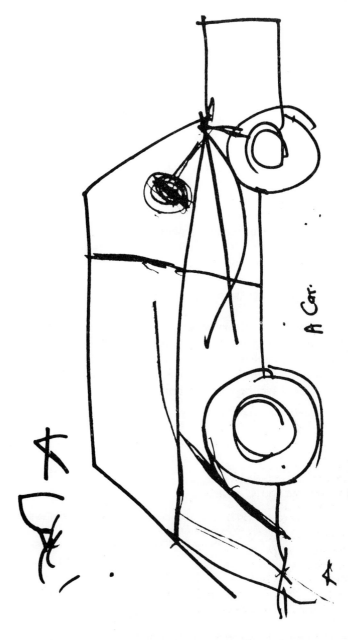

Fig. 43 A car, by M.A. (4½ years).

speech is slowly developing as an accompaniment to action. Social adjustment is improving; he is beginning to enjoy joint activities.'

Conclusions

Childhood autism is still a condition of which the causes and the most satisfactory methods of treating are somewhat obscure. But detailed knowledge and careful observations of autistic children have increased in recent years. Successful teaching methods have been reported, and accounts of autistic children who have improved sufficiently to be able to attend ordinary school, have been published in the scientific journals.

For instance, Mittler et al. (1965), in a follow-up study of children discharged from Smith Hospital, found that about one-third showed considerable improvements in behaviour.

The majority, however, especially those with combined mental retardation (about 50 per cent) will, as far as our present knowledge goes, be likely to remain dependent, in a sheltered or semi-sheltered environment. The quality of their lives within such an environment will be greatly influenced by the treatment and education they receive; and sustained efforts are needed to improve the effectiveness of treatment techniques.

Organizations and literature

The National Society for Autistic Children has done a great deal to publicize the problems and educational needs of these children. Books, pamphlets, general guidance and advice about schooling and after-school facilities can be obtained from:

The National Society for Autistic Children,
1A Golders Green Road, London NW11 8EA.

REFERENCES

Creak, M. (1961) The schizophrenic syndrome in childhood. Progress report of a working party. *British Medical Journal*, 2, 889.

Everard, M. P. (Ed.) (1976) *An Approach to Teaching Autistic Children*. Oxford: Pergamon.

Folstein, S. & Rutter, M. (1977) Infantile autism: a genetic study of 21 twin pairs. *Journal of Child Psychology and Psychiatry*, 4, 297–321.

Howlin, P. et al. (1978) A home visiting programme. In *Autism*. Ed. Rutter, M. & Schopler, E. New York: Plenum Press.

Minski, L. Shepperd, M. J. (1970) *Non-communicating Children*. London: Butterworth.

Mittler, P., Gillies, S. & Jukes, E. (1965) Report of a follow-up study. *Journal of Mental Deficiency Research*, 10, 73–83.

O'Gorman, G. (1967) *The Nature of Childhood Autism*. London: Butterworth.

Rutter, M., Bartak, L. & Newman, S. (1971) Autism: a central disorder of cognition and language? In *Infantile Autism*. Ed. Rutter, M. Edinburgh: Churchill Livingstone.

Schopler, E. (1976) Towards reducing behaviour problems. In *Early Childhood Autism*. Ed. Wing, L. Oxford: Pergamon Press.

Taylor, J. (1976) An approach to teaching cognitive skills. In *An Approach to Teaching Autistic Children*. Ed. Everard, M. P. Oxford: Pergamon.

Wing, J. K., O'Connor, N. & Lotter, V. (1967) Autistic conditions in early childhood: a survey in Middlesex. *British Medical Journal*, 3, 389.

Wing, L. (Ed.) (1976) *Early Childhood Autism*. Oxford: Pergamon Press.

7

Children with handicaps in developing countries

In Chapter 1 we outlined the change in attitude and growth in people's understanding and expertise concerning the handicapped which has taken place during the course of history. But it was not until the twentieth century that the State began to acknowledge that the needs of the handicapped are the responsibility of the community as a whole. The most recent development in attitudes is that help for the handicapped should be offered as a right and not as a charitable 'hand-out' and that, where necessary, legal codes must enforce these rights. These developments in the West are the outcome of a whole complex of medical and scientific developments, in addition to religious, moral and legal changes; they also have the backing of considerable economic growth, due largely to industrialization.

The background situation in many developing countries is obviously very different. In many such countries there are far too many people, especially children, in spite of infant mortality rates that are ten times higher than those in the West. Economic resources are often limited, poverty and malnutrition being particularly widespread when the crops fail. Diseases then spread easily, some of which lead to the kind of chronic handicapping conditions which have been largely controlled in the West, such as poliomyelitis. What are the prospects for handicapped children in such a setting?

In Chapter 1 we mentioned a dilemma: to help children with handicaps, we must first identify them, in order to plan the services we need; but 'identification' marks out certain children as being different, which tends to make integration and acceptance into society more difficult. In developing countries there is a more dramatic dilemma. Should the chronically handicapped be helped at all, at this stage, when there are so many able-bodied children lacking important facilities—housing, food, water, medical care, education, jobs, etc? Why bother with the handicapped when there are so many urgent problems affecting the able-bodied? The answer is simple; the question is invalid, and riddled with hidden value judgements. It presumes that the world can be conveniently divided up into the 'able-bodied' on the one hand, and the 'handicapped' on the other, and further assumes that the latter are 'second-class' citizens who must wait at the back of the queue until the needs of the 'first-class' citizens have been met. We do not believe that these assumptions are acceptable. We use the term 'handicapped children' purely for convenience in expressing our ideas and achieving some sort of focus. But when it comes to the rights to services, we believe that all children should have equal rights. Better services are needed for all, in many developing countries, and there are encouraging signs of growing services for children with chronic handicaps throughout the developing world. There is also an answer in terms of expediency—the right kinds of help given to the handicapped, especially at an early age, can make them more productive and less dependent on the rest of the community.

In this brief Chapter we can offer only a few examples centering on what we see as the two major problems:

1. What is special about the situation of the handicapped in developing countries, over and above the general problems that are continually mentioned, poverty, poor nutrition, high birth rates, high rates of infection, etc. (See Boutourline Young, 1970, and Morley, 1973, for excellent reviews of medical work in several developing countries.)
2. How Western ideas and practices can help (or perhaps hinder in certain situations) the building up of better services for chronically handicapped children—which must always be integrated into the existing culture. (See Malin, 1974, and Gardner, 1977, for brief outlines of some of the problems.)

Attitudes to the handicapped

In developing countries additional factors, for example religion and superstition, complicate social attitudes towards the handicapped. In parts of Africa, illness and handicap are thought to be caused by witches, ancestral spirits or malevolent gods (Norman-Taylor, 1961) who must not be offended lest they become angry and make matters worse. Rituals will be practised to placate the evil spirits and Western experts should not try to interfere with such deeply ingrained ideas, when offering their more scientific kinds of treatment. Nor should they be indifferent to the traditional local practitioner (sometimes referred to as a 'witch doctor') who plays an important part in the mental life of a community that is often struck by disasters almost unimaginable to people in the West. The Western practitioner must do his bit within the existing social structure, offering a complementary service that may eventually become an alternative service, if it is seen to be effective.

In India, the Hindu religion has particular ideas concerning the handicapped. It stresses the importance of philanthropy and mutual aid as a duty. But the doctrine of 'Karma', a fatalistic concept involving ideas of reincarnation, regards handicap as a retribution for sins committed by the family in previous generations. It follows that handicap might be regarded as a slur on the family name and that efforts by outsiders to improve the condition of one of its members might upset the balance of divine justice. Therefore, the local religious leader's (Guru) agreement often needs to be sought.

In the Islamic world the influence of religious ideas is even stronger. Islamic law decrees that mutilation be the punishment for some crimes (e.g. by severing a thief's right hand), and this has the unfortunate effect of linking handicap with criminality. The scope for conflict between such laws and the tremendous influx of Western ideas and techniques in the oil-rich countries such as Saudi Arabia is considerable. Saudi Arabia's vast economic resources and relatively small population offer tremendous opportunities for preventive work, and many superbly equipped, centralized hospitals have been provided. But these services are no substitute for the more community-based ones that are needed for chronically handicapped children. Assessment and educational services are available for the blind and the deaf, but more are needed for other chronically handicapped children, especially the physically handicapped.

Other factors that can lead to negative attitudes towards handicap are the roles that many handicapped persons play as beggars in some developing countries. In very poor sections of society, a family can become quite dependent on the income derived from their handicapped child's begging, and therefore resist efforts to give him schooling and treatment. To help such a child, one must simultaneously help the family, and the costs involved are quite trivial by Western standards. Another difficulty is 'fear of contamination'. Some illiterate groups fear that a handicapping condition such as cerebral palsy might be contagious and, therefore, should be avoided—a fear which is understandable in countries where diseases are common. The public education problem here is vast.

Fig. 44 Neurological examination in Saudi Arabia.

The importance of the family

The Westerner, coming from cultures where the size and importance of the family have been rapidly declining in recent decades,
must realize that families are still very large and very important
in most S.E. Asian countries. This often means that many people,
spanning several generations on both the husband and wife's side,
have to be consulted when decisions are to be made concerning
a handicapped child. On balance there is much to be said for the
'extended family', especially in respect of the support it offers the
child and its parents. So many parents are sadly isolated in the
West and highly dependent on paid professional support. The disadvantage is that older generations tend to be more set in their
ways, and have particular difficulties in adjusting to modern ideas
about the education and treatment of handicapped children (which
include encouraging independence, more integration into society,
use of aids and equipment, etc.). Another tendency is for males
to consider that handicapped children are especially the province

of females, and to have little to do with them. This is based partially on the notion that females are responsible for causing handicap. This can add to the mother's sense of shame, and lead to what
is virtually a hiding away of the handicapped child from public
gaze and very much needed treatment. Parent-founded organizations such as the Indian Spastics Society have run several courses
with particular reference to getting fathers more involved, and
spelling out ways in which they can help. Some aspects of the
'parental-involvement' schemes that we have previously mentioned could also prove helpful.

The growth of services in developing countries

The growth of services for handicapped children in developing
countries tends to follow the same sequence as in the West. The
more obviously educable children, such as the deaf and the blind,
are usually the first groups to receive schooling, followed by the
physically handicapped and then the mentally retarded (see
Taylor and Taylor, 1970, for an excellent account of the development of such services in India).

Taking the physically handicapped group (including children
affected by polio, cerebral palsy, amputation, congenital absence
of limbs) as an example, the first forms of help are usually by charitable missions, setting up homes, and offering care and protection
but little effective treatment or education. In countries such as

Fig. 45 Bombay: end of term party at the Indian Spastics Society's Centre for
Special Education.

India, the medical profession has improved these over the last 25 years. Through the efforts of orthopaedic surgeons and others they have set up school groups within the hospital setting and brought together many of the necessary disciplines, therapists, social workers, psychologists, etc. Recently, the movement has advanced still further by agencies such as parent-formed groups, especially those intent on building up special schools, e.g. for the deaf and the cerebral palsied. They are endeavouring to prove that special education can reduce many of the effects of the handicap, and have, further, given families of handicapped children much needed social and economic support.

Special education in developing countries

It is encouraging to see how the availability and organization of up-to-date educational facilities has improved in many developing countries in recent years. The International Cerebral Palsy Society, for example, is in touch with dozens of voluntary groups, most of which are parent-formed, in all continents. And the Deaf and Spastics Societies in India, in collaboration with various Indian and Western experts, have set up several first-rate schools which are comparable to almost anything available in the West—despite the difficulties posed by the multiplicity of languages and dialects. In Bombay and Calcutta, for instance, instruction has to be given in several languages.

The main problem, however, is how to form enough of these

Fig. 46 Calcutta: the Oral School for the Deaf.

excellent centres throughout the subcontinent, which has a population of over 600 million. The Spastics Society of India has a Five-Year plan to extend its facilities. At present it has only three schools. The first started in Bombay in 1973, followed by one in Calcutta, and more recently one in Delhi. Each provides for about 45 children with cerebral palsy and associated handicaps, open to families of all socio-economic levels, fees being waived in the case of the poor. This reminds us that handicap can cut across the usual 'class and caste' boundaries. The school in Bombay, known as the Centre for Special Education, has eight teachers, two physiotherapists, two speech therapists, an occupational therapist and a medical social worker; and visiting medical consultants and psychologists help with preliminary and on-going assessment and advisory work. The school also provides an 'out-patient' service, e.g. for children who cannot be admitted to the school on a regular basis, because of transport difficulties.

Since some of the problems arising from cerebral palsy are universal, such as the need to improve speech (in any language), sitting balance (for sitting on the floor, if chairs are rarely used), for improving perceptual skills (for whatever shapes are common in the particular culture), and generally adapting the educational environment to match the pattern of learning difficulties that handicap brings about—some of the expertise gained in the West in recent decades is useful.

The difficult part of the exercise is finding out how best to transfer such Western ideas to Indian circumstances. For example, it would be useless for Western educationalists to advocate expensive programmes involving sophisticated teaching machines for handicapped children, not simply because of the expense, but because many Indian teachers might find such equipment alien to their methods of teaching children and the kind of rapport they prefer to have with them.

Similarly, it would be wrong for a Western 'integrationist' to advocate placement of all handicapped children in normal rather than special schools, failing to realize that most normal schools in India are simply not ready to deal with such a challenge. In many areas in India the teaching staff are already overloaded with large classes, and confined to a rigidly prescribed curriculum that would not allow for the individualized and small group approaches that are essential for many handicapped children—even if the staff had sufficient knowledge of the special techniques necessary for children with special learning difficulties. The integration of children into normal schools in any society presupposes that a fair

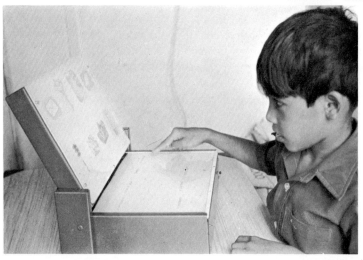

Fig. 47 Bombay Centre for Education: pupil with the Meldreth A4 Tutor, a low cost teaching aid, using inexpensive home-made programmes for perceptual discrimination—matching shapes, words, pictures, numbers, etc.

proportion of the staff has a basic interest in, and sympathy for handicapped children and some knowledge of their special problems. They must also have access to educational advisers and psychologists who can offer them help. This is coming, but it is certainly not available yet.

Teacher training

The training of staff is a vital consideration in any developing country, and in Bombay the first one-year course for the training of graduate teachers in the education of physically handicapped children was started in 1977.

The traditional approach has been for such staff to go abroad for training, such as to the UK and the USA—an approach which will always continue to have some uses, but will not get to the root of the problem of how to adapt Western techniques to African or Indian conditions and how to take the valuable parts of Western experience and technical competence and merge them into a culture that is likely in many respects to be much less technically minded in its approach to handicapped children and their needs. The West has much to learn about keeping its science and technology as useful servants instead of allowing them to dominate so much of its outlook.

The following abstract from a brochure produced by the Indian

Spastics Society gives a brief description of the course held in Bombay. This is a course which could perhaps serve as a model for other courses in other developing countries, provided the basic content is adapted to suit the differing conditions.

The following diploma course for teachers in the education of the physically handicapped child has been organized by the Spastics Society with the support of the Central Government and in collaboration with the Bombay Institute of Education and experts from the Spastics Society, UK, and London University, Institute of Education.

Types of children studied

Types of children to be studied include: the cerebrally palsied (which exemplifies much of the work, including the consideration of specific learning difficulties, perceptual problems, language disorders, subtle sensory defects etc.), the orthopaedically handicapped, the minimally brain damaged, epileptic, polio, spina bifida, amputees, congenital absence of limbs. Visual, hearing and intellectual retardation problems and problems of emotionally disturbed/deprived children are also to be considered, since they are often associated with conditions such as cerebral palsy, but they will not be dealt with in depth.

Qualifications for admission

Preferably graduates or trained teachers, but other applicants with suitable qualifications will be considered.

Type of course

The objective is to familiarize the students with developments in Special Education over recent years, with special reference to physically handicapped children, especially the cerebrally palsied and similar conditions with 'brain dysfunctioning' that give rise to a variety of learning difficulties, calling for both special educational treatment and special understanding.

Children without brain damage, such as those who have suffered polio or amputations, will also be dealt with, especially when the conditions are severe enough to cause communication, educational and social difficulties. The emphasis will be on highlighting how handicaps can interfere with normal learning and how educational intervention can reduce much of the interference. The wider family and community context surrounding the children will also be considered.

Course outline

The course is for one academic year, August 1st to April 30, and is divided into three sections:

1. Lectures and tutorials.
2. Practical work.
3. Special assignments.

1. The lectures and tutorials will cover the following topics:

a. Normal psychology and child development, including methods in psychology: theories of learning, individual differences, cognitive development and human intelligence, behaviour modification, perception, emotional and social factors. In child development, besides a general view, specific attention will be paid to language and motor development.

b. The psychology of handicap: individual and social: the assessment of exceptional children, learning disorders, communication difficulties.

c. Medical aspects of child development: normal and handicapped, including basic anatomy and neurophysiology. Causes, types and treatment of various physical handicaps.

d. Educational aspects: history and philosophy of normal and special education. The national and international scene. Teaching strategies and curriculum development (language and communication systems, perceptual development, reading and number work).

   Physically handicapped children—specific learning disabilities, diagnosis and evaluation of classroom difficulties and their remediation. Specialized aids, teaching materials and educational tests.

e. Therapies and P.H. children: physiotherapy, occupational therapy, speech therapy, aids and appliances. The integration of the various therapies. Early diagnostic intervention and treatment programmes.

f. Social and community aspects: the role of the social worker. The family and the handicapped child. Services for the child and family—present and future, in various parts of India, urban and rural.

Fig. 48 Teacher training. Lecturer and students at the Indian Spastics Society course on the education of physically handicapped children at the Bombay Institute of Education.

2. *Practical work*, including visits to various schools and clinics: teaching practice with P.H. children: case studies of at least four children.
3. *Special assignments:* periodic essay writing and reviews of selected publications: one applied research dissertation of 10 000 words. Guidance will be given in the selection of a topic during the early months of the course.

The course in Bombay has an output of ten trained teachers each year, and similar courses are planned in Calcutta and several other cities—to provide the necessary staff to allow the expansion of special educational facilities as part of the Indian Spastics Society's Five Year plan.

The need for a planned approach
Efforts to help the handicapped in developing countries cannot be left to small groups 'working their own patch', however dedicated they may be. A wider, long-term plan providing for all aspects of handicap is essential. The Indian Spastics Society's Five Year plan has been drawn up to include the following relevant aims:

1. To provide more special schools (initially in the major cities) with proper assessment, advisory and counselling facilities for physically handicapped children and their families.
2. To use these schools as resource centres from which visiting/mobile services can be sent out to the villages (where over 80 per cent of the population of India lives and where the incidence of handicap is high).
3. To build hostel accommodation, attached to the day schools for physically handicapped children who are isolated in remote areas, and for very deprived, handicapped children, living in slums and orphanages. Preliminary surveys in these areas have already been carried out by the students on the teacher training course.
4. To develop teacher training courses in several cities along the lines of the course in Bombay, to provide the essential staff for special schools, and soon, for units attached to ordinary schools. The latter often function under difficult conditions and much planning, advice and support will be needed if they are to integrate successfully even moderately handicapped children.
5. To implement research, often in collaboration with other agencies, to acquire the accurate information on the incidence of physical handicaps essential to the proper planning of services. Research is also planned on the application of Western assessment techniques to Indian populations, involving

problems of differing languages, motivation, etc. (see Kamat, 1967).

6. To develop services for school leavers, including further education and vocational training, and sheltered workshops for handicapped people, giving the latter a chance to play their part in the economic life of the country.

7. To improve the public's understanding of, and attitudes towards, people with a handicap through both electronic and print media.

8. To increase professional education in prevention and management through conferences, both national and international. This would involve specialists from many disciplines—orthopaedists, gynaecologists, paediatricians, neurologists, psychologists, therapists, educationalists, social workers. A primary consideration would be how to bring these various professionals together, and in partnership with parents. The papers from the first conferences on prevention and management of cerebral palsy, held in Delhi and Bombay, are available (Chib, 1978).

Conclusions

We have briefly described a few of the problems facing the handicapped in developing countries, giving examples mainly from sources in India, where the backcloth of other problems—poverty, disease, population pressures, religious attitudes, village remoteness and urban squalor—frequently seems overwhelming. In spite of these, small groups of pioneers have made important advances in recent years, altering attitudes, building up excellent examples of services, and persuading Governments and industrialists to spare some of their resources for work with the handicapped. Enlightened officials agree that the needs of the handicapped and their families are too urgent and pressing to be made to wait until the problems of the able-bodied are solved. The two processes have to move forward in parallel, helping people to help themselves, instead of remaining a burden.

As we have mentioned, the scope for preventive work such as preventing blindness due to infections, eradicating polio and similar diseases that plagued the West until this century, and the scope for expanding much needed services for the large numbers of existing persons with handicaps, are tremendous in developing countries.

It must be remembered that it has taken the West hundreds of years to develop such services to what might be regarded as an acceptable level. It is to be hoped that some of the expertise gained in this process will be of use to experts in the developing countries—and that the economic resources essential to their expansion become available on a more generous scale than at present. For example, the UK Overseas Development Administration offers technical, medical and educational services in nearly all developing countries (over 800 million people) and has to do so on a budget that is almost identical to the amount of money spent on confectionery alone in the UK. Clearly this is not enough, and far greater resources are required.

The organizations below are involved in a variety of ways in the interchange of information and expertise through publications, conferences and training schemes, as well as in the exchange of personnel and provision of funds.

International Cerebral Palsy Society,
5A Netherhall Gardens,
London NW3.

Rehabilitation International
 Information Service,
c/o Stiftung Rehabilitation,
6900 Heidelberg 1,
P.O. Box 101 409,
Federal Republic of Germany.

Royal Commonwealth Society for the
 Blind,
Commonwealth House,
Haywards Heath,
Sussex.

United Nations Educational, Scientific
 and Cultural Organization
(UNESCO),
Place de Fonteney
75700 Paris,
France.

World Health Organization (WHO),
Geneva,
Switzerland.

REFERENCES

Boutourline Young, H. (1970) Socio-economic factors and child development. In *Malnutrition is a Problem of Ecology*. Ed. Kline, O. L. & Gyorgy, P. Munich: Karger.

Chib, M. (Ed.) (1978) *Action for the Handicapped*: papers from the International Conference on Prevention and Management in Cerebral Palsy, obtainable from: The Spastics Society of India, Centre for Special Education, Upper Colaba Road, Colaba, Bombay.

Chib, M. (1978) Cerebral palsy in India. *International Cerebral Palsy Society Bulletin* (June).

Gardner, L. (1977) 'A passage to India'. *International Cerebral Palsy Society Bulletin* (Jan.).

Kamat, V. V. (1967) *Measuring the Intelligence of Indian Children*. Oxford: OUP (India).

Malin, A. J. (1974) Special education in India. In *Educational Equality for the Handicapped*, papers from 5th International Seminar, Australian Council for Rehabilitation.

Morley, D. (1973) *Paediatric Priorities in the Developing World*. London: Butterworth.

Norman-Taylor, W. (1961) Witchcraft, sorcery and mental health. *Health Education Journal*, **19**, 30–38.

Taylor, W. W. & Taylor, I. W. (1970) *Services for the Handicapped in India*. Rehabilitation International, New York.

8

The handicapped child in the family and the community

Throughout this book our concern has been with children presenting certain physical handicaps, but the problems of the parents caring for such children have constantly been in the forefront of our minds and the impact of these children on the rest of the family and the special adjustments necessary in family life are matters of first consideration. We have tried primarily to be informative and practical. We have given facts and figures, stated the known causes of the conditions, described in some detail the methods of treatment, training and education that have proved to be of value. We have made it clear that in most instances one cannot think in terms of cure, but only in terms of amelioration, compensation, support and guidance. The handicapped child and his family learn to live with the particular disability, make a reasonable adjustment, and discover potentials and limitations in the situation, provided expert treatment, sympathetic understanding and practical help are offered when needed.

Some children are multi-handicapped. They have several of the handicapping conditions that have been described in various sections of this book, and the associated problems are not a simple addition of the effects of, say, blindness plus deafness plus motor handicap, but their multiplying effect—such as blindness preventing lip-reading, motor handicap preventing written expression, and so on. In cases with multiple handicap, it is sometimes even difficult to decide what the main special educational needs are, or even which organization to turn to for help. But, fortunately, various voluntary societies, including those for the deaf, the blind and the spastic in the UK, have been alert to the problem for some years and have provided some 'multi-handicap' facilities. There are also organizations specifically set up for dual handicaps, such as for children who are both deaf and blind.

It goes without saying that the responsibilities of parents of children with multi-handicap are very great, and their burdens must be shared.

Family and community care

There are many people who try to give help to the parents of a multi-handicapped child—the nurse, the doctor, the health visitor, the social worker, the psychologist, the psychiatrist and more especially the relatives, friends and neighbours. But it does not help such a mother to be told glibly 'not to worry, it could be worse'; or bluntly 'better forget about him. Why not put him in a home and adopt a baby'; or unrealistically 'You never can tell. See another specialist. His blindness (or spasticity) might be curable; miracles do happen.' Such well-meaning but almost invariably invalid advice is becoming more rare as public, and professional, education improves.

Probably all mothers, sometime during their pregnancy, have presentiments and fears about the baby they are carrying, that all might not go well. The arrival of a baby who is recognized as abnormal, who does not move his limbs, or look or listen, or who has an unsightly birthmark, who is premature, whose delivery may have been prolonged or difficult, who is a blue baby or severely jaundiced, is usually a very great shock to the mother. This is not always recognized, but clearly she needs immediate support, sympathy and help. Feelings of anguish, guilt, inadequacy or depression may almost overwhelm her. She may blame herself, her husband or the hospital or all three. She may turn away from the child, unable to face the fact of his disablement, and sometimes unable to feed him. She may cling to her husband for support, or she may turn against him, regarding him as responsible, and a happy marriage may end in separation or divorce.

More usually, fortunately, a disabled baby calls forth natural maternal solicitude. His urgent needs are recognized from the start. It is especially hard for the mother if the baby has to spend the first few weeks in an oxygen tent, or if he is unable to suckle because of his physical disability. It is damaging to the early close relationship of mother and child, if she cannot feed and cuddle him in these early weeks of his life. But many mothers seem able to overcome this difficulty and begin to build up a close emotional tie to their baby. This close involvement of mother and child may mean that at least temporarily the husband and other children take second place in her affections. It is unfortunate if this attachment remains so close that the rest of the family feel excluded. It is from this situation that acute feelings of hostility and jealousy may arise among the siblings. The handicapped child, in their view, always seems to take first place. Special allowances have to be made for him, special treats foregone and it may not be so easy to entertain friends or go on holidays as before.

Support services

Clearly a wide variety of support services is necessary from the start if negative reactions such as these are to be avoided. Two factors seem to be of especial importance:

1. Coming to terms with reality, through the airing of anxieties.
2. Sharing the day-to-day care.

Parents may experience feelings of shock, sadness and sometimes guilt over the diagnosis of their child's handicap. The sadness may be thought of as a kind of mourning for the 'lost' normal child that might have been.

This grieving may take a long time, periods of resignation alternating with denial of problems or hopes for a 'miracle cure'. The person with whom the parents share their grief becomes a vital link in helping them to come to terms with the reality of the handicap. Whoever this supporting person is, he or she must combine sympathy with realism and, above all, have the time to listen.

Initial counselling may be most appropriate with someone already known and trusted within the community, be it priest, health visitor or family doctor. However, parents often express a wish to confide in someone 'who really knows what it's like from the inside'. To fulfil this need parents of babies suffering from Down's syndrome (mongolism) have started up groups whose aim is to make contact and give support in the blackest early days after the diagnosis is made.

In a baby with a severe physical handicap, it may be the physiotherapist who can best help the parents at this crucial juncture. By discovering with the mother the best ways of handling and stimulating the baby, the expert demonstrates to the mother that she can be the best 'therapist' for her own child. In this way, a parent can be given back the confidence in her own mothering abilities, which has been dealt a body blow by the very fact of giving birth to a 'damaged' child.

At the same time as she is helping the mother with practical matters of handling, the wise therapist, by involving the siblings in the 'treatment' activities, will encourage the mother to be aware of the needs of the other members of the family. This approach, of looking at the day-to-day management problems within the family set-up, is described in detail in the book *Handling the Young CP Child at Home* (Finnie, 1974). The advice and ingenious suggestions for adapting the home environment to the needs of the handicapped child are chiefly applicable to those with a physical disability, but the emphasis on the often overlooked emotional needs of siblings applies to all families with a handicapped member. For a detailed account of the disruptive effect that a disabled child can have on family relationships see *Handicap and Family Crisis* (Kew, 1975).

Some centres that provide treatment or nursery facilities for handicapped children offer parents opportunities for discussion on a regular basis. This approach of providing on-going family support was pioneered by such organizations as the Invalid Children's Aid Association (ICAA) and is being increasingly adopted by local authorities (through weekly meetings with a social worker, for mothers with a child in a special care unit), as well as by specialized child development centres (see Jolly *et al.*, 1977).

Sharing the day-to-day care

In addition to the need to talk through their anxieties and to have some guidance about handling, the whole family may welcome the opportunity for occasional outings, as a unit, without having to make constant allowances for the handicapped member. Workers with such families, however, do quite often make the observation that an exhausted and over-wrought mother may hesitate to accept an offer of 'baby sitting' or an overnight stay in a special children's hostel, claiming that they can 'manage on their own' or that 'no-one could be expected to cope with their child'.

In looking at the possible reasons for this refusal to accept proffered help, let us consider the attitude, in the same situation, of a mother with her first normal baby. The same feelings of total responsibility and physical exhaustion may apply, but the husband usually insists that an evening out will do her good. The mother is encouraged to think of her own needs, as well as those of her husband. On returning home to find that the baby-minder has coped with any problems and that the baby is 'still in one piece' the young mother has taken a big step forward, in discovering that the baby is able to survive without her constant presence and that she can take time off, occasionally, to be herself. By sharing the care of her baby with others she is also beginning to realize that he has a place as the newest cherished member of an extended family and of the neighbourhood, and that he can give much delight to others.

This sense of pride and the sharing of joy is often missing with a very obviously handicapped baby. Both parents and friends, for fear of causing embarrassment, avoid asking questions or making comments about the baby's development. There is a conspiracy of tactful silence. Because he seems 'different', relatives may be hesitant about handling him, and over the months the mother's feeling that only she can manage him (with his floppy limbs or his 'funny turns') may become a reality. Because they lack experience with handling the baby, friends and relatives may begin to feel he is too 'fragile' and difficult for them to manage. The mother in her uncertainty may connive with this, feeling that her child is so great a burden, she may eventually reach the position that she refuses the chance of expert relief care.

After visiting several such caring, conscientious families, Rosemary Evans, a research psychologist, made a plea for small community-based homes that can provide weekend or relief care for very handicapped babies. She feels this is particularly needed for those with other young children, with no relatives nearby or for those with a severely handicapped or behaviourally disturbed child. Her article 'Sharing the caring' (Evans, 1977) emphasizes the necessity for practical support *before* the family shows signs of stress. This would help to prevent family break-down and lessen the need for long-term institutional placement. See Stone and Taylor (1977) for an excellent description of the range of voluntary and statutory organizations that can offer support.

Turning, now, to the handicapped child himself: it is sometimes difficult to know how he feels about his situation. He may be very demanding, constantly seeking to monopolize the attention of adults, feeling the need for limelight and compensation. Often he must feel keen frustration. 'They run off and leave me, they know I can't keep up'; 'I never get a chance of kicking the ball or scoring a goal myself'. 'Oh how I wish I could be a ballet dancer', or 'learn to drive a car', or 'be a pilot' or 'ride a horse'—such remarks reveal inner feelings. Tantrums or fits of depression are common. Retreat and withdrawal are a means of defence. Over-compensation by phantasy, fabrications or over-ambitious plans for a career are typical of the adolescent facing the immense problems of growing up with a handicap. But all along the road, such children can be helped by the family and by the community. School achievements with the help of specially designed aids, braille, the Possum typewriter, the loop system linked with a hearing aid, to name just a few, mean a great deal to children with very special needs. Adventure playgrounds and holiday clubs for handicapped children build up confidence and improve social adjustment. Vocational guidance centres for the disabled, sheltered workshops and special facilities in industry for handicapped adults offer employment prospects. There are now very many voluntary and state organizations in industrialized countries which are actively providing special help. But is this enough?

The future for children with a handicap in our society

'Just because I can't speak properly they think I am stupid'—the bitterness with which this sort of remark is made by intelligent, physically handicapped adolescents is a sign of the humiliating effect of prejudice. Such prejudice is sometimes more crippling than the disability itself. One of the most fundamental aspects of handicap is the psychological one of its effects on human relationships. As we discussed in Chapter 1, very few people feel at ease in the presence of a handicapped person: the origins of the feelings of uneasiness are very complex but seem to reflect, on the whole, a failure to regard someone with a handicap as a person. He is labelled, instead, in terms of the handicap: in other words the handicap is assumed to extend to all aspects of his personality and to affect all aspects of his behaviour. His worth as a person, his capacities for ordinary thought, feelings and activities, are assumed to be very reduced or completely lacking and consequently he is regarded as an 'outsider', as far as the main stream of social life is concerned. We will not try to pass over the fact that a small percentage of disabled are so severely handicapped both mentally and physically that they more or less remain 'infantilized' throughout their lives, in spite of early treatment and education. The degree to which they can form relationships amongst themselves and with other people is extremely limited and some kind of 'segregated' placement, should the parents wish, is probably the kindest alternative. Injustice arises when the majority are treated in such a way.

Whereas most societies in the past (and some in the present) have tended to exclude or segregate the handicapped, in recent decades attitudes to handicapped people have improved. This is due to a whole combination of factors, e.g. the educational effects of voluntary society work in disseminating information, pioneering proper services and research, and to the increased state and local authority concern with welfare, as part of the general trend. This has been more specifically expressed in UK legislation such as the Morris Act (Chronically Sick and Disabled Persons Act 1970) which established the rights of the handicapped to certain facilities such as housing, access to buildings, home help and other provision. General trends in social attitudes, towards greater tolerance of individual and group differences, although regarded as 'over-permissive' by some, have also helped towards increasing social acceptance of the handicapped.

Persons with a handicap are no longer a neglected group in most countries and in this book we have been able to describe the growing facilities that are promoting earlier and more comprehensive assessment, treatment and education. Older disabled people were denied such facilities and the severity of the handicaps that many of them now possess is a result of this neglect. Our next task is to explore the extent to which early recognition and help can improve the quality of life of the handicapped and help to break down the barriers erected by previous generations to exclude and segregate them. A great deal of research is urgently needed, to examine the effectiveness of the facilities provided and to find out the best ways of promoting progress.

Parents and professionals

As we have noted, conditions as complex as these call for a large team of professional workers—in education, medicine, health visiting, psychology, social work, physiotherapy, speech and occupational therapy, vocational guidance and community work, and one very important lesson has been the realization that *the most important members of the team are the parents*. Without their unconditional love and understanding, encouragement and guidance, the child's chance of reaching his maximum possible degree of integration within the normal community is seriously diminished. It is essential that professional workers should give a great deal of thought to the kinds of help that parents and children need and to realize that much of this help is best channelled through the parents: and that as the child becomes older, his self-help and independence must be encouraged. Care must be taken not to undermine parents' confidence in themselves as parents, by overwhelming them with advice and allowing no scope for their own ideas. As the child becomes older, he gains confidence in himself, in his abilities to explore the limits to which he can become independent and to appreciate situations where he cannot be so, and then to accept help.

Professional workers have to learn to eschew paternalistic attitudes. Skilled and well-trained professionals are aware of this danger and are therefore in a position to contribute a great deal of help—in making objective assessments and reasonable predictions based on hard-won experience, and within the framework of this, making available the best methods of treatment, training, education, therapy, counselling and vocational and other services. Professional workers are learning to work together in clinics, centres, classrooms and in the wider community. They bring much needed expertise to bear: they also bring much needed emotional support to parents and children in times of crisis.

Professional workers, alongside the parents, have another important part to play: that of helping to educate the public about the nature and consequences of handicap. Integration of the handicapped, complete or partial, within the normal community depends basically on the attitudes of the public. The services, the clinics, centres and schools, the local and central government facilities and statutes are vital in promoting the welfare of the handicapped—but they are no substitute for considerable thought and action concerning every person's deeper feelings and attitudes about handicap. As one parent of a multi-handicapped child put it: 'He gave me the key to unlock reserves of strength buried so deep inside me that I never knew they existed. The challenge was not to concentrate on my own suffering or that of my child but the suffering of other people and how this might be resolved.'

REFERENCES

Cooper, L. & Henderson, R. (Eds.) (1973) *Something Wrong?* London: Arrow.
Evans, R. E. (1978) Sharing the caring. *Child: Care, Health and Development*, **4.**
Finnie, N. R. (1974) *Handling the Young Cerebral Palsied Child at Home.* London: Heinemann.
Hewett, S. (1970) *The Family and the Handicapped Child.* London: Allen & Unwin.
Jolly, H. *et al.* (1977) The Charing Cross Hospital Child Development Centre. *Child: Care, Health and Development*, **3.**
Kew, S. (1975) *Handicap and Family Crisis.* London: Pitman.
Stone, J. & Taylor, F. (1977) *A Handbook for Parents with a Handicapped Child.* London: Arrow.
Younghusband, E. (1970) *Living with Handicap.* London: National Children's Bureau.

(The National Children's Bureau also publishes a series of clearly written booklets entitled *Helping the Handicapped Child.*)

Author Index

Subject Index